ToyShop's ACTION FIGURE

PRICE GUIDE

EDITED BY ELIZABETH A. STEPHAN

Front Cover:
All price are for figures in Mint in Package condition

B.A. Baracus, A-Team, Galoob, 1984, $25
Cowardly Lion, Wizard of Oz, Mego, 1973, $50
Captain America, Famous Covers, Toy Biz, $20
Spawn from Spawn Alley, Spawn: The Movie, McFarlane;
    value for play set, $20
Darth Maul (Jedi Duel), Hasbro, $9
Gowron the Klingon, Star Trek: The Next Generation,
    Playmates, $25

Daggit (Brown), Battlestar Galactica, Mattel, $30
Bride of Frankenstein, Universal Monsters, Sideshow
    Toys, $20
Spider-Man, Wold's Greatest Super-Heros, Mego, $50-100
G.I. Joe, 1960s era, $300-350

Back Cover:
John Lennon, Yellow Submarine, McFarlane, $10

krause publications
700 East State Street • Iola, WI 54990-0001
715/445-2214 • FAX: 715/445-4087   www.krause.com

Published by
700 E. State St.
Iola, WI 54990-0001
Telephone 715-445-2214
www.krause.com

Please call or write for our free catalog. Our toll-free number to place an order
or obtain a free catalog is 800-258-0929 or please use our regular business
telephone 715-445-2214 for editorial comment and further information.

Library of Congress Catalog Number: 00-102692

ISBN: 0-87341-917-0

Printed in the United States of America

Contents

Introduction

Once upon a time, in a world far, far away, action figures were based on superheroes and fictional television characters—Superman, Spider-Man, Captain America, Obi Wan and Boba Fett, Transformers, and of course, G.I. Joe. Things are different now. Action figures of aging rock stars KISS and the Animal Planet's Crocodile Hunter have changed how manufacturers and collectors view these one-time kid's toys.

An Action Figure was Born

For many action figure collectors, time began in the 1960s. While boys had played with toy soldiers for hundreds of years, these were typically iron or lead figures with no movable parts. The same held true for the hard plastic Marx figures of the 1950s. By definition, however, the term "action figure" was born in the 1960s.

From 1961 to 1963, toy makers watched with envy and despair as Mattel's Barbie, aided by TV, took the world of girls' toys by storm. Of course, no one would dream of selling dolls to boys, so this barrier seemed insurmountable. But the wheels of industry would not be easily stopped, and the simple solution to this dilemma ranks as one of the greatest marketing spins of all time. If boys won't play with dolls, why not rename them "action figures?"

Along Came Joe

G.I. Joe, the twelve-inch action figure made especially for boys, debuted New York's International Toy Fair in 1964. Toy buyers and retailers were skeptical about Hasbro's new figure. Could it be sold to the public as a military action figure? Or would it be perceived as a doll for boys? Hasbro gambled a sizable investment to launch an extensive advertising campaign portraying G.I. Joe as "America's Moveable Fighting Man."

In retrospect, we can see how much G.I. Joe influenced the world of action figures. Hasbro single-handedly broke the stigma of boys playing with a doll-like figure by creating an articulated, movable man-of-action figure. G.I. Joe did for boys what his female counterpart, Barbie, did for girls—allowed them to role play any situation imaginable.

G.I. Joe Timeline

- **February 9, 1964**—This was the magical date in G.I. Joe history. This was the beginning of New York's International Toy Fair and the day Hasbro introduced G.I. Joe to a few select toy buyers. Even though Merrill Hassenfeld, president of Hasbro, was able to convince buyers that G.I. Joe was an action figure and not a doll, they were still skeptical. New York City was chosen as the initial test market for G.I. Joe; the figures sold out in a week. Hasbro put their new toy into limited national distribution in August and September of 1964.

- **1967**—Hasbro attempted to capture the girls' market by introducing the G.I. Nurse. She couldn't compete with Mattel's Barbie doll and boys didn't want to introduce a girl into their adventures. Because so few were sold, G.I. Nurse is now one of the most valuable and sought after G.I. Joe action figures.

- **1968**—As public sentiment turned against the military action in Southeast Asia, many parents did not want their children playing with "war" toys of any kind. Hasbro recognized the need for change, and G.I. Joe saw his last year of military service in 1968.

- **1969**—G.I. Joe became a civilian adventurer in 1969. He was an Aquanaut, an Astronaut, a Frogman and an Underwater Diver.

- **1970-1976**—The Adventure Team was the next step for G.I. Joe. Hasbro introduced Man of Action, Talking Commander, Black Adventurer and Land, Air, and Sea Adventurers which joined the G.I. Joe ranks.

- **1978**—Due to rising oil prices, Hasbro could no longer economically produce a twelve-inch action figure.

- **1982**—Joe was reborn as a 3-3/4-inch action figure. Over the next few years several hundred figures and vehicles were produced. This product line consisted primarily of futuristic adventures and were tied into comic books and television cartoon series.

- **1991**—Hasbro introduced the Hall of Fame Series, twelve-inch models of their 3-3/4-inch counterparts. The popularity of the "new" twelve-inch figures prompted Hasbro to expand the Hall of Fame series to include additional figures, accessories and vehicles. Electronic Talking Battle Command Duke became part of the Hall of Fame line in 1993, the first talking G.I. Joe since the original debuted in the 1960s.

- **1994**—Hasbro marked G.I. Joe's 30th Anniversary in 1994 at New York's International Toy Fair by introducing a special line of twelve- and 3-3/4-inch action figures. G.I. Joe Action Soldier, Action Sailor, Action Marine, and Action Pilot were released to commemorate Joe's anniversary. This was to be the last year of the 3-3/4-inch figure.

- **1996**—Hasbro introduced the Classic Collection that would grow over the years to include figures like Theodore Roosevelt, George Washington.

- **1999**—G.I. Joe turned 35. He is the only action figure to have reached this milestone, and few toys have reflected changes in the United States and the rest of the world like Joe.

- **2000**—JFK G.I. Joe was added to the Classic Collection. Hasbro also honored some of the unsung heroes of WWII, including Navaho Code Talker and Tuskegee Airman. The 3-3/4-inch figure was reintroduced.

GI JOE ®

America's Movable Fighting Man ™

© 1965

G. I. JOE® DIVISION. HASSENFELD BROS., INC., PAWTUCKET, RHODE ISLAND

Hasbro started it all when they introduced G.I Joe in 1964. This cover of Hasbro's 1964 G.I. Joe catalog shows Joe in action.

G.I. Joe may have been the first true fully-articulated action figure, but he wouldn't be alone for long. A.C. Gilbert introduced James Bond figures in 1965, but for the first time in his career, Ian Fleming's super spy failed in his mission. Marx also entered the ring with the Best of the West series, but G.I. Joe had a seemingly limitless arsenal of battle-geared appeal.

The first reasonably successful challenge to G.I. Joe came from Ideal's Captain Action. While Joe's identity was well established, Captain Action was a man of many faces. Ideal designed Captain Action to establish not only his own identity, but also to capitalize on those of many popular superheroes. Joe was just Joe, but Captain Action could become Spider-Man, Batman, the Phantom, Green Hornet and others. Today,

Captain Action figures and sets command some of the highest prices in the action figure market.

Ideal's brief foray into the world of superhero action figures paved the way for many to come. By 1969, Ideal tired of Captain Action's complex licensing agreements and discontinued the series, but another company was waiting in the wings. It was Mego.

Mighty Mego

In 1972, Mego released its first superhero series, the six-figure set of Official World's Greatest Super Heroes. These eight-inch tall cloth and plastic figures were joined by twenty-eight others by the time the series ended ten years later. Mego sup-

G.I. Joe's first major competitor in the action figure world was Ideal's Captain Action. Photo from 1968 Ideal catalog.

plemented this superhero line with licensed film and TV characters from, most notably, *Planet of the Apes*, *Star Trek* and *The Dukes of Hazzard*, as well as historic figures representing the Old West and the World's Greatest Super Knights.

Star Wars

Another milestone in action figure—and toy—history took place in 1977. Out of nowhere, George Lucas's *Star Wars* had become a worldwide smash, but nobody except Kenner had bothered to secure rights to merchandise toys. (Mego was offered the license, but due to the lack of interest in other sci-fi toys, they passed.) When Kenner realized the magnitude of *Star Wars'* potential, it rushed toys through production, but it didn't have time to get action figures on the shelves by Christmas. Instead, Kenner essentially presold the figures as the mail-order Early Bird set.

By Christmas 1978, the line had grown to seventeen figures and the first wave of a deluge of accessories and related toys. The *Star Wars* frenzy continues. When *Star Wars: Episode I* was released in 1999, the toys caused a frenzy at local toy stores. Many retailers opened at midnight on May 3, allowing collectors to be the first on their block to get their hands on a twelve-inch Darth Maul or a 3-3/4-inch Obi Wan Kenobi. Less than twelve months later, many of the same toys were sitting in the clearance aisles of many stores. Many of the toys were

overproduced, but that didn't matter to the die-hard *Star Wars* collector—he still searches for every figure ever made.

The *Star Wars* figures also established a third standard size for action figures. G.I. Joe and Captain Action were twelve-inch figures, Mego figures measured eight inches, and Kenner's *Star Wars* figures were just 3-3/4 inches tall. Their tremendous popularity cemented that size as a new standard that holds to this day.

The release of *Star Wars* marked the birth of the second generation of action figure collectors. The new generation learned to buy two of each figure—one to play with and one to keep in the pack.

Enter the 1980s

Next came the six-inch figure set by Mattel's highly successful and lucrative 1981 Masters of the Universe series. This series was the first to be reverse licensed; in other words, Mattel made the toys first, and then sold the licensing to television and film, not the other way around. Mattel also upped the manufacturing ante by endowing the figures with action features such as punching and grabbing movements, thus enhancing their play value and setting another standard in the process.

Hasbro then scored again with the 1985 introduction of the next level in the evolution of action figures, the transforming

Ideal's Comic Heroine Posin' Dolls, a.k.a. the Super Queens, are four of the most sought-after action figures on the market. Photo from 1968 Ideal catalog.

May the Force be With You

The *Star Wars* trilogy—the top grossing trilogy of all time—spawned a line of toys that changed the face of the industry. Before *Star Wars*, large-sized action figures were anywhere from six to twelve inches tall. But Lucasfilm, along with Kenner (the major licensee of *Star Wars* toys), decided that smaller was better. The 3-3/4-inch size became the industry standard, making larger action figures seem bulky in comparison.

Why this change in size was made is open to speculation, but here's something to consider—how big would your Millennium Falcon have to be to fit your twelve-inch Han Solo action figure into the cockpit? (And how many kids would it take to lift it?) While Kenner's plastic Millennium Falcon was not produced to true scale, it still allowed a figure to sit in the cockpit with room for more in the main hold.

But what makes *Star Wars* toys so great? If you're not impressed with their smaller size or the way they revolutionized the licensing market, then consider their position as one of the most venerable toy lines of the millennium. While there was a period between 1984 and 1995 when *Star Wars* toys seemed to cool and few if any new items appeared on the market, the news that George Lucas would update the old movies and would soon begin scripting the three prequels renewed industry interest in this merchandising gold mine. New lines of *Star Wars* action figures were released by Kenner in July 1995, and Galoob began issuing *Star Wars* Micro Machines in 1996.

But how collectible are the new *Star Wars* toys? Well, remember that the main reason the original toys are so collectible is because they were taken out of the package—children enamored with the latest *Star Wars* movie were not going to leave their Luke Skywalker with telescoping lightsaber in his blisterpack. As is the case with most hobbies, items are collectible because they are rare. While children will play with

their Darth Maul and Qui-gon Jinn action figures, their parents will stash Mint, unopened toys in the attic. But since ninety percent of all collectors will be doing the same thing, don't expect your Obi-Wan action figure to put your kids through college.

The new toys don't have great collectible value—all of the Episode I toys can be found on the secondary market. Darth Maul—the new cult favorite—is the most popular character, and could easily have eclipsed Boba Fett as the current favorite character of true fans if Hasbro hadn't overproduced the new toys. Some characters, namely Jar Jar Binks, were so unpopular among collectors that their toys have no secondary market value. Because so many collectors will be stashing away their Mint on Card figures, the new toys won't bring thousands of dollars at an auction. With any luck, the toy will make its way into the hands of a child who will play with it. Then, and only then, will the long-term value increase.

Star Wars will eventually fade from the memories of collectors, just as it did through the late 1980s and early 1990s. But since there are two more movies planned tentatively for release in 2002 and 2005, it will be some time before this fade-out occurs. On average, prices on early *Star Wars* toys will never vary much from their current levels and the collectible value of the new crop of toys is uncertain, although expect the values of *Episode I* toys (and any toys from the other prequels) to stay low. That's not to say that people will stop buying into the *Star Wars* merchandising craze. While certain prequel products have languished on the shelves, new licensees such as Lego have been hard-pressed to keep up with demand. *Star Wars* and its toys will endure, even if the movies are considered financial failures, but the days of the $8,000 action figure are long gone.

figure. The aptly-named Transformers did just that, changing from innocuous-looking vehicles into menacing robots with a few deft twists, and then back again. Hasbro's mutating robots also transformed the toy industry, spawning numerous competitors and introducing the element of interchangeability into toy design. Hasbro, however, did not invent the transforming robot. That credit, as far as research shows, goes to a Japanese line called GoDaiKins. But Hasbro perfected the mass merchandising of the concept.

Masters of the Universe and Transformers are both becoming more popular and valuable with collectors. The kids that played with them in the '80s are grown-ups with disposable income.

McFarlane Toys produces figures are aimed at the adult collector. How many teen-age kids even remember Bob and Doug McKenzie? Or the Hanson Brothers? It would be safe to say not many. But they do know Austin Powers and Spawn. McFarlane is able to bridge some of generation gap and appeal to the non-collector with niche figures like Janis Joplin and Where the Wild Things Are.

Action figures are big business, and hot series like Spawn and The Simpsons are now regularly ranked in the top twenty

best selling lines by industry trade magazines. An enduring character identity is a key to continued demand and future appreciation.

Collectibility

In the past, action figures were seen as a plaything, but by the 1980s, that attitude began to change.

To say that *Star Wars* altered the world of collectible toys would be an understatement. In the early 1980s, it was evident that the *Star Wars* trilogy was a mega-hit, and fans wanted the toys—Mint in Box. The value of these original toys skyrocketed, and by the end of the decade, they were valued in the thousands.

When it became evident that figures would be worth more in the package, kids, parents and collectors could be heard uttering the phrase, "Don't take it out of the pack! You'll ruin the value." And now, in the year 2000, one rarely sees an action figure that is out of its packaging.

Pre-Star Wars action figures that are Mint in Pack are rare and highly coveted. Mint in Pack figures released within the last ten years are much more common. That's not to say they aren't valuable, but sixty dollars would be considered valuable for a recent figure, whereas the same value for one of Mego's "Super Queens" would be laughable.

Some action figures like Power Rangers, one of the best-selling action figure lines ever, don't have a lot of collector appeal. Based on a children's television show, the figures are popular with the show's viewership. Will these figures be popular with these kids when they grow up? Only time will tell.

Buyer Beware

As veteran collectors can tell you, education is the best way not to get ripped off. Know what you want and what you are looking for. Get to know the hobby.

Invest in a number of different resource guides and get to know other collectors. Attend shows and see what's out there and ask questions. Collectors love to talk about their collections! Don't be afraid to ask.

Toy Shop magazine has regular coverage of new action figures in the New Products section. New and old figures are covered in the monthly "Figure This" column written by John Marshall.

Price guides can help, but they can be frustrating. By the time you hold this book in your hand, some of the values given may be out of date. That's the nature of the price guide business. A price guide is not a bible; it is a guide and only a guide. If you are selling a figure, remember that a dealer will not give you book price; they have to make a profit, too.

The price grades used in this book are standard for the hobby. MIP or MIB stand for Mint in Pack and Mint in Box, respectively. MNP and MNB mean Mint no Pack and Mint no Box, respectively.

Acknowledgements

Numerous people helped produce the book you hold in your hands.

John Marshall, Corey LeChat and Michael Zolotorow all lent their expertise to the listings. Lenny Lee, publisher of *Lee's Action Figure News & Toy Review* provided many of the photographs that appear throughout the book.

Many thanks go out to Paul Kennedy and Mark Williams. They each went above and beyond the call of duty to make sure this book happened.

Sharon Korbeck, editor of *Toy Shop*, was there for me when I needed help.

Merry Dudley, associate editor of *Toy Cars & Vehicles*, is a Star Wars fanatic and was able to answer all my Star Wars-related questions.

Mark Rich, Tom Michael and Mike Jacquart provided the figures used on the cover. Ross Hubbard, Kris Kandler, and Bob Best photographed the cover; Chris Pritchard designed the cover; and Tom Nelsen designed the inside pages.

Contributors

John Marshall
P.O. Box 340
Rancocas, NJ 08073
Jmars@toyzilla.com
www.toyzilla.com
Marshall collects all types of action figures and writes "Figure This" and "G.I. Joe," regular columns for *Toy Shop* magazine.

Corey LeChat
P.O. Box 40135
Pittsburgh, PA 15201
email: the1999guy@aol.com
LeChat is a collector and expert on *Space: 1999, Battlestar Galactica, Doctor Who* and other late '60s and '70s character related sci-fi toys.

Michael Zolotorow
email: Zolotoro@localnet.com
Zolotorow is a collector of all action figures, especially Masters of the Universe figures.

A-Team (Galoob, 1984)
12" Figures

	MNP	MIP
Mr. T, non-talking	30	65
Mr. T, talking	40	75

3-3/4" Figures and Accessories

Armored Attack Adventure with B.A. Figure	25	55
A-Team Four Figure Set	40	65
Bad Guys Figure Set: Viper, Rattler, Cobra, Python	35	60
Combat Headquarters with four A-Team figures	30	60
Corvette with Face Figure	25	50
Interceptor Jet Bomber with Murdock	30	60
Motorized Patrol Boat	15	35
Tactical Van Play Set	25	45

6-1/2" Figures and Accessories

Amy Allen	10	30
B.A. Baracus	8	25
Cobra	6	15
Face	6	25
Hannibal	6	25
Murdock	8	25
Off Road Attack Cycle	8	20
Python	6	15
Rattler	6	15
Viper	6	15

Action Jackson (Mego, 1974)
8" Figures

Action Jackson, Black version	25	60
Action Jackson, blond, brown, or black beard	15	30
Action Jackson, blond, brown, or black hair	15	30

Accessories

Fire Rescue Pack	5	15
Parachute Plunge	5	15
Strap-On Helicopter	5	15
Water Scooter	5	15

Outfits

Air Force Pilot	7	15
Army Outfit	7	15
Aussie Marine	7	15
Baseball	7	15
Fisherman	7	15
Football	7	15
Frog Man	7	15
Hockey	7	15
Jungle Safari	7	15
Karate	7	15
Navy Sailor	7	15
Rescue Squad	7	15
Scramble Cyclist	7	15
Secret Agent	7	15
Ski Patrol	7	15
Snowmobile Outfit	7	15
Surf and Scuba Outfit	7	15
Western Cowboy	7	15

Play Sets

Jungle House	40	85
Lost Continent Play Set	40	85

Vehicles

Adventure Set	40	85

A-Team—Armored Attack Adventure with B.A. Figure, Galoob

	MNP	MIP
Campmobile	40	85
Dune Buggy	30	60
Formula Racer	30	60
Mustang	30	60
Rescue Helicopter	40	85
Safari Jeep	40	85
Scramble Cycle	20	40
Snowmobile	15	30

Addams Family (Playmates, 1992)
Figures

Gomez	4	15
Granny	4	15
Lurch	4	15
Morticia	5	18
Pugsley	4	15
Uncle Fester	4	15

Addams Family (Remco, 1964)
Figures

Lurch	150	450
Morticia	160	500
Uncle Fester	160	500

Alien (Kenner, 1979)
18" Figure

Alien	200	500

Aliens (Kenner, 1992-94)
Accessories

Evac Fighter	7	20
Hovertread	5	20
Power Loader	5	20
Stinger XT-37	5	20

Series 1, 1992

Apone	5	15
Bull Alien	7	15
Drake	5	15
Gorilla Alien	8	15
Hicks	5	15
Queen Alien	10	25
Ripley	5	15
Scorpion Alien	7	15

Series 2, 1993

Alien vs. Predator	15	30
Flying Queen Alien	5	15

ALIENS

Alien—Alien, Kenner, Photo Courtesy

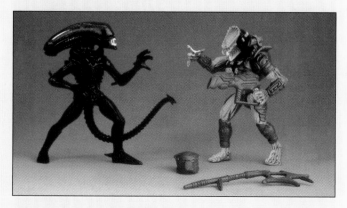

Aliens—Alien vs. Predator, Kenner

Aliens—Hudson, Kenner

Aliens—O'Malley, Kenner

Aliens—Swarm Alien (electronic), Kenner

	MNP	MIP
Queen Face Hugger	5	15
Snake Alien	5	15

Series 3, 1994

Arachnid Alien	6	25
Atax	5	20
Clan Leader Predator	5	25
Cracked Tusk Predator	5	15
Hudson (foreign release)	15	40
Invisible Predator (mail-in)	20	40
Kill Krab Alien	5	15
King Alien	10	25
Lasershot Predator (electronic)	15	30
Lava Predator	5	15
Mantis Alien	5	15
Night Cougar Alien	5	15
Night Storm Predator	6	15
O'Malley (foreign release)	20	40
Panther Alien	5	15
Rhino Alien	7	15
Spiked Tail Predator	4	15
Stalker Predator	4	15
Swarm Alien (electronic)	15	25
Vasquez (foreign release)	15	40
Wild Boar Alien	4	15

Alpha Fight (Toy Biz, 1999)
5" Figures

Northstar & Aurora	3	12

	MNP	MIP
Sasquatch & Vindicator	3	12
Snowbird & Puck	3	12

American West (Mego, 1973)
8" Figures

Buffalo Bill Cody, boxed	40	75
Buffalo Bill Cody, carded	40	100
Cochise, boxed	40	75
Cochise, carded	40	100
Davy Crockett, boxed	70	110
Davy Crockett, carded	70	140
Shadow (horse), boxed	70	140
Sitting Bull, boxed	45	90
Sitting Bull, carded	45	125
Wild Bill Hickok, boxed	40	75
Wild Bill Hickok, carded	40	125
Wyatt Earp, boxed	40	75
Wyatt Earp, carded	40	125

Play Sets

Dodge City Play Set, vinyl	100	200

ANTZ (Playmates, 1998)
Figures

Colonel Cutter	2	4
General Mandible	2	4
Princess Bala	2	4
Weaver	2	4
Z	2	4

ANTZ—Z, Playmates

ANTZ

Archies—by Marx. Left to Right: Archie; Jughead

Archies (Marx, 1975)
Figures

	MNP	MIP
Archie	15	75
Betty	15	75
Jughead	15	75
Veronica	15	75

ARCHIE

Astronauts—Jane Apollo Astronaut, Marx

Armageddon (Mattel, 1998)
Figures

	MNP	MIP
A.J. Frost	3	10
Harry Stamper	3	10

Astronauts (Marx, 1969)
Figures

Jane Apollo Astronaut	65	125
Johnny Apollo Astronaut	125	200
Kennedy Space Center Astronaut	65	140

Austin Powers (McFarlane, 1999-2000)
Series 1

Austin in Union Jack underwear	3	8
Austin in Union Jack Underwear, "dirty version"	5	15
Austin in velvet suit	3	8
Austin in velvet suit, "dirty version"	5	15
Dr. Evil with Mr. Bigglesworth	3	10
Dr. Evil with Mr. Bigglesworth, "dirty version"	5	15
Fat Bastard	25	50
Felicity Shagwell	3	8
Felicity Shagwell, "dirty version"	10	25
Mini-Me	10	25

Series 2

Austin Powers in striped suit	3	8
Austin Powers, "dirty version"	3	10
Dr. Evil and Mini-Me with Mini-Mobile	8	20
Dr. Evil, Moon Mission	4	12
Fembot	3	8
Mini-Me, Moon Mission	8	20
Scott Evil, says "A trillion is worth more than a billion, numbnuts"	3	10

Austin Powers—Felicity Shagwell, McFarlane Toys

	MNP	MIP
Scott Evil, says "Get away from me, you lazy-eyed psycho"	3	8
Vanessa Kensington	4	12

Austin Powers (Trendmasters, 1999)
12" Figures

	MNP	MIP
Austin Powers	4	12
Dr. Evil	4	12
Fembot	8	20

Avengers (Toy Biz, 1997-present)
12" Collectors Series

	MNP	MIP
Captain America, 2000	5	15
Hawkeye, 2000	5	15
Tigra, 2000	5	15

6" Figures

	MNP	MIP
Iron Man, 1997	4	8
Loki, 1997	4	8
Scarlett Witch, 1997	4	8
The Mighty Thor, 1997	4	8

Series I, 5" Figures

	MNP	MIP
Ant-Man, 2000	4	8
Captain America, 2000	4	8
Ultron, 2000	4	8
Vision, 2000	4	8
Wasp, 2000	4	8

Series II, 5" Figures

	MNP	MIP
Falcon, 2000	4	8
Hawkeye, 2000	4	8
Kang, 2000	4	8
Tigra, 2000	4	8
Wonder Man, 2000	4	8

Series III, 5" Figures

	MNP	MIP
Ant-Man, 2000	4	8
Hawkeye, 2000	4	8
Iron Man, 2000	4	8
Remnant I, 2000	4	8
Thor, 2000	4	8

Shape Shifters

	MNP	MIP
Ant-Man transforms into Armored Ant	4	8

Avengers—The Mighty Thor, Toy Biz

Avengers—Scarlet Witch, Toy Biz

AVENGERS

Avengers—Iron Man, Toy Biz

Avengers—Loki, Toy Biz

	MNP	MIP
Captain America transforms into American Eagle.............4		8
Hawykeye transforms into Armored Hawk......................4		8
Thor transforms into Flying Horse.................................4		8

Team Gift Pack

Hulk, Iron Man, Thor, Ant-Man/Giant Man, The Wasp 8		20

Banana Splits (Sutton, 1970)
Figures

Bingo the Bear...45		125
Drooper the Lion 45		125
Fleagle Beagle 45		125
Snorky the Elephant 45		125

Batman & Robin (Kenner, 1997-1998)
12" Figures

Batgirl 30		70
Batman...25		50
Ice Battle Batman (WB Exclusive) 20		50

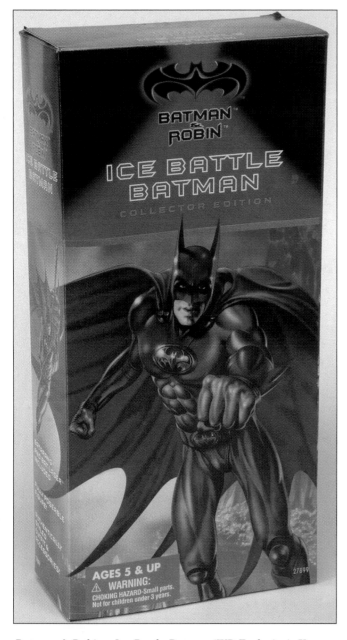

Batman & Robin—Ice Battle Batman (WB Exclusive), Kenner

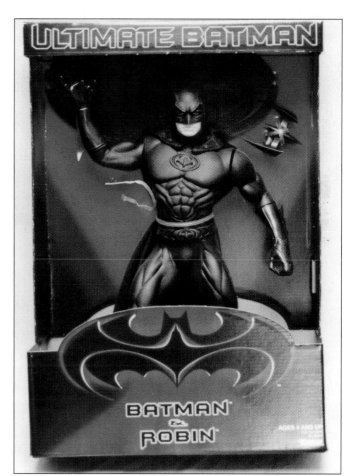

Batman & Robin—Ultimate Batman, Kenner

	MNP	MIP
Mr. Freeze...20		40
Robin 25		45
Ultimate Batman...15		40
Ultimate Robin 15		40

5" Figures

Bane, Leather Impact 5		15
Batgirl 5		10
Batman, Ambush Attack 5		15
Batman, Battle Board with Ring 5		15
Batman, Heat Scan 5		15
Batman, Hover Attack 5		15
Batman, Ice Blade 5		15
Batman, Ice Blade with Ring 5		25
Batman, Laser Cape with Ring 5		15
Batman, Mail Away from Fuji...............................45		n/a
Batman, Neon Armor 5		15
Batman, Neon Armor with Ring 5		25
Batman, Rotoblade with ring 5		25
Batman, Sky Assault with ring..............................5		25
Batman, Snow Tracker 5		15
Batman, Thermal Shield with ring 5		25
Batman, Wing Blast...5		15
Batman, Wing Blast with ring 5		25
Bruce Wayne, Battle Gear 5		15
Frostbite 5		15
Jungle Venom Poison Ivy 5		10
Mr. Freeze, Ultimate Armor 10		25
Robin, Attack Wing 5		15
Robin, Blade Blast..5		15

AVENGERS

Batman & Robin by Kenner—Left to Right: Jungle Venom Poison Ivy; Batgirl

Batman & Robin—Ice Blade Batman, Kenner

Batman & Robin—Ambush Attack Batman, Kenner

Batman & Robin—Wing Blast Batman, Kenner

BATMAN & ROBIN

Batman & Robin—Blade Blast Robin, Kenner

Batman & Robin—Talon Strike Robin, Kenner

	MNP	MIP
Robin, Iceboard	5	10
Robin, Razor Skate	5	10
Robin, Talon Strike	5	10
Robin, Talon Strike with ring	5	25
Robin, Tripple Strike	5	10
Robin, Tripple Strike with ring	5	25

Deluxe Figures, 1997

	MNP	MIP
Batgirl with Icestrike Cycle	20	40
Batman	10	20
Batman, Blast Wing	10	15
Batman, Rooftop Pursuit	10	15
Mr. Freeze, Ice Terror	10	15
Robin	10	20
Robin, Blast Wing	10	15
Robin, Glacier Battle	10	25
Robin, Redbird Cycle	20	40

Two Pack Figures, 1998

	MNP	MIP
Batman vs Poison Ivy	25	75

Two-Pack Figures, 1998

	MNP	MIP
A Cold Night At Gotham	10	20
Batmobile	15	40
Batmobile, Sonic	15	30
Brain vs. Brawn	10	20
Changelers Of The Night	20	30
Cryo Freeze Chamber	5	15
Guardians Of Gotham	10	20
Ice Fortress	10	15
Ice Hammer	20	40
Jet Blade	15	40
Night Hunter Robin vs. Evil Entrapment Poison Ivy	10	15
NightSphere	20	50
Wayne Manor Batcave	45	105

Batman Forever—Batman vs. The Riddler, 1997, Kenner

BATMAN & ROBIN

Batman Dark Knight—Bruce Wayne, Kenner

Batman Forever—Riddler, Kenner

Batman Crime Squad (Kenner, 1995)

Accessories

	MNP	MIP
Attack Jet	7	15

Figures

	MNP	MIP
Air Assault Batman	5	15
Land Strike Batman	5	15
Piranha Blade Batman	5	15
Sea Claw Batman	5	15
Ski Blast Robin	5	15
Stealthwing Batman	5	15
Torpedo Batman	5	15

Batman Dark Knight (Kenner, 1990-91)

Figures

	MNP	MIP
Blast Shield Batman	12	25
Bruce Wayne	7	20
Claw Climber Batman	12	25
Crime Attack Batman	7	15
Iron Winch Batman	7	15
Knockout Joker	25	75
Night Glider Batman	20	35
Power Wing Batman	12	25
Shadow Wing Batman	7	15

	MNP	MIP
Sky Escape Joker	10	30
Thunder Whip Batman	12	25
Wall Scaler Batman	7	15

Batman Forever (Kenner, 1995)

Figures

	MNP	MIP
Batman vs. The Riddler, Batman Forever, 1997	5	15
Blast Cape Batman	5	10
Fireguard Batman	5	10
Hydro Claw Robin	5	10
Manta Ray Batman	5	10
Night Hunter Batman	5	10
Riddler	10	15
Sonar Sensor Batman	4	10
Street Biker Robin	4	10
Transforming Bruce Wayne	4	10
Transforming Dick Grayson	4	10
Two Face	10	15

Batman Returns (Kenner, 1992-94)

Figures

	MNP	MIP
Aerostrike Batman	5	15
Air Attack Batman	4	15
Arctic Batman	4	15
Batman vs. Catwoman, Batman Movie Collection, 1997	5	15

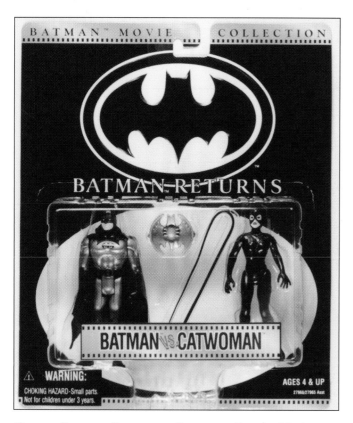

Batman Returns—Batman vs. Catwoman, Batman Movie Collection, 1997, Kenner

	MNP	MIP
Batman, 12"	25	75
Bola Strike Batman	4	15
Bruce Wayne	10	20
Catwoman	10	25
Claw Climber Batman	4	15
Crime Attack Batman	4	15
Deep Dive Batman	5	15
Glider Batman	4	15
High Wire Batman	4	15
Hydrocharge Batman	4	15
Jungle Tracker Batman	4	15
Laser Batman	4	15

Batman Returns—Catwoman, Kenner

Batman: Knight Force Ninjas—Tornado Blade Riddler, Kenner

	MNP	MIP
Night Climber Batman	4	15
Penguin	15	40
Penguin Commandos	10	25
Polar Blast Batman	4	15
Power Wing Batman	6	15
Robin	10	25
Shadow Wing Batman	4	15
Sky Winch Batman	4	15
Thunder Strike Batman	4	15
Thunder Whip Batman	5	15

Vehicles

	MNP	MIP
B.A.T.V. Vehicle	5	15
Bat Cycle	5	25
Batmobile	20	70
Bat-Signal Jet	3	15
Bruce Wayne Custom Coupe	12	50
Camo Attack Batmobile	30	100

Batman: Knight Force Ninjas (Hasbro, 1998-99)

Figures

	MNP	MIP
Batman Ally Azrael	3	10
Batman vs. The Joker	8	20
Fist Fury Batman	3	10

*Batman: Legends of the Dark Knight—
Bat Attack Batman, Kenner*

*Batman: Legends of the Dark Knight—
Batgirl, Kenner*

*Batman: Legends of the Dark Knight—
Lava Fury Batman, Kenner*

*Batman: Legends of the Dark Knight—
Lethal Impact Bane, Kenner*

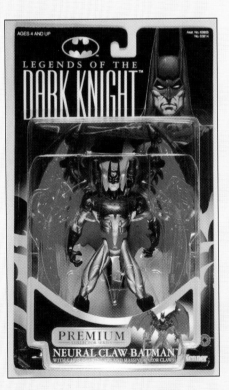

*Batman: Legends of the Dark Knight—
Neutral Claw Batman, Kenner*

*Batman: Legends of the Dark Knight—
Spline Cape Batman, Kenner*

BATMAN: LEGENDS OF THE DARK KNIGHT

Batman: Legends of the Dark Knight—Underwater Assault Batman, Kenner

	MNP	MIP
Karate Chop Batman	3	10
Multi-Blast Batman	3	10
Power Kick Batman!	3	10
Side Strike Robin	3	10
Tail Whip Killer Croc	3	10
Thunder Kick Batman	3	10
Tornado Blade Riddler	3	10

Vehicles

	MNP	MIP
Knight Force Batmobile	5	15

Batman: Legends of the Dark Knight
(Kenner, 1997-Present)
Figures

	MNP	MIP
Assault Gauntlet Batman	3	10
Bat Attack Batman	3	10
Batgirl	5	15
Batman The Dark Knight	8	25
Clayface	8	25
Dark Knight Detective Batman	8	25
Dive Claw Robin	5	15
Glacier Shield Batman	3	10
Jungle Rage Robin	3	10

	MNP	MIP
Laughing Gas Joker	5	15
Lava Fury Batman	3	8
Lethal Impact Bane	3	10
Man-Bat	5	15
Neutral Claw Batman	5	15
Panther Prowl Catwoman	5	15
Penguin	3	10
Shatter Blade Batman	5	15
Spline Cape Batman	5	15
Twister Strike Scarecrow	3	10
Underwater Assault Batman	3	8

Batman: The Animated Series
(Kenner, 1993-95)
Accessories

	MNP	MIP
Batcycle	10	20
Batmobile	10	65
Bat-Signal Jet	3	6
Hoverbat Vehicle	5	15
Joker Mobile	6	20
Robin Dragster	75	325
Street Jet	15	25
Turbo Batplane	6	20

Figures

	MNP	MIP
Anti-Freeze Batman	4	15

Batman: The Animated Series—Batcycle, Kenner

Left: Batman: The Animated Series— Anti-Freeze Batman, Kenner

Right: Batman: The Animated Series— Dick Grayson/Robin, Kenner

Left: Batman: The Animated Series— Poison Ivy, Kenner

Right: Batman: The Animated Series— Riddler, Kenner

BATMAN: THE ANIMATED SERIES

	MNP	MIP
Bane	10	20
Bruce Wayne	10	20
Catwoman	7	25
Clay Face	7	25
Combat Belt Batman	7	40
Dick Grayson/Robin	5	15
Ground Assault Batman	5	10
Infrared Batman	5	10
Jet Pack Joker (green face)	10	25
Jet Pack Joker (white face)	10	25

	MNP	MIP
Joker	7	20
Killer Croc	8	20
Knight Star Batman	4	10
Lightning Strike Batman	4	10
Manbat	7	25
Mechwing Batman	4	10
Mr. Freeze	8	15
Ninja Power Pack Batman and Robin	10	25
Ninja Robin	8	15
Parawing Robin	8	15

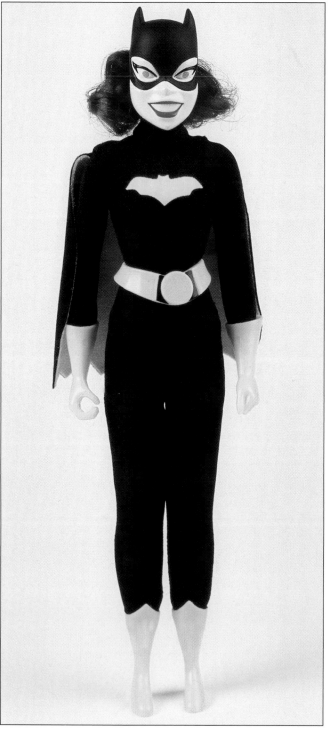

Batman: The New Batman Adventures—Batgirl, Hasbro

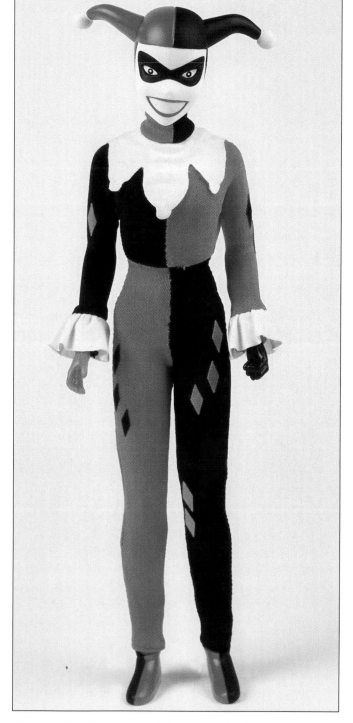

Batman: The New Batman Adventures—Harley Quinn, Hasbro

	MNP	MIP
Penguin	12	85
Phantasm	15	30
Poison Ivy	20	30
Power Vision Batman	8	15
Riddler	10	40
Scarecrow	7	25
Skydive Batman	5	10
Total Armor Batman	4	10
Turbojet Batman	7	15
Two Face	7	25
Ultimate Batman (15")	25	75

Batman: The New Batman Adventures (Hasbro, 1998-99)
12" Figures

	MNP	MIP
Batgirl	10	50
Batman	10	40

	MNP	MIP
Harley Quinn	10	40
Joker	10	40
Nightwing	10	30
Robin	10	40

Figures

	MNP	MIP
Anti-Blaze Batman	3	8
Arctic Blast Robin	3	10
Cave Climber Batman	3	8
Crime Fighter Robin	4	12
Crime Solver Nightwing	4	12
Dark Knight Detective Batman	8	20
Desert Attack Batman	3	8
Force Shield Nightwing	3	8
Glider Strike Batman	3	8
Heavy Artillery Batman	3	8
Insect-Body Mr.Freese	3	10
Jungle Tracker Batman	3	10

Batman: The New Batman Adventures—Nightwing, Hasbro

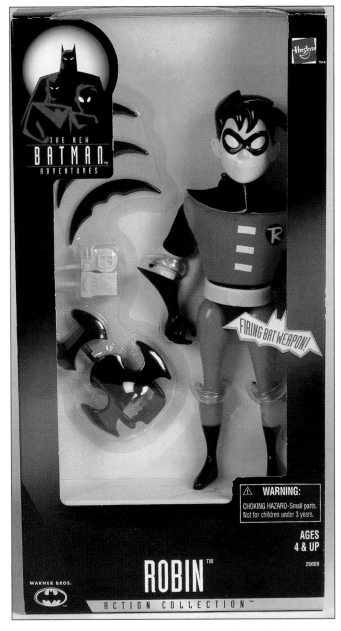

Batman: The New Batman Adventures—Robin, Hasbro

BATMAN: THE NEW ADVENTURES

*Batman: The New Batman Adventures—
Cave Climber Batman, Hasbro*

*Batman: The New Batman Adventures—
Crime Fighter Robin, Hasbro*

*Batman: The New Batman Adventures—
Crime Solver Nightwing, Hasbro*

*Batman: The New Batman Adventures—
Glider Strike Batman, Hasbro*

*Batman: The New Batman Adventures—
Insect-Body Mr. Freeze, Hasbro*

*Batman: The New Batman Adventures—
Mad Hatter, Hasbro*

Batman: The New Batman Adventures—Slalom Racer Batman, Hasbro

	MNP	MIP
Knight Glider Batman	3	8
Mad Hatter	5	15
Rumble Ready Riddler	3	8
Shatter Blade Batman	3	8
Slalom Racer Batman	3	8
Speedboat Batman	3	8
The Creeper	3	8
Undercover Bruce Wayne	3	10
Wildcard Joker	5	15

Battlestar Galactica (Mattel, 1978-79)

12" Figures

	MNP	MIP
Colonial Warrior	30	85
Cylon Centurian	30	95

Series 1, 3-3/4" Figures, 1978

	MNP	MIP
Commander Adama	15	40
Cylon Centurian	15	40
Daggit (brown)	15	30
Daggit (tan)	15	30
Imperious Leader	15	30
Ovion	12	35
Starbuck	15	40

Series 2, 3-3/4" Figures, 1979

	MNP	MIP
Baltar	30	75
Boray	30	75

Battlestar Galactica by Mattel—Left to Right: Colonial Warrior; Cylon Centurian

Battlestar Galactica—Daggit (brown), Mattel

BATTLESTAR GALACTICA

Battlestar Galactica—Ovion, Mattel

Battlestar Galactica—Lucifer, Mattel

Battlestar Galactica by Mattel—Left to Right: Imperious Leader; Commander Adams; Boray

Battlestar Galactica by Mattel—Left to Right: Imperious Leader; Daggit (tan)

Best of the West—by Marx. Left to Right: Best of the West Johnny West; Johnny West Covered Wagon with horse and harness

	MNP	MIP
Cylon Commander	55	110
Lucifer	55	110

Beavis & Butthead (Moore, 1998)
Figures

Beavis	4	10
Butt-head	4	10
Cornholio	5	12

Beetlejuice (Kenner, 1989-90)
Accessories

Creepy Cruiser	5	25
Phantom Flyer	7	15
Snake Mask	7	15
Vanishing Vault	10	20

Figures

Adam Maitland	8	20
Exploding Beetlejuice	5	10
Harry the Haunted Hunter	8	20
Old Buzzard	8	20
Otho the Obnoxious	8	20
Shipwreck Beetlejuice	5	15
Shish Kabab Beetlejuice	5	15
Showtime Beetlejuice	5	15
Spinhead Beetlejuice	5	15
Street Rat	8	20
Talking Beetlejuice, 12" tall	35	75
Teacher Creature	10	20

Best of the West (Marx, 1960s)
Figures

Bill Buck, 1967	300	475
Buckboard with Horse and Harness	100	225
Chief Cherokee, 1965	150	200
Daniel Boone, 1965	100	200
Davy Crockett	175	250
Fighting Eagle, 1967	150	225
General Custer, 1965	100	200
Geronimo and Pinto	150	200
Geronimo, 1967	100	150
Jamie West, 1967	50	100
Jane West, 1966	60	120
Janice West, 1967	50	100

Best of the West—Fighting Eagle, Marx

BEST OF THE WEST

Best of the West—Daniel Boone, Marx

Best of the West—Sheriff Garrett, Marx

	MNP	MIP
Jay West, 1967	50	100
Johnny West Covered Wagon, with horse and harness	100	225
Johnny West with Comanche	80	125
Johnny West, 1965	75	150
Josie West, 1967	50	100
Pancho Horse, for 9" figures, 1968	50	75
Princess Wildflower, 1974	100	175
Sam Cobra, 1972	100	200
Sheriff Garrett, 1973	150	200
Thunderbolt Horse	75	125
Zeb Zachary, 1967	200	300

Big Jim (Mattel, 1973-76)
Accessories

Baja Beast	10	20
Boat and Buggy Set	10	25

Best of the West—Pancho Horse, Marx

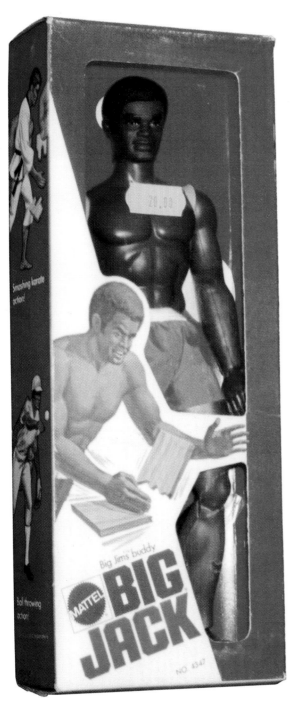

Big Jim—Big Jack, Mattel

	MNP	MIP
Camping Tent	5	15
Camping Tent	5	20
Devil River Trip	15	30
Jungle Truck	15	30
Motorcross Honda	20	50
Rescue Rig	20	50
Rugged Rider	15	30
Sky Commander	20	40
Sport Camper	20	50

Figures

Big Jack	7	25
Big Jeff	7	25
Big Josh	7	25
Dr. Steel	10	30

Big Jim's P.A.C.K. (Mattel, 1976-77)
Accessories

	MNP	MIP
Beast	45	100
BlitzRig	60	120
Howler	30	60
LazerVette	45	100

Figures

Big Jim, window box	40	90
Dr. Steel, window box	30	75
Warpath, widow box	35	80
Whip, The, window box	35	80

Bill & Ted's Excellent Adventure (Kenner, 1991)
Accessories

Phone Booth	10	20
Wild Stallyns Speaker and Tape	7	20

Figures

Abe Lincoln	15	30
Bill	10	20
Bill & Ted Jam Session, two pack	20	40
Billy The Kid	10	25
Genghis Khan	10	25
Grim Reaper	25	50
Rufus	10	25
Ted	10	20

Bionic Six (LJN, 1986)
Figures

Bunji	4	12
Chopper	4	12
Dr. Scarab	4	12
Eric	4	12
FLUFFI	8	20
Glove	4	12
Helen	4	12
J.D.	4	12
Jack	4	12
Klunk	4	12
Madame O	4	12
Mechanic	4	12
Meg	4	12

Bionic Woman (Kenner, 1976-77)
12" Figures

Fembot	70	160
Jamie Sommers	40	100
Jamie Sommers with purse	50	125

Accessories

Beauty Salon	30	70
Carriage House	55	140
Classroom	100	200
Dome House	55	140
Sports Car	40	100

Black Hole (Mego, 1979-80)
12" Figures

Captain Holland	40	75
Dr. Alex Durant	40	75
Dr. Hans Reinhardt	40	75
Harry Booth	45	85
Kate McCrae	50	95

BLACK HOLE

Black Hole by Mego—Left to Right: Maximillian; Sentry Robot; V.I.N.cent

Black Hole by Mego—Left to right: Kate McCrae; Dr. Alex Durant; Dr. Hans Reinhardt

	MNP	MIP
Pizer	40	75

3-3/4" Figures

Captain Holland, 1979	5	25
Dr. Alex Durant, 1979	5	25
Dr. Hans Reinhardt, 1979	5	25
Harry Booth, 1979	5	25
Humanoid, 1980	200	750
Kate McCrae, 1979	5	25
Maximillian, 1979	20	75
Old B.O.B., 1980	60	200
Pizer, 1979	10	50
S.T.A.R., 1980	85	350
Sentry Robot, 1980	15	75
V.I.N.cent., 1979	15	70

Blackstar (Galoob, 1984)

Accessories

Ice Castle	35	75
Triton	25	50
Warlock	25	50

Figures

Blackstar	15	40
Blackstar with Laser Light	10	35
Devil Knight with Laser Light	25	45
Gargo	10	35
Gargo with Laser Light	10	35
Kadray	10	35
Kadray with Laser Light	10	35

	MNP	MIP
Klone with Laser Light	15	45
Lava Loc with Laser Light	15	45
Mara	30	60
Meuton	10	35
Neptul	25	50
Overlord	15	45
Overlord with Laser Light	15	40
Palace Guard	15	40
Palace Guard with Laser Light	10	35
Togo	10	35
Togo with Laser Light	10	35
Vizir with Laser Light	10	35
White Knight	10	35

Blade (Toy Biz, 1998)

6" Figures

Blade	10	30
Deacon Frost	10	30
Vampire Blade	8	20
Whistler	8	20

Blade Vampire Hunter (Toy Biz, 1998)

Figures

Blade	2	8
Deacon Frost	2	8
Vampire Blade	2	8
Whistker	2	8

Bob & Doug McKenzie (McFarlane, 2000)

Figures

Bob McKenzie with half of Great White North stage set	5	15
Doug McKenzie with half of Great White North stage set	5	15

Bonanza (American Character, 1966)

Accessoires

4 in 1 Wagon	40	100
Ben's Palomino	35	75
Hoss' Stallion	35	75
Little Joe's Pinto	35	75

Figures

Ben	50	150
Ben with Palomino	80	225
Hoss	70	150
Hoss with Stallion	70	200
Little Joe	50	150
Little Joe with Pinto	70	200
Outlaw	50	150

BraveStarr (Mattel, 1996)

Figures

BraveStarr and Thirty/Thirty, two-pack	15	50
Col. Borobot	7	25
Deputy Fuzz	7	25
Handle Bar	7	25
Laser-Fire BraveStarr	7	25
Laser-Fire Tex Hex	10	30
Marshal BraveStarr	7	25
Outlaw Skuzz	7	25
Sand Storm	7	25
Skull Walker	5	20
Tex Hex	10	30
Thunder Stick	10	30

Left: Blade—Blade, Toy Biz

Right: Blade— Deacon Frost, Toy Biz

Left: Blade— Whistler, Toy Biz

Right: Blade— Vampire Blade, Toy Biz

BLADE

Bob McKenzie with half of Great White North stage set, McFarlane Toys

Doug McKenzie with half of Great White North stage set, McFarlane Toys

Bruce Lee
(Sideshow Toys, 1999-Present)
8" Figures

	MNP	MIP
Bruce Lee, bare chested	7	15
Bruce Lee, traditional outfit	7	15

Buck Rogers (Mego, 1979)
12" Figures

	MNP	MIP
Buck Rogers	30	90
Doctor Huer	30	80
Draco	30	80
Draconian Guard	30	80
Killer Kane	30	80
Tiger Man	30	125
Twiki	30	60

3-3/4" Figures

	MNP	MIP
Ardella	6	15
Buck Rogers	35	60
Doctor Huer	6	20
Draco	6	20
Draconian Guard	10	20
Killer Kane	6	15
Tiger Man	10	25

	MNP	MIP
Twiki	20	45
Wilma Deering	12	25

3-3/4" Play Sets

	MNP	MIP
Star Fighter Command Center	35	100

3-3/4" Vehicles

	MNP	MIP
Draconian Marauder	25	50
Land Rover	20	40
Laserscope Fighter	20	40
Star Fighter	25	50
Star Searcher	30	60

Buffy the Vampire Slayer
(Diamond Select, 1999)
Figures

	MNP	MIP
Angel	3	15
Buffy	3	15
Willow	3	15

Buffy the Vampire Slayer
(Moore Action Collectibles, 1999)
Figures

	MNP	MIP
Angel	3	15

Buck Rogers—Draconian Guard, Mego

	MNP	MIP
Buffy	3	15
Master, The	3	15
Willow	3	15

Bug's Life, A (Mattel, 1998)
Figures

Enemy Hopper	2	5
Enemy Molt	2	5
Francis & Slim	2	5
Hang Glider Flik	2	5
Inventor Flik	2	5
Princess Atta	2	5
Tuck & Roll	2	5
Warrior Flik	2	5

Butch and Sundance: The Early Days (Kenner, 1979)
Accessories and Vehicles

Bluff, Butch's horse	20	50
Mint Wagon	25	60
Saloon Play Set	45	110
Spurs, Sundance's horse	20	50

Figures

Butch Cassidy	12	30
Marshall LeFors	12	30
O.C. Hanks	12	30
Sheriff Bledsoe	12	30
Sundance Kid	12	30

Cadillacs and Dinosaurs (Tyco, 1994)
Figures

	MNP	MIP
Hammer Terhune	2	5
Hannah Dundee	4	10
Hermes	2	5
Jack Cadillac Tenrec	2	5
Jungle Fighting Jack Tenrec	3	8
Kentrosaurus	5	15
Mustapha Cairo	2	5
Snake Eyes	5	15
Vice Terhune	3	8
Zeke	2	5

Captain & Tennille (Mego, 1970s)
Figures

Daryl Dragon (Captain)	40	75
Toni Tennille	40	75

Captain Action (Ideal, 1966-68)
12" Figures

Captain Action, parachute offer on box, 1967	275	700
Captain Action, photo box, 1966	300	900
Captain Action, with blue-shirted Lone Ranger on box, 1966	200	500
Captain Action, with red-shirted Lone Ranger on box, 1966	200	500
Dr. Evil, 1967	300	1200

Captain & Tennille—Toni Tennille, Mego

Captain Action with parachute offer on box, 1967, Ideal

Captain Action—Dr. Evil, 1967, Ideal

Captain Action—Robin, 1967, Ideal

Captain Action with red-shirted Lone Ranger on box, 1966, Ideal

9" Figures

	MNP	MIP
Action Boy, 1967	275	900
Action Boy, with space suit, 1968	350	1100

Accessories

	MNP	MIP
Action Cave Carrying Case, vinyl, 1967	400	700
Directional Communicator Set, 1966	110	300
Dr. Evil Sanctuary, 1967	2500	3500
Jet Mortar, 1966	110	300
Parachute Pack, 1966	100	225
Power Pack, 1966	125	250
Quick Change Chamber, Cardboard, Sears Exclusive, 1967	750	900

Captain Action—Aquaman, 1966, Ideal

Captain Action—Batman, 1966, Ideal

Captain Action—Phantom, 1966, Ideal

Captain Action—Steve Canyon, 1966, Ideal

CAPTAIN ACTION

Captain Action—Green Hornet, 1967, Ideal

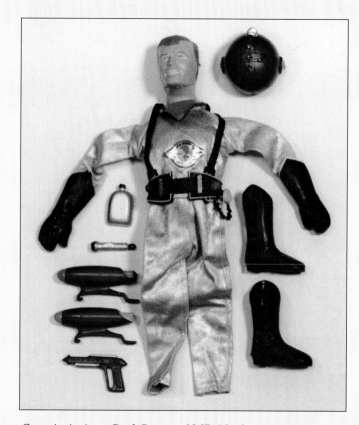

Captain Action—Buck Rogers, 1967, Ideal

Captain Action by Playing Mantis—Left to Right: Dr. Evil; Captain Action. Photo Courtesy Playing Mantis

	MNP	MIP
Silver Streak Amphibian, 1967	800	1200
Silver Streak Garage (with Silver Streak Vehicle, Sears Exclusive)	1500	2000
Survival Kit, twenty pieces, 1967	125	275
Vinyl Headquarters Carrying Case, Sears Exclusive, 1967	200	500
Weapons Arsenal, ten pieces, 1966	110	225

Action Boy Costumes

	MNP	MIP
Aqualad, 1967	300	900
Robin, 1967	300	1200
Superboy, 1967	300	1000

Captain Action Costumes

	MNP	MIP
Aquaman, 1966	160	600
Aquaman, with flasher ring, 1967	180	950
Batman, 1966	225	700

	MNP	MIP
Batman, with flasher ring, 1967	250	1100
Buck Rogers, with flasher ring, 1967	450	2700
Captain America, 1966	220	900
Captain America, with flasher ring, 1967	225	1200
Flash Gordon, 1966	200	600
Flash Gordon, with flasher ring, 1967	225	800
Green Hornet, with flasher ring, 1967	2000	7500
Lone Ranger, blue shirt, with flasher ring, 1967	500	1000
Lone Ranger, red shirt, 1966	200	700
Phantom, 1966	200	750
Phantom, with flasher ring, 1967	250	900
Sergeant Fury, 1966	200	800
Spider-Man, with flasher ring, 1967	550	8000
Steve Canyon, 1966	200	700
Steve Canyon, with flasher ring, 1967	225	850
Superman, 1966	200	700

 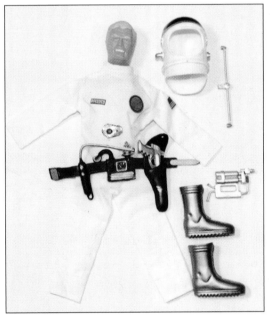

Captain Action by Ideal— Left to Right: Captain America; Flash Gordon

 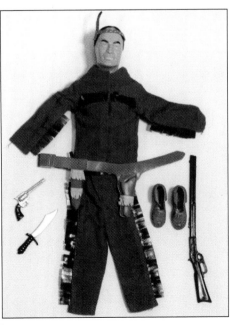

Captain Action by Ideal— Left to Right: Lone Ranger, red shirt; Tonto

CAPTAIN ACTION

Captain Action by Playing Mantis—Left to right: Lone Ranger; Tonto. Photo courtesy Playing Mantis

CAPTAIN ACTION

	MNP	MIP
Superman, with flasher ring, 1967	225	1100
Tonto, with flasher ring, 1967	375	1100

Captain Action (Playing Mantis, 1998-99)
Figures and Costumes

	MNP	MIP
Captain Action	15	20
Dr. Evil	15	20
Flash Gordon	15	20
Green Hornet	15	25
Kato	15	20
Lone Ranger	15	25
Ming the Merciless	15	35
Tonto	15	25

Captain Power and the Soldiers of the Future (Mattel, 1987-88)
Accessories

	MNP	MIP
Dread Stalker	8	15
Interlocker	10	20
Magna Cycle	12	25
Phantom Striker	12	25
Power Base	25	50
Power Jet XT-7	20	50
Power on Energizer with figure	5	15
Trans-Field Base Station	15	30
Trans-Field Communication Station	10	20

Series I

	MNP	MIP
Blastarr Ground Guardian	5	15
Captain Power	10	20
Lord Dread	5	15
Lt. Tank Ellis	10	20
Major Hawk Masterson	5	15

	MNP	MIP
Soaron Sky Sentry	5	15

Series II

	MNP	MIP
Col. Stingray Johnson	12	25
Cpl. Pilot Chase	10	20
Dread Commander	45	90
Dread Trooper	45	90
Sgt. Scout Baker	10	20
Tritor	15	35

Captain Scarlett (Pedigree, 1967)
12" Figure

	MNP	MIP
Captain Scarlet	150	300

Captain Scarlett (Vivid Imaginations, 1993-94)
12" Figures

	MNP	MIP
Captain Black	25	50
Captain Scarlett	25	50

3-3/4" Figures

	MNP	MIP
Captain Black	3	8
Captain Blue	3	8
Captain Scarlett	4	10
Colonel White	3	8
Destiny Angel	5	12
Lieutenant Green	3	8

Chaos! (Moore Action Collectibles, 1997-present)
Series I, 12" Figures

	MNP	MIP
Lady Death	10	30
Royal Lady Death	10	30

Charlie's Angels—Sabrina (Kate Jackson), Hasbro

Series I

	MNP	MIP
Evil Earnie	3	12
Evil Ernie, glow in the dark	8	25
Lady Death	3	12
Lady Death, chrome	10	30
Lady death, glow in the dark	10	30
Lady Demon	3	12
Lady Demon, glow in the dark	10	30
Purgatori	3	12
Purgatori, metallic	8	25

Series II

Cremator	8	20
Cremator	3	12
Lady Death in Battle Armor	3	12
Lady Death, Azure	10	30
Lady Death, bronze	10	30

Charlie's Angels (Hasbro, 1977)

8-1/2" Figures

Jill—Farrah Fawcett	50	100
Kelly—Jaclyn Smith	40	75
Kris—Cheryl Ladd	40	75
Sabrina—Kate Jackson	40	75
Sabrina, Kris and Kelly Gift Set	75	200

CHiPs (Mego, 1979)

3-3/4" Figures and Accessories

Jimmy Squeaks	5	15
Jon	10	20
Launcher with Motorcycle	25	50
Motorcycle, boxed	5	30
Ponch	8	20

Comic Heroine Posin' Dolls (Super Queens) by Ideal—Left to Right: Supergirl; Batgirl; Mera; Wonder Woman

Comic Heroine Posin' Dolls (Super Queens)—Batgirl, Ideal

	MNP	MIP
Sarge	10	30
Wheels Willie	5	15

8" Figures and Accessories

	MNP	MIP
Jon	20	50
Motorcycle	30	75
Ponch	15	40
Sarge	25	50

Chuck Norris (Kenner, 1986-87)
6" Figures

	MNP	MIP
Chuck Norris Battle Gear	8	15
Chuck Norris Kung Fu Training	6	12
Chuck Norris Undercover Agent	8	15

	MNP	MIP
Kimo	6	12
Ninja Master	6	12
Ninja Serpent	6	12
Ninja Warrior	6	12
Super Ninja	6	12
Tabe	6	12

Clash of The Titans (Mattel, 1980)
Figures

	MNP	MIP
Calibos	20	50
Charon	30	75
Kraken	75	250
Pegasus	25	75
Perseus	20	50
Perseus and Pegasus, two-pack	50	105
Thallo	20	50

Comic Action Heroes (Mego, 1975)
3-3/4" Figures

	MNP	MIP
Aquaman	30	75
Batman	20	75
Captain America	20	75
Green Goblin	22	125
Hulk	20	50
Joker	20	75
Penguin	20	75
Robin	20	65
Shazam	20	75
Spider-Man	20	75
Superman	20	65
Wonder Woman	20	65

Accessories

	MNP	MIP
Collapsing Tower (with Invisible Plane & Wonder Woman)	100	200
Exploding Bridge with Batmobile	100	200
Fortress of Solitude with Superman	100	200
Mangler	125	300

Comic Heroine Posin' Dolls (Ideal, 1967)
12" Boxed Figures

	MNP	MIP
Batgirl, 1967	1000	5500
Mera, 1967	600	4500
Supergirl, 1967	600	4500
Wonder Woman, 1967	600	4500

Commander Power (Mego, 1975)
Figure with Vehicle

	MNP	MIP
Commander Power with Lightning Cycle	20	40

Commando (Diamond, 1985)
18" Figures

	MNP	MIP
Arnold Schwarzenegger, black box	80	200
Arnold Schwarzenegger, red box	80	300

3-3/4" Figures

	MNP	MIP
Blaster	10	25
Chopper	10	25
Lead Head	10	25
Matrix	40	150
Psycho	10	25
Sawbones	10	25
Spex	10	25
Stalker	10	25

6" Figures

	MNP	MIP
Blaster	15	40
Chopper	15	40
Lead Head	15	40
Matrix	35	90
Pyscho	15	40
Sawbones	15	40
Spex	15	40
Stalker	15	40

Conan (Hasbro, 1994)

Asst. I

	MNP	MIP
Conan the Adventurer with Star Metal Slash	10	20
Conan the Warrior with Slashing Battle Action	10	20
Wrath-Amon with Serpent Slash	10	20
Zulu with Dart Firing Crossbow	10	20

Asst. II

	MNP	MIP
Conan the Exlporer with Two-fisted Chopping Action	10	20
Greywolf with Cyclone Power Punch	10	35
Ninja Conan with Katana Chop	10	20
Skulkur with Zombie Tornado Slash	10	20

Conan (Remco, 1984)

Figures

	MNP	MIP
Conan the Warrior	15	40
Devourer of Souls	15	40
Jewel Man	15	40
Throth Amon	15	40

Coneheads (Playmates, 1995)

Figures

	MNP	MIP
Agent Seedling	2	4

	MNP	MIP
Beldar in flight uniform	2	4
Beldar in street clothes	2	4
Connie	2	4
Prymaat in flight uniform	2	4
Prymaat in street clothes	2	4

Congo (Kenner, 1995)

Figures

	MNP	MIP
Amy	3	5
Blastface	3	5
Bonecrucher, Deluxe	4	8
Kahega	2	4
Karen Ross	2	4
Mangler	2	4
Monroe	2	4
Monroe, Deluxe	4	8
Peter Elliot	2	4

Vehicles

	MNP	MIP
Net trap Vehicle	4	8
Trail Hacker Vehicle	4	8

Danger Girl (McFarlane, 1999)

Figures

	MNP	MIP
Abbey Chase	8	20
Major Maxim	3	8
Natalia Kassle	8	20
Sydney Savage	8	20

DC Comics Super Heroes (Toy Biz, 1989)

Figures

	MNP	MIP
Aquaman	10	15
Batman	5	10

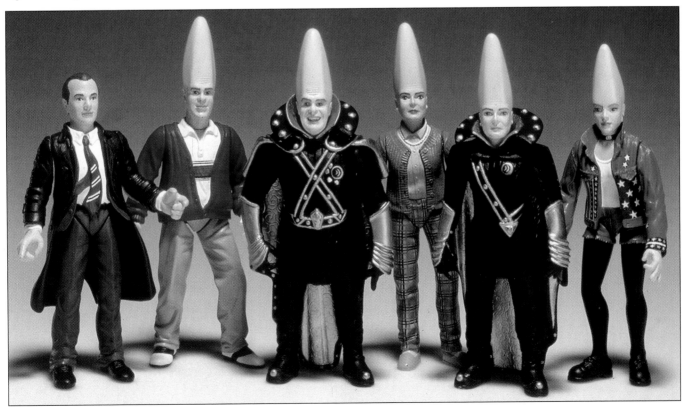

Coneheads by Playmates—Left to Right: Coneheads Agent Seedling; Beldar in street clothes; Beldar in flight uniform; Prymaat in street clothes; Prymaat in flight uniform; Connie

Danger Girl—Abbey Chase, McFarlane Toys

Danger Girl—Major Maxim, McFarlane Toys

Danger Girl—Natalia Kassle, McFarlane Toys

Danger Girl—Sydney Savage, McFarlane Toys

	MNP	MIP
Bob The Goon	10	20
Flash	7	15
Flash II with Turbo Platform	10	15
Green Lantern	15	30
Hawkman	15	30
Joker, no forehead curl	5	15
Joker, with forehead curl	10	15
Lex Luthor	5	10
Mr. Freeze	8	15
Penguin, long missile	15	25

	MNP	MIP
Penguin, short missile	15	30
Penguin, umbrella-firing	5	15
Riddler	7	15
Superman	20	50
Two Face	15	20
Wonder Woman	8	15

Defenders of the Earth (Galoob, 1985)
Figures

	MNP	MIP
Flash Gordon	8	25
Garaz	8	25
Lothar	8	25
Mandrake	8	25
Ming	8	20
Phantom, The	10	30

Vehicles

	MNP	MIP
Claw Copter	8	25

*DC Comics Super Heroes by Toy Biz—Left to Right:
Aquaman; Hawkman*

*DC Comics Super Heroes by Toy Biz—Top row, left to right:
Riddler; Mr. Freeze. Bottom row: Lex Luthor*

Dick Tracy—Breathless Mahoney, Playmates

Dick Tracy—The Blank, Playmates

Dick Tracy—Flattop, Playmates

	MNP	MIP
Flash Swordship 8		25
Garax Swordship 8		25
Phantom Skull Copter 10		35

Dick Tracy (Playmates, 1990)

Figures, large

	MNP	MIP
Breathless Mahoney 25		50
Dick Tracy 25		50

Figures, small

	MNP	MIP
Al "Big Boy" Caprice 8		15
Blank, The 50		150
Brow, The 6		12
Dick Tracy 8		15
Flattop 6		12
Influence 6		12
Itchy 8		15
Lips Manlis 6		12
Mumbles 6		12
Pruneface 6		12
Rodent, The 8		15
Sam Catchem 6		12
Shoulders 6		12
Steve the Tramp 6		12

Die-Cast Super Heroes (Mego, 1979)

6" Figures

	MNP	MIP
Batman 30		125
Hulk 25		75
Spider-Man 30		125
Superman 30		95

Doctor Who (Dapol, 1988-95)

Figures

	MNP	MIP
Ace with bat and pack 4		8
Cyberman 4		8
Dalek, black and gold, with friction drive 5		10
Dalek, black and silver, with friction drive 5		10
Dalek, gold, with friction drive 5		10
Dalek, gray and black, with friction drive 5		10

Doctor Who—K-9, Denys Fisher. Photo Courtesy Corey LeChat

Doctor Who—Cyberman, Denys Fisher. Photo Courtesy Corey LeChat

Doctor Who (4th) in an Italian Box, Denys Fisher. Photo Courtesy Corey LeChat

Doctor Who—Giant Robot, Denys Fisher. Photo Courtesy Corey LeChat

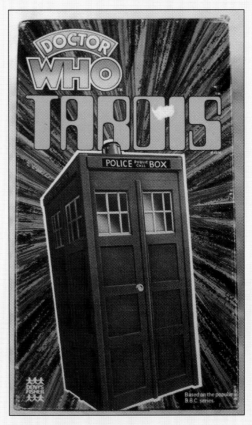

Doctor Who—Leela, Denys Fisher. Photo Courtesy Corey LeChat

DOCTOR WHO

Doctor Who— Dalek, Talking, Palitoy. Photo Courtesy Corey LeChat

Doctor Who—K-9, Talking, Palitoy. Photo Courtesy Corey LeChat

DOCTOR WHO

Doctor Who—Leela, Denys Fisher. Photo Courtesy Corey LeChat

	MNP	MIP
Dalek, gray and black, with friction drive	5	10
Dalek, red and black, with friction drive	5	10
Dalek, red and gold, with friction drive	5	10
Dalek, white and gold, with friction drive	5	10
Doctor Who (3rd), Jon Pertwee	5	10
Doctor Who (4th), Tom Baker	4	8
Doctor Who (7th) with gray coat	5	10
Doctor Who (7th), The, with brown coat	5	10
Ice Warrior	4	8
K9 with motor action	5	10
Master, The	4	8
Mel, blue shirt	4	8
Mel, pink shirt	4	8
Melkur	5	10
Sea Devil with cloth outfit	5	10
Silurian	4	8
Silurian, armored	4	8
Sontaran	5	10
Sontaran Captain with helmet	5	10
Tetrap	5	10
Time Lords, brown	5	10
Time Lords, burgundy	5	10
Time Lords, gray	5	10
Time Lords, off-white	5	10

Play Sets

	MNP	MIP
Doctor Who (3rd) Play Set	20	55

Vehicles and Accessories

	MNP	MIP
Dalek Play Set	18	35
Tardis with flashing light	12	25

Doctor Who
(Denys Fisher, 1976)
Figures

	MNP	MIP
Cyberman	200	400
Dalek	150	325
Doctor Who (4th)	100	225
Giant Robot	165	375
K-9	150	300
Leela	200	400

Vehicles

	MNP	MIP
Tardis	150	300

Doctor Who (Palitoy, 1976)
Figures

	MNP	MIP
Dalek, Talking	250	475
K-9, Talking	150	300

Dukes of Hazzard (Mego, 1981-82)
3-3/4" Carded Figures

	MNP	MIP
Bo Duke	8	15
Boss Hogg	8	20
Cletus	15	30
Cooter	15	30
Coy Duke	15	30
Daisy Duke	12	25
Luke Duke	8	20
Rosco Coltrane	15	30
Uncle Jesse	15	30
Vance Duke	15	30

3-3/4" Figures with Vehicles

	MNP	MIP
Daisy Jeep with Daisy, 1981, boxed	25	50
General Lee Car with Bo and Luke, 1981, boxed	25	50

8" Carded Figures

	MNP	MIP
Bo Duke	15	30
Boss Hogg	20	40
Coy Duke (card says Bo)	25	50
Daisy Duke	25	50
Luke Duke	15	30
Vance Duke (card says Luke)	25	50

Dune (LJN, 1984)
Figures

	MNP	MIP
Baron Harkonnen	20	40
Feyd	20	40
Paul Atreides	20	40
Rabban	20	40
Sardauker Warrior	25	50
Stilgar the Freman	20	40

Vehicles

	MNP	MIP
Sand Crawler	20	40
Sand tracker	20	40
Sandworm	25	50
Spice Scout	25	50

Dungeons & Dragons (LJN, 1983-84)
Monsters

	MNP	MIP
Dragonne	20	40
Hook Horror	20	40
Timat	90	200

Mounts

	MNP	MIP
Bronze Dragon	20	40
Destrier	15	30
Nightmare	15	30

Play Sets

	MNP	MIP
Fortress of Fangs	65	130

Series I, 3-3/4" Figures, 1983

	MNP	MIP
Elkhorn	15	30
Kelek	15	30
Melf	15	35
Mercion	15	35

	MNP	MIP
Peralay	15	30
Ringlerun	15	30
Strongheart	15	30
Warduke	15	30
Zarak	15	30

Series I, 5" Figures, 1983

	MNP	MIP
Northlord	20	45
Ogre King	20	45
Young Male Titan	15	30

Series II, 3-3/4" Figures, 1984

	MNP	MIP
Bowmarc	40	90
Deeth	55	120
Drex	55	120
Elkhorn	20	50
Grimsword	30	70
Hawkler	50	100
Strongheart	20	45
Warduke	20	45
Zarak	20	45
Zorgar	60	120

Series II, 5" Figures, 1984

	MNP	MIP
Mandoom	60	120
Mettaflame	60	120
Northland	50	100
Ogre King	65	130
Young Male Titan	50	100

Dungeons & Dragons—Warduke, LJN

DUNGEONS & DRAGONS

Dungeons & Dragons—Zarak, LJN

Dungeons & Dragons—Warduke, LJN

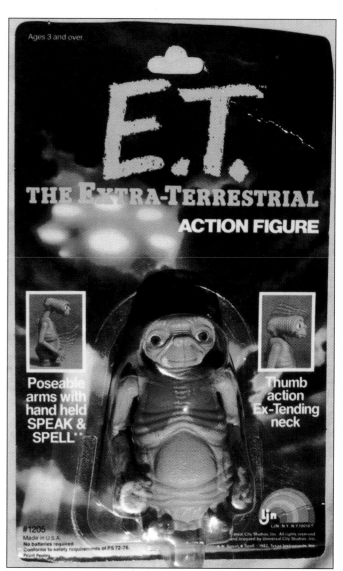

E.T. with Speak and Spell

E.T. the Extra-Terrestrial (LJN, 1982-83)
Figures

	MNP	MIP
E.T and Elliot with bike	10	20
E.T. with dress and hat	6	12
E.T. with robe	6	12
E.T. with Speak and Spell	6	12
E.T., talking	15	35
E.T., walking	12	25

Earthworm Jim (Playmates, 1995)
Figures

Bob	5	12
Earthworm Jim with Battle Damage	5	8
Earthworm Jim with Snott	5	8
Hench Rat with Evil Cat	5	10
Monstrous Peter Puppy	5	8
Peter Puppy	5	8
Pocket Rocket	5	8
Princess What's-Her-Name	7	12
Psycrow with Major Mucus	4	8

Earthworm Jim—Pocket Rocket, Playmates

Earthworm Jim—Psycrow, Playmates

*Earthworm Jim by Playmate Toys—Left to Right: Earthworm
Jim with Battle Damage; Princess What's-Her-Name;
Earthworm Jim with Snott. Photo Courtesy Playmates*

Emergency (LJN, 1973)
Figures

	MNP	MIP
John	35	100
Roy	35	100

Vehicles

Rescue Truck	35	100

Evel Knievel (Ideal, 1973-74)
Figures

Evel Knievel, blue suit	20	50
Evel Knievel, red suit	20	50
Evel Knievel, white suit	20	50
Robby Knievel	25	60

Vehicles and Accessories

Arctic Explorer set	35	75

*Evel Knievel by Ideal—Left to Right: Robby Knievel,
Evel Knievel with blue suit*

	MNP	MIP
Chopper	35	75
Evel Knievel Canyon Stunt Cycle	40	80
Evel Knievel Dragster	50	110
Evel Knievel Stunt and Crash Car	45	100
Evel Knievel Stunt Cycle	35	75
Explorer Set	20	40
Racing Set	20	40
Rescue Set	20	40
Road and Trail Set	50	125
Scramble Van	30	75
Skull Canyon Play Set	50	125
Stunt Stadium	40	100
Tail Bike	35	60

ExoSquad (Playmates, 1993-95)

Exoconverting Series

	MNP	MIP
J.T. Marsh with Exoconverting E-frame	8	15

ExoWalking Series

	MNP	MIP
Marsala with ExoWalking E-frame	8	15

General Purpose E-Frames with Figure, Original Series

	MNP	MIP
Alec DeLeon with Field Communications	8	15
J.T. Marsh with Aerial Attack E-Frame	8	15
Pheaton with Command E-Frame	8	15
Typhonus with High Speed Stealth E-Frame	8	15

General Purpose E-Frames with Figure, Secondary Series

	MNP	MIP
Draconis with Interrogator E-frame	8	15
Jinx Madison with Fire Warrior E-frame	8	15
Jonas Simbacca with Pirate Captain E-frame	8	15
Nara Burns with Reconnaissance E-frame	8	15
Peter Tanaka with Samurai E-frame	8	15
Rita Torres with Field Sergeant E-frame	8	15
Sean Napier with police Enforcer E-frame	8	15
Wolf Bronski with Ground Assault E-frame	8	15

General Purpose E-Frames with Figure, Third Series

	MNP	MIP
J.T. Marsh with Gridiron Command E-frame	8	15
Kaz Takagi with Gorilla E-frame	8	15
Marsala with Sub-Sonic Scout E-frame	8	15
Wolf Bronski with Medieval Knight E-frames	8	15

Jumptroops

	MNP	MIP
Captain Avery Butler	4	8

	MNP	MIP
Gunnery Sergeant Ramon Longfeather	4	8
Lance Corporal Vince Pelligrino	4	8
Lieutenant Colleen O'Reilly	4	8

Light Attack E-frames

	MNP	MIP
Livanus with Troop Transport E-frame	12	25
Maggie Weston with Field Repair E-frame	12	25
Marsala with Rapid Assault E-frame	12	25
Shiva with Amphibious Assault E-frame	12	25

Mini Exo-Command Battle Sets

	MNP	MIP
Alec DeLeon and Phaeton with Vesta Space Port Battleset	4	8
J.T. Marsh and Typhonus with Resolute II Hangar Battleset	4	8
Phaeton and J.T. Marsh with Olympus Mons Command Ship Bridge Battleset	4	8

Neo warriors

	MNP	MIP
Neo Cat	4	8
Neo Lord	4	8

Robotech Series, 3" figures

	MNP	MIP
Excaliber	2	4
Gladiator	2	4
RaidarX	2	4
Spartan	2	4

Robotech Series, 7" figures

	MNP	MIP
Excaliber MK VI	5	10
Gladiator Destroid	5	10

Extreme Ghostbusters—Eduardo, Trendmasters

Extreme Ghostbusters—Eduardo, Trendmasters

*Extreme Ghostbusters—Deluxe Edition
Eduardo, Trendmasters*

*Extreme Ghostbusters—Deluxe Edition
Kylie, Trendmasters*

*Extreme Ghostbusters—Deluxe Edition
Egon, Trendmasters*

*Extreme Ghostbusters—House Ghost,
Trendmasters*

*Extreme Ghostbusters—Egon,
Trendmasters*

*Extreme Ghostbusters—Mouth Critter,
Trendmasters*

EXTREME GHOSTBUSTERS

Extreme Ghostbusters—Deluxe Edition Roland,
Trendmasters

Extreme Ghostbusters—Roland, Trendmasters

Extreme Ghostbusters—Slimer, Trendmasters

Extreme Ghostbusters—Sam Hain,
Trendmasters

	MNP	MIP
RaidarX	5	10
Spartan Destroid	5	10
Zentraedi Power Armor Botoru Battalion	5	10
Zentraedi Power Armor Quadrono Battalion	5	10

Robotech Series, Vehicles

	MNP	MIP
VeriTech Hover Tank	12	24
VF-IS Veritech Fighter	8	15

Space Series

	MNP	MIP
Exocarrier Resolute II with Mini E-frames	12	25
Kaz Takagi with ExoFighter Space E-frame	12	25
Thrax with NeoFighter Space E-frame	12	25

Special Mission E-frames

	MNP	MIP
Alec DeLeon with All-Terrain Special Mission E-frame	8	15
J.T. Marsh with Deep Space Special Mission E-frame	8	15
Typhonus with Deep Submergence Special Mission E-frame	8	15
Wolf Ronski with Subterranean Special Mission E-frame	8	15

Extreme Ghostbusters (Trendmasters, 1997-98)

Figures

	MNP	MIP
Eduardo	2	4
Eduardo, Deluxe Edition	2	4
Egon	2	4
Egon, Deluxe Edition	2	4
House Ghost	2	4
Kylie	2	4
Kylie, Deluxe Edition	2	4

Fantastic Four––Invisible Woman, Toy Biz

Fantastic Four—Mr. Fantastic, Toy Biz

	MNP	MIP
Mouth Critter	2	4
Roland	2	4
Roland, Deluxe Edition	2	4
Sam Hain	2	4
Slimer	2	4

Vehicles and Accessories

	MNP	MIP
Ecto 1	12	24
Eduardo with Motorcycle	4	8
Roland and Gyro-Copter	4	8

Fantastic Four (Toy Biz, 1995)

10" Boxed Figures

	MNP	MIP
Dr. Doom	6	12
Human Torch	6	12
Silver Surfer	10	15

5" Figures

	MNP	MIP
Annihilus	3	10
Attuma	3	10
Black Bolt	3	10
Blastaar	3	10
Dr. Doom	3	10
Dragon Man	3	10
Firelord	3	10

FANTASTIC FOUR

Fantastic Four—The Thing, Toy Biz

	MNP	MIP
Gorgon	3	10
Human Torch	3	10
Invisible Woman	10	20
Mole Man	5	10
Mr. Fantastic	3	10
Namor the Sub-Mariner	3	10
Silver Surfer	6	10
Super Skrull	3	10
Terrax	3	10
Thanos	3	10
Thing	5	10
Thing II	5	10
Triton	3	10

Electronic 14" Figures

	MNP	MIP
Galactus	10	40
Talking Thing	10	20

Vehicles

	MNP	MIP
Fantasticar	7	15
Mr. Fantastic Sky Shuttle	7	15
The Thing's Sky Cycle	7	15

Flash Gordon (Mego, 1976)

9" Figures

	MNP	MIP
Dale Arden	35	85
Dr. Zarkow	55	110
Flash Gordon	55	110
Ming	30	85

Play Sets

	MNP	MIP
Flash Gordon Play Set	55	125

Flintstones (Mattel, 1994)

Figures

	MNP	MIP
Betty and Bamm Bamm	4	8
Big Shot Fred	3	6
Evil Cliff Vandercave	4	8
Filling Station Barney	3	6
Hard Hat Fred	3	6
Lawn Bowling Barney	3	6
Licking Dino	4	8
Wilma and Pebbles	4	8

Vintage (1960-70s)

Action Girl Series

Figure Sets

	GOOD	EX	MIP
G.I. Nurse, Red Cross hat and arm band, white dress, stockings, shoes, crutches, medic bag, stethescope, plasma bottle, bandages and splints., 1967, No. 8060 1750	2000	4000

Action Marine Series

Figure Sets

	GOOD	EX	MIP
Action Marine, fatigues, green cap, boots, dog tags, insignias and manual, 1964, No. 7700 125	145	375

G.I. Nurse, Action Girl Series, 1967

Front Row, left to right: G.I. Joe Action Marine, Action Marine Series, 1964; G.I. Joe Action Sailor, Action Sailor Series, 1964. Back row, left to right: G.I. Joe Eight Ropes of Danger Set, Adventure Team, 1970; G.I. Joe Fantastic Freefall Set, Adventure Team, 1970

	GOOD	EX	MIP
Marine Medic Series, Red Cross helmet, flag and arm bands, crutch, bandages, splints, first aid pouch, stethoscope, plasma bottle, stretcher, medic bag, belt with ammo pouches, 1967, No. 90711 325	425	3250
Talking Action Marine, 1967, No. 7790 175	200	850
Talking Adventure Pack and Tent Set, 1968, No. 90711 275	325	3250
Talking Adventure Pack with Field Pack Equipment, 1968, No. 90712 275	325	3250

Uniform/Equipment Sets

	GOOD	EX	MIP
Beachhead Assault Field Pack Set, M-1 rifle, bayonet, entrenching shovel and cover, canteen with cover, belt, mess kit with cover, field pack, flamethrower, first aid pouch, tent, pegs and poles, tent camo and camo, 1964, No. 7713 100	175	325
Beachhead Assault Tent Set, tent, flame-thrower, pistol belt, first-aid pouch, mess kit with utensils and manual, 1964, No. 7711 100	200	475
Beachhead Fatigue Pants, 1964, No. 7715 15	30	200
Beachhead Fatigue Shirt, 1964, No. 7714 20	30	225
Beachhead Field Pack, cartridge belt, rifle, grenades, field pack, entrenching tool, canteen and manual, 1964, No. 7712 ...40	65	150
Beachhead Flamethrower Set, reissue, 1967, No. 7718 15	30	225
Beachhead Flamethrower Set, 1964, No. 7718 15	30	125

G.I. Joe Beachhead Assault Tent Set, Action Marine Series, 1964

	GOOD	EX	MIP
Beachhead Mess Kit Set, 1964, No. 7716 25		40	275
Beachhead Rifle Set, bayonet, cartridge belt, hand grenades and M-1 rifle, 1964, No. 7717 30		50	150
Beachhead Rifle Set, reissue, 1967, No. 7717 30		50	225
Communications Field Radio/Telephone Set, reissue, 1967, No. 7703 35		60	275
Communications Field Set, 1964, No. 7703...35		50	175
Communications Flag Set, flags for Army, Navy, Air Corps, Marines and United States, 1964, No. 7704...................200		250	475
Communications Poncho, 1964, No. 7702 35		50	250
Communications Post and Poncho Set, field radio and telephone, wire roll, carbine, binoculars, map, case, manual, poncho, 1964, No. 7701 125		175	475
Dress Parade Set, Marine jacket, trousers, pistol belt, shoes, hat, M-1 rifle and manual, 1964, No. 7710 125		225	450
Dress Parade Set, reissue, 1968, No. 7710 ...125		225	750
Jungle Fighter Set, reissue, 1968, No. 7732 450		700	2750

	GOOD	EX	MIP
Jungle Fighter Set, bush hat, jacket with emblems, pants, flamethrower, field telephone, knife and sheath, pistol belt, pistol, holster, canteen with cover and knuckle knife, 1967, No. 7732 450		700	3500
Marine Automatic M-60 Machine Gun Set, 1967, No. 7726 35		75	325
Marine Basics Set, 1966, No. 7722 55		85	275
Marine Bunk Bed Set, 1966, No. 7723...........55		80	375
Marine Bunk Bed Set, reissue, 1967, No. 7723 55		80	475
Marine Demolition Set, reissue, 1968, No. 7730 50		100	450
Marine Demolition Set, mine detector and harness, land mine, 1966, No. 7730 50		100	350
Marine First Aid Set, reissue, 1967, No. 7721 45		85	225
Marine First Aid Set, first-aid pouch, arm band and helmet, 1964, No. 7721 45		85	125
Marine Medic Set, with crutch, etc., 1965, No. 7720 25		40	125
Marine Medic Set, reissue, 1967, No. 7720 25		40	225

	GOOD	EX	MIP
Marine Medic Set with stretcher, first-aid shoulder pouch, stretcher, bandages, arm bands, plasma bottle, stethoscope, Red Cross flag, and manual, 1964, No. 7719 175	300	850
Marine Mortar Set, 1967, No. 7725 60	80	350
Marine Weapons Rack Set, 1967, No. 7727 75	145	625
Paratrooper Camouflage Set, netting and foliage, 1964, No. 7708 20	35	65
Paratrooper Helmet Set, 1964, No. 7707 20	40	85
Paratrooper Parachute Pack, 1964, No. 7709 30	80	125
Paratrooper Small Arms Set, reissue, 1967, No. 7706 30	75	225
Tank Commander Set, includes faux leather jacket, helmet and visor, insignia, radio with tripod, machine gun, ammo box, 1967, No. 7731 325	500	1750
Tank Commander Set, reissue, 1968, No. 7731 325	500	1525

Action Pilot Series

Figure Sets

	GOOD	EX	MIP
Action Pilot, orange jumpsuit, blue cap, black boots, dog tags, insignias, manual, catalog and club application, 1964, No. 7800 130	165	600
Talking Action Pilot, 1967, No. 7890 190	245	1500

Uniform/Equipment Sets

	GOOD	EX	MIP
Air Academy Cadet Set, reissue, 1968, No. 7822 225	450	1150
Air Academy Cadet Set, deluxe set with figure, dress jacket, shoes, and pants, garrison cap, saber and scabbard, white M-1 rifle, chest sash and belt sash, 1967, No. 7822 225	450	1250
Air Force Basics Set, reissue, 1967, No. 7814 30	55	275
Air Force Basics Set, 1966, No. 7814 30	55	200
Air Force Mae West Air Vest & Equipment Set, 1967, No. 7816 85	125	325
Air Force Police Set, reissue, 1967, No. 7813 70	150	325
Air Force Police Set, 1965, No. 7813 70	150	250
Air Force Security Set, Air Security radio and helmet, cartridge belt, pistol and holster, 1967, No. 7815 275	350	590
Air/Sea Rescue Set, reissue, 1968, No. 7825 325	550	2500
Air/Sea Rescue Set, includes black air tanks, rescue ring, buoy, depth gauge, face mask, fins, orange scuba outfit, 1967, No. 7825 325	550	2500
Astronaut Set, reissue, 1968, No. 7824 100	200	1250

	GOOD	EX	MIP
Astronaut Set, helmet with visor, foil space suit, booties, gloves, space camera, propellant gun, tether cord, oxygen chest pack, silver boots, white jumpsuit and cloth cap, 1967, No. 7824 100	200	3000
Communications Set, 1964, No. 7812 55	100	225
Crash Crew Set, fire proof jacket, hood, pants and gloves, silver boots, belt, flashlight, axe, pliers, fire extinguisher, stretcher, strap cutter, 1966, No. 7820 125	250	450
Dress Uniform Jacket Set, 1964, No. 7804 ...40	65	250
Dress Uniform Pants, 1964, No. 7805 20	35	200
Dress Uniform Set, Air Force jacket, trousers, shirt, tie, cap and manual, 1964, No. 7803 225	450	3000
Dress Uniform Shirt & Equipment Set, 1964, No. 7806 25	40	200
Fighter Pilot Set, working parachute and pack, gold helmet, Mae West vest, green pants, flash light, orange jump suit, black boots, 1967, No. 7823 400	650	2500
Fighter Pilot Set, reissue, 1968, No. 7823 ...400	650	2650
Scramble Communications Set, reissue, 1967, No. 7812 35	75	250
Scramble Communications Set, poncho, field telephone and radio, map with case, binoculars and wire roll, 1965, No. 7812 35	75	175
Scramble Crash Helmet, reissue, 1967, No. 7810 65	90	225
Scramble Crash Helmet, helmet, face mask, hose, tinted visor, 1964, No. 7810 65	90	125
Scramble Flight Suit, 1967, No. 7808 50	75	400
Scramble Flight Suit, gray flight suit, 1964, No. 7808 50	300	225
Scramble Parachute Set, 1964, No. 7811 20	40	150
Scramble Parachute Set, reissue, 1967, No. 7809 20	40	250
Scramble Set, deluxe set, gray flight suit, orange air vest, white crash helmet, pistol belt with .45 pistol, holster, clipboard, flare gun and parachute with insert, 1964, No. 7807 125	225	950
Survival Life Raft Set, raft with oar and sea anchor, 1964, No. 7802 45	90	325
Survival Life Raft Set, raft with oar, flare gun, knife, air vest, first-aid kit, sea anchor and manual, 1964, No. 7801 75	125	550

Vehicle Sets

	GOOD	EX	MIP
Crash Crew Fire Truck Set, 1967, No. 8040 950	1700	3500
Official Space Capsule Set, space capsule, record, space suit, cloth space boots, space gloves, helmet with visor, 1966, No. 8020 175	225	350
Official Space Capsule Set with flotation, Sears exclusive with collar, life raft and oars, 1966, No. 5979 200	325	700

G.I. JOE – VINTAGE

Action Sailor Series

Figure Sets

	GOOD	EX	MIP
Action Sailor, white cap, denim shirt and pants, boots, dog tags, navy manual and insignias, 1964, No. 7600	125	225	350
Navy Scuba Set, Adventure Pack, 1968, No. 7643-83	300	450	3250
Talking Action Sailor, 1967, No. 7690	200	330	1250
Talking Landing Signal Officer Set, Talking Adventure Pack, 1968, No. 90621	325	350	3500
Talking Shore Patrol Set, Talking Adventure Pack, 1968, No. 90612	200	450	3500

Uniform/Equipment Sets

	GOOD	EX	MIP
Annapolis Cadet, reissue, 1968, No. 7624	275	375	1350
Annapolis Cadet, garrison cap, dress jacket, pants, shoes, sword, scabbard, belt and white M-1 rifle, 1967, No. 7624	275	375	1350
Breeches Buoy, yellow jacket and pants, chair and pulley, flare gun, blinker light, 1967, No. 7625	325	425	1500
Breeches Buoy, reissue, 1968, No. 7625	325	425	1450
Deep Freeze, white boots, fur parka, pants, snow shoes, ice axe, snow sled with rope and flare gun, 1967, No. 7623	250	375	1600
Deep Freeze, reissue, 1968, No. 7623	250	375	1500

G.I. Joe Annapolis Cadet, Action Sailor Series, 1967

	GOOD	EX	MIP
Deep Sea Diver Set, underwater uniform, helmet, upper and lower plate, sledge hammer, buoy with rope, gloves, compass, hoses, lead boots and weight belt, 1965, No. 7620	325	425	2000
Deep Sea Diver Set, reissue, 1968, No. 7620	325	425	2000
Frogman Scuba Bottoms, 1964, No. 7604	20	35	100
Frogman Scuba Tank Set, 1964, No. 7606	25	40	100
Frogman Scuba Top Set, 1964, No. 7603	25	45	125
Frogman Underwater Demolition Set, headpiece, face mask, swim fins, rubber suit, scuba tank, depth gauge, knife, dynamite and manual, 1964, No. 7602	175	250	1500
Landing Signal Officer, jumpsuit, signal paddles, goggles, cloth head gear, headphones, clipboard (complete), binoculars and flare gun., 1966, No. 7621	225	350	575
Navy Attack Helmet Set, shirt and pants, boots, yellow life vest, blue helmet, flare gun binoculars, signal flags, 1964, No. 7610	35	75	150
Navy Attack Life Jacket, 1964, No. 7611	20	45	120
Navy Attack Set, life jacket, field glasses, blinker light, signal flags, manual, 1964, No. 7607	60	125	425
Navy Attack Work Pants Set, 1964, No. 7609	25	40	150
Navy Attack Work Shirt Set, 1964, No. 7608	25	40	175
Navy Basics Set, 1966, No. 7628	25	55	125
Navy Dress Parade Rifle Set, 1965, No. 7619	35	65	125
Navy Dress Parade Set, billy club, cartridge belt, bayonet and white dress rifle, 1964, No. 7619	45	80	175
Navy L.S.O. Equipment Set, helmet, headphones, signal paddles, flare gun, 1966, No. 7626	40	80	150
Navy Life Ring Set, U.S.N. life ring, helmet sticker, 1966, No. 7627	25	45	150
Navy Machine Gun Set, MG and ammo box, 1965, No. 7618	40	80	175
Sea Rescue Set, life raft, oar, anchor, flare gun, first-aid kit, knife, scabbard, manual, 1964, No. 7601	95	135	500
Sea Rescue Set, reissued with life preserver, 1966, No. 7622	95	135	500
Shore Patrol, reissued with radio and helmet and shoes, 1967, No. 7612	1000	2000	3500
Shore Patrol, dress shirt, tie and pants, helmet, white belt, .45 and holster, billy club, boots, arm band, sea bag, 1964, No. 7612	500	1000	2000

G.I. Joe Official Sea Sled and Frogman Set, Action Sailor Series, 1966

	GOOD	EX	MIP
Shore Patrol Dress Jumper Set, 1964, No. 7613 75	125	225
Shore Patrol Dress Pant Set, 1964, No. 7614 40	75	175
Shore Patrol Helmet and Small Arms Set, white belt, billy stick, white helmet, .45 pistol, 1964, No. 7616 40	75	150
Shore Patrol Sea Bag Set, 1964, No. 7615 25	50	125

Vehicle Sets

| Official Sea Sled and Frogman Set, Sears, with figure and underwater cave, orange scuba suit, fins, mask, tanks, sea sled in orange and black, 1966, No. 5979 ......175 | 325 | 650 |
| Official Sea Sled and Frogman Set, without cave, 1966, No. 8050 ....150 | 300 | 550 |

Action Soldier Series

Figure Sets

Action Soldier, fatigue cap, shirt, pants, boots, dog tags, army manual and insignias, helmet, belt with pouches, M-1 rifle, 1964, No. 7500 100	175	350
Black Action Soldier, 1965, No. 7900 450	800	2500
Canadian Mountie Set, Sears exclusive, 1967, No. 5904 850	1500	4000
Desert Patrol Attack Jeep Set, Desert Fighter figure, jeep with steering wheel, spare tire, tan tripod, gun and gun mount and ring, black antenna, tan jacket and shorts, socks, goggles, 1967, No. 8030 400	1250	2000
Forward Observer Set, Sears exclusive, 1966, No. 5969 200	375	750

G.I. Joe Action Soldier, Action Soldier Series, 1964

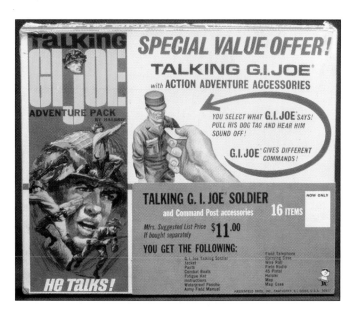

G.I. Joe Talking Adventure Pack, Command Post Equipment, Action Soldier Series, 1968

	GOOD	EX	MIP
Green Beret, field radio, bazooka rocket, bazooka, green beret, jacket, pants, M-16 rifle, grenades, camo scarf, belt pistol and holster, 1966, No. 7536	275	400	3000
Machine Gun Emplacement Set, Sears exclusive, 1965, No. 7531	150	275	1250
Talking Action Soldier, 1967, No. 7590	85	135	825
Talking Adventure Pack, Bivouac Equipment, 1968, No. 90513	275	325	3000
Talking Adventure Pack, Command Post Equipt., 1968, No. 90517	275	375	3000
Talking Adventure Pack, Mountain Troop Series, 1968, No. 7557-83	375	650	3500
Talking Adventure Pack, Special Forces Equip., 1968, No. 90532	275	500	3500

Uniform/Equipment Sets

	GOOD	EX	MIP
Adventure Pack with twelve items, Adventure Pack Footlocker, 1968, No. 8006.83	75	125	600
Adventure Pack with twelve items, Adventure Pack Footlocker, 1968, No. 8005.83	75	125	600
Adventure Pack with fourteen pieces, Adventure Pack Footlocker, 1968, No. 8008.83	75	125	600
Adventure Pack with sixteen items, Adventure Pack Footlocker, 1968, No. 8007.83	75	125	600
Adventure Pack, Army Bivouac Series, 1968, No. 7549-83	225	450	3500
Air Police Equipment, gray field phone, carbine, white helmet and bayonet, 1964, No. 7813	40	95	200
Basic Footlocker, wood tray with cardboard wrapper, 1964, No. 8000	35	75	125

	GOOD	EX	MIP
Bivouac Deluxe Pup Tent Set, M-1 rifle and bayonet, shovel and cover, canteen and cover, mess kit, cartridge belt, machine gun, tent, pegs, poles, camoflage, sleeping bag, netting, ammo box, 1964, No. 7513	115	225	450
Bivouac Machine Gun Set, reissue, 1967, No. 7514	25	40	225
Bivouac Machine Gun Set, machine gun set and ammo box, 1964, No. 7514	25	40	125
Bivouac Sleeping Bag, zippered bag, 1964, No. 7515	20	30	125
Bivouac Sleeping Bag Set, mess kit, canteen, bayonet, cartridge belt, M-1 rifle, manual, 1964, No. 7512	25	30	150
Combat Camouflaged Netting Set, foliage and posts, 1964, No. 7511	25	40	85
Combat Construction Set, orange safety helmet, work gloves, jack hammer, 1967, No. 7572	325	400	575
Combat Demolition Set, 1967, No. 7573	65	100	525
Combat Engineer Set, pick, shovel, detonator, dynamite, tripod and transit with grease gun, 1967, No. 7571	125	175	625

G.I. Joe Black Action Soldier, Action Soldier Series, 1965

G.I. Joe Combat Camouflaged Netting Set, Action Soldier Series, 1964

G.I. Joe Combat Rifle Set, Action Soldier Series, 1967, Photo Courtesy

	GOOD	EX	MIP
Combat Fatigue Pants Set, 1964, No. 7504 ...15		25	110
Combat Fatigue Shirt Set, 1964, No. 7503 20		30	125
Combat Field Jacket, 1964, No. 7505 45		65	325
Combat Field Jacket Set, jacket, bayonet, cartridge belt, hand grenades, M-1 rifle and manual, 1964, No. 7501 65		100	525
Combat Field Pack & Entrenching Tool, 1964, No. 7506 25		45	125
Combat Field Pack Deluxe Set, field jacket, pack, entrenching shovel with cover, mess kit, first-aid pouch, canteen with cover, 1964, No. 7502 75		125	325
Combat Helmet Set, with netting and foliage leaves, 1964, No. 7507 20		35	75
Combat Mess Kit, plate, fork, knife, spoon, canteen, etc., 1964, No. 7509 20		45	85
Combat Rifle Set, bayonet, M-1 rifle, belt and grenades, 1967, No. 7510 55		100	325
Combat Sandbags Set, three bags per set, 1964, No. 7508 10		40	85
Command Post Field Radio and Telephone Set, field radio, telephone with wire roll and map, 1964, No. 7520 35		70	135
Command Post Field Radio and Telephone Set, reissue, 1967, No. 7520 35		70	400

	GOOD	EX	MIP
Command Post Poncho, on card, 1964, No. 7519 30		45	225
Command Post Poncho Set, poncho, field radio and telephone, wire roll, pistol, belt and holster, map and case and manual, 1964, No. 7517 85		125	400
Command Post Small Arms Set, holster and .45 pistol, belt, grenades, 1964, No. 7518 ...30		60	100
Dress Parade Adventure Pack, Adventure Pack with thirty-seven pieces, 1968, No. 8009.83 750		1250	3500
Green Beret and Small Arms Set, reissue, 1967, No. 7533 85		100	425
Green Beret and Small Arms Set, 1966, No. 7533 85		110	300
Green Beret Machine Gun Outpost Set, Sears exclusive with two figures and equipment, 1966, No. 5978 225		450	1500
Heavy Weapons Set, mortar launcher and shells, M-60 machine gun, grenades, flak jacket, shirt and pants, 1967, No. 7538 175		325	1750
Heavy Weapons Set, reissue, 1968, No. 7538 175		325	1500
Military Police Duffle Bag Set, 1964, No. 7523 25		40	85
Military Police Helmet and Small Arms Set, 1964, No. 7526 35		75	125

G.I. JOE - VINTAGE

G.I. Joe Command Post Field Radio and Telephone Set, Action Soldier Series, 1964

G.I. Joe Military Police Ike Pants, Action Soldier Series, 1964

	GOOD	EX	MIP
Military Police Helmet and Small Arms Set, reissue, 1967, No. 7526	35	75	250
Military Police Ike Jacket, jacket with red scarf and arm band, 1964, No. 7524	40	60	125
Military Police Ike Pants, matches Ike jacket, 1964, No. 7525	20	30	100
Military Police Uniform Set, includes green or tan uniform, black and gold MP Helmet, billy club, belt, pistol and holster, MP armband and red tunic, 1967, No. 7539	450	1650	3500
Military Police Uniform Set, reissue, 1968, No. 7539	450	900	3000
Military Police Uniform Set, includes Ike jacket and pants, scarf, boots, helmet, belt with ammo pouches, .45 pistol and holster, billy club, armband, duffle bag, 1964, No. 7521	450	1650	3000
Mountain Troops Set, snow shoes, ice axe, ropes, grenades, camoflage pack, web belt, manual, 1964, No. 7530	90	175	350
Sabotage Set, dingy and oar, blinker light, detonator with strap, TNT, wool stocking cap, gas mask, binoculars, green radio and .45 pistol and holster, 1967, No. 7516	125	250	2000
Sabotage Set, reissued in photo box, 1968, No. 7516	125	250	1700
Ski Patrol Deluxe Set, White parka, boots, goggles, mittens, skis, poles and manual, 1964, No. 7531	170	350	1250
Ski Patrol Helmet and Small Arms Set, reissue, 1967, No. 7527	75	125	250
Ski Patrol Helmet and Small Arms Set, 1965, No. 7527	35	75	135
Snow Troop Set, reissue, 1967, No. 7529	20	45	225
Snow Troop Set, snow shoes, goggles and ice pick, 1966, No. 7529	20	45	150
Special Forces Bazooka Set, 1966, No. 7528	35	45	225
Special Forces Bazooka Set, reissue, 1967, No. 7528	35	45	325
Special Forces Uniform Set, 1966, No. 7532	200	375	1000
West Point Cadet Uniform Set, dress jacket, pants, shoes, chest and belt sash, parade hat with plume, saber, scabbard and white M-1 rifle, 1967, No. 7537	250	475	1500
West Point Cadet Uniform Set, reissue, 1968, No. 7537	250	375	1200

Vehicle Sets

	GOOD	EX	MIP
Amphibious Duck, Irwin, 26" long, 1967, No. 5693	175	375	700

	GOOD	EX	MIP
Armored Car, Irwin, friction powered, 20" long, 1967, No. 5397 150		300	500
Helicopter, Irwin, friction powered, 28" long, 1967, No. 5395 150		300	500
Jet Fighter Plane, Irwin, friction powered, 30" long, 1967, No. 5396 225		475	800
Military Staff Car, Irwin, friction powered, 24" long, 1967, No. 5652 200		400	750
Motorcycle and Sidecar, Irwin, 14" long, khaki, with decals, 1967, No. 5651 75		150	325
Official Combat Jeep Set, trailer, steering wheel, spare tire, windshield, cannon, search light, shell, flag, guard rails, tripod, tailgate and hood, without Moto-Rev Sound, 1965, No. 7000 200		375	550
Official Jeep Combat Set, With Moto-Rev sound, 1965, No. 7000 225		400	650
Personnel Carrier/Mine Sweeper, Irwin, 26" long, 1967, No. 5694 300		350	700

Action Soldiers of the World

Figure Sets

	GOOD	EX	MIP
Australian Jungle Fighter, standard set with action figure uniform, no equipment, 1966, No. 8205 150		275	1200

G.I. Joe Snow Troop Set, Action Soldier Series, 1966

G.I. Joe Mountain Troops Set, Action Soldier Series, 1964

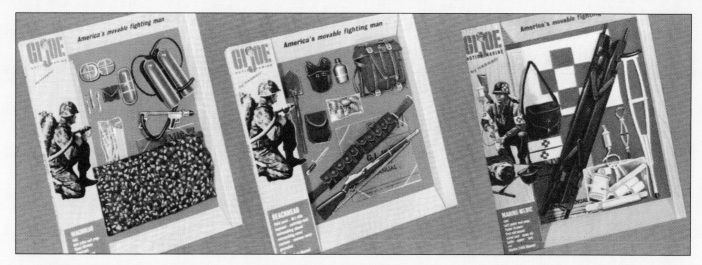

Action Marine accessories. Left to right: Beachhead Assault Tent Set, 1964; Beachhead Field Pack, 1964; Marine Medic Set with stretcher, 1964. Photo from Hasbro's 1965 G.I. Joe Catalog

Action Soldier accessories. Left to Right: Combat Field Jacket Set, 1964; Combat Field Pack Deluxe Set, 1964; Bivouac Sleeping Bag Set, 1964. Photo from Hasbro's 1965 G.I. Joe Catalog

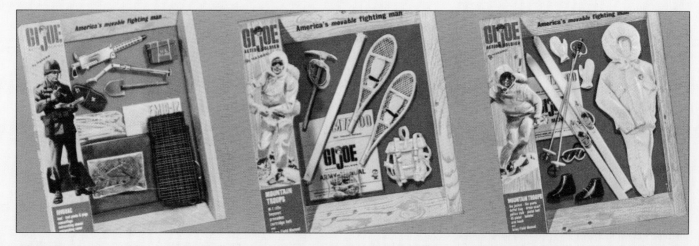

Action Soldier accessories. Left to Right: Bivouac Deluxe Pup Tent Set, 1964; Mountain Troops Set, 1964; Ski Patrol Deluxe Set, 1964. Photo from Hasbro's 1965 G.I. Joe Catalog.

	GOOD	EX	MIP
Australian Jungle Fighter, action figure with jacket, shorts, socks, boots, bush hat, belt, "Victoria Cross" medal, knuckle knife, flamethrower, entrenching tool, bush knife and sheath, 1966, No. 8105	250	400	2500
British Commando, standard set with no equipment, 1966, No. 8204	150	275	1750
British Commando, deluxe set with action figure, helmet, night raid green jacket, pants, boots, canteen and cover, gas mask and cover, belt, Sten sub machine gun, gun clip and "Victoria Cross" medal, 1966, No. 8104	300	425	2500
Foreign Soldiers of the World, Talking Adventure Pack, 1968, No. 8111-83	750	825	5000
French Resistance Fighter, deluxe set with figure, beret, short black boots, black sweater, denim pants, "Croix de Guerre" medal, knife, shoulder holster, pistol, radio, sub machine gun and grenades, 1966, No. 8103	200	250	2250
French Resistance Fighter, Standard set with action figure and equipment, 1966, No. 8203	125	225	1250
German Storm Trooper, Standard set with no equipment, 1966, No. 8200	275	325	1300
German Storm Trooper, deluxe set with figure, helmet, jacket, pants, boots, Luger pistol, holster, cartridge belt, cartridges, "Iron Cross" medal, stick grenades, 9MM Schmeisser, field pack, 1966, No. 8100	275	425	2500
Japanese Imperial Soldier, Standard set with equipment, 1966, No. 8201	300	325	1425
Japanese Imperial Soldier, deluxe set with figure, Arisaka rifle, belt, cartridges, field pack, Nambu pistol, holster, bayonet, "Order of the Kite" medal, helmet, jacket, pants, short brown boots, 1966, No. 8101	425	675	2700
Russian Infantry Man, deluxe set with action figure, fur cap, tunic, pants, boots, ammo box, ammo rounds, anti-tank grenades, belt, bipod, DP light machine gun, "Order of Lenin" medal, field glasses and case, 1966, No. 8102	275	400	2250
Russian Infantry Man, standard set with no equipment, 1966, No. 8202	315	400	1250
Uniforms of Six Nations, 1967, No. 5038	750	950	2500

Uniform/Equipment Sets

	GOOD	EX	MIP
Australian Jungle Fighter Set, 1966, No. 8305	25	50	250
British Commando Set, Sten submachine gun, gas mask and carrier, canteen and cover, cartridge belt, rifle, "Victoria Cross" medal, manual, 1966, No. 8304	125	200	325

	GOOD	EX	MIP
French Resistance Fighter Set, shoulder holster, Lebel pistol, knife, grenades, radio, 7.65 submachine gun, "Croix de Guerra" medal, counter-intelligence manual, 1966, No. 8303	25	50	275
German Storm Trooper, 1966, No. 8300	125	175	325
Japanese Imperial Soldier Set, field pack, Nambu pistol and holster, Arisaka rifle with bayonet, cartridge belt, "Order of the Kite" medal, counter-intelligence manual, 1966, No. 8301	175	275	625
Russian Infantry Man Set, DP light machine gun, bipod, field glasses and case, anti-tank grenades, ammo box, "Order of Lenin" medal, counter-intelligence medal, 1966, No. 8302	175	220	325

Adventure Team
Figure Sets

	GOOD	EX	MIP
Air Adventurer, includes figure with Kung Fu grip, orange flight suit, boots, insignia, dog tags, rifle, boots, warranty, club insert, 1970, No. 7403	120	375	300
Air Adventurer, life-like body figure, uniform and equipment, 1976, No. 7282	75	100	200
Air Adventurer, with Kung Fu grip, 1974, No. 7282	95	125	325
Black Adventurer, with life-like body and Kung Fu grip, 1976, No. 7283	85	125	225
Black Adventurer, includes figure, shirt with insignia, pants, boots, dog tags, shoulder holster with pistol, 1970, No. 7404	125	150	375
Bulletman, 1976, No. 8026	50	75	150
Eagle Eye Black Commando, 1976, No. 7278	85	125	250
Eagle Eye Land Commander, 1976, No. 7276	65	80	150
Eagle Eye Man of Action, 1976, No. 7277	65	80	165
Intruder Commander, 1976, No. 8050	50	75	150
Intruder Warrior, 1976, No. 8051	50	75	175
Land Adventurer, 1976, No. 7280	35	50	150
Land Adventurer, 1976, No. 7270	20	50	180
Land Adventurer, includes figure, camo shirt and pants, boots, insignia, shoulder holster and pistol, dog tags and team inserts, 1970, No. 7401	45	75	200
Land Adventurer, with life-like body and Kung Fu grip and uniform set, 1974, No. 7280	50	65	225
Man of Action, includes figure, shirt and pants, boots, insignia, dog tags, team inserts, 1970, No. 7500	50	75	225
Man of Action, 1976, No. 7274	25	45	175

G.I. Joe Danger of the Depths Set,
Adventure Team, 1970

	GOOD	EX	MIP
Man of Action, figure with life-like body and Kung Fu grip, 1974, No. 7284 45		75	200
Mike Powers/Atomic Man, figure with "atomic" flashing eye, arm that spins hand-held helicopter, 1975, No. 8025 20		45	150
Sea Adventurer, 1976, No. 7271 40		75	250
Sea Adventurer, 1976, No. 7281 55		85	200
Sea Adventurer, includes figure, shirt, dungarees, insignia, boots, shoulder holster and pistol, 1970, No. 7402 45		70	245
Sea Adventurer, with life-like body and Kung Fu grip and uniform with equipment, 1974, No. 7281 55		75	225
Secret Mountain Outpost, 1975, No. 8040 50		85	150
Talking Adventure Team Black Commander, 1973, No. 7406 150		225	600
Talking Adventure Team Black Commander, with Kung Fu grip, 1974, No. 7291 85		350	750
Talking Adventure Team Commander, with Kung Fu grip, 1974, No. 7290 75		200	500
Talking Adventure Team Commander, includes figure, two-pocket green shirt, pants, boots, insignia, instructions, dog tag, shoulder holster and pistol, 1970, No. 7400 65		125	400

	GOOD	EX	MIP
Talking Astronaut, 1970, No. 7590 90		175	650
Talking Black Commander, 1976, No. 7291 125		300	600
Talking Commander, 1976, No. 7290 75		115	500
Talking Man of Action, 1976, No. 7292 75		120	525
Talking Man of Action, with life-like body and Kung Fu grip, 1974, No. 7292 75		200	650
Talking Man of Action, shirt, pants, boots, dog tags, rifle, insignia, instructions, 1970, No. 7590 75		125	350

Uniform/Equipment Sets

	GOOD	EX	MIP
Adventure Team Headquarters Set, Adventure Team playset, 1972, No. 7490 ...50		125	200
Adventure Team Training Center Set, rifle rack, logs, barrel, barber wire, rope ladder, three tires, two targets, escape slide, tent and poles, first aid kit, respirator and mask, snake, instructions, 1973, No. 7495 75		125	225
Aerial Reconnaissance Set, jumpsuit, helmet, aerial recon vehicle with built-in camera, 1971, No. 7345 75		125	225
Attack at Vulture Falls, super deluxe set, 1975, No. 7420 75		150	275
Black Widow Rendezvous, super deluxe set, 1975, No. 7414 125		200	350

	GOOD	EX	MIP
Buried Bounty, deluxe set, 1975, No. 7328-5 10	25	85
Capture of the Pygmy Gorilla Set, 1970, No. 7437 100	175	325
Challenge of Savage River, deluxe set, 1975, No. 8032 100	175	350
Chest Winch Set, 1972, No. 7313 10	15	40
Chest Winch Set, reissue, 1974, No. 7313 10	15	75
Command Para Drop, deluxe set, 1975, No. 8033 200	300	550
Copter Rescue Set, blue jumpsuit, red binoculars, 1973, No. 7308-3 15	20	30
Danger of the Depths Set, 1970, No. 7412 100	175	325
Danger Ray Detection, magnetic ray detector, solar communicator with headphones, two-piece uniform, instructions and comic, 1975, No. 7338-1 45	90	225
Dangerous Climb Set, 1973, No. 7309-2 20	35	75
Dangerous Mission Set, green shirt, pants, hunting rifle, 1973, No. 7608-5 20	35	75
Demolition Set, armored suit, face shield, bomb, bomb disposal box, extension grips, 1971, No. 7370 20	45	125
Demolition Set, with land mines, mine detector and carrying case with metallic suit, 1971, No. 7371 75	100	250
Desert Explorer Set, 1973, No. 7309-5 20	40	80
Desert Survival Set, 1973, No. 7308-6 20	40	80
Dive to Danger, Mike Powers set, orange scuba suit, fins, mask, spear gun, shark, buoy, knife and scabbard, mini sled, air tanks, comic, 1975, No. 8031 150	250	450
Diver's Distress, 1975, No. 7328-6 35	70	125
Drag Bike Set, three-wheel motorcycle brakes down to backpack size, 1971, No. 7364 25	65	125
Eight Ropes of Danger Set, 1970, No. 7422 125	225	375
Emergency Rescue Set, shirt, pants, rope ladder and hook, walkie talkie, safety belt, flashlight, oxygen tank, axe, first aid kit, 1971, No. 7374 45	75	150
Equipment Tester Set, 1972, No. 7319-5 15	20	40
Escape Car Set, 1971, No. 7360 30	60	85
Escape Slide Set, 1972, No. 7319-1 15	25	40
Fangs of the Cobra, deluxe set, 1975, No. 8028-2 125	200	375
Fantastic Freefall Set, 1970, No. 7423 125	200	375
Fight For Survival Set, with blue parka, 1970, No. 7431 300	550	2500

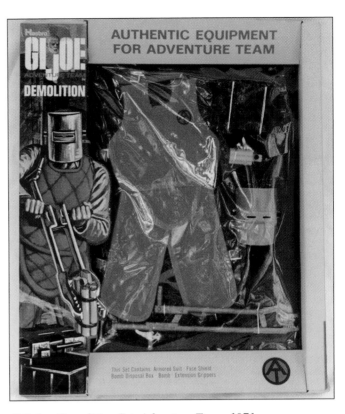

G.I. Joe Demolition Set, Adventure Team, 1971

	GOOD	EX	MIP
Fight for Survival Set, brown shirt and pants, machete, 1973, No. 7308-2 20	30	45
Fight for Survival Set with Polar Explorer, 1969, No. 7982 250	450	850
Fire Fighter Set, 1971, No. 7351 20	30	55
Flying Rescue Set, 1971, No. 7361 35	60	85
Flying Space Adventure Set, 1970, No. 7425 400	600	1000
Footlocker, green plastic with cardboard wrapper, 1974, No. 8000 35	70	225
Green Danger, 1975, No. 7328-4 30	45	60
Hidden Missile Discovery Set, 1970, No. 7415 100	200	450
Hidden Treasure Set, shirt, pants, pick axe, shovel, 1973, No. 7308-1 15	25	40
High Voltage Escape Set, net, jumpsuit, hat, wrist meter, wire cutters, wire, warning sign, 1971, No. 7342 40	75	150
Hurricane Spotter Set, slicker suit, rain measure, portable radar, map and case, binoculars, 1971, No. 7343 55	80	175
Jaws of Death, super deluxe set, 1975, No. 7421 325	500	650
Jettison to Safety, infrared terrain scanner, mobile rocket pack, two-piece flight suit, instructions and comic, 1975, No. 7339-2 85	200	275
Jungle Ordeal Set, 1973, No. 7309-3 15	25	45

	GOOD	EX	MIP
Jungle Survival Set, 1971, No. 7373 15	25	45
Karate Set, 1971, No. 7372 35	70	125
Laser Rescue Set, hand-held laser with backpack generator, 1972, No. 7311 20	35	45
Laser Rescue Set, reissue, 1974, No. 7311 20	35	100
Life-Line Catapult Set, 1971, No. 7353 15	25	40
Long Range Recon, deluxe set, 1975, No. 7328-3 10	20	35
Magnetic Flaw Detector Set, 1972, No. 7319-2 10	20	30
Mine Shaft Breakout, sonic rock blaster, chest winch, two-piece uniform, netting, instructions, comic, 1975, No. 7339-3 70	125	250
Missile Recovery Set, 1971, No. 7340 40	55	85
Mystery of the Boiling Lagoon, Sears, pontoon boat, diver's suit, diver's helmet, weighted belt and boots, depth gauge, air hose, buoy, nose cone, pincer arm, instructions, 1973, ...150	200	225
Night Surveillance, deluxe set, 1975, No. 7338-2 35	45	90
Peril of the Raging Inferno, fireproof suit, hood and boots, breathing apparatus, camera, fire extinguisher, detection meter, gaskets, 1975, No. 7416 85	150	275
Photo Reconnaissance Set, 1973, No. 7309-4 20	30	45
Race for Recovery, 1975, No. 8028-1 20	35	125

	GOOD	EX	MIP
Radiation Detection Set, jumpsuit with belt, "uranium ore," goggles, container, pincer arm, 1971, No. 7341 30	50	85
Raging River Dam Up, 1975, No. 7339-1 60	90	150
Rescue Raft Set, 1971, No. 7350 15	20	65
Revenge of the Spy Shark, super deluxe set, 1975, No. 7413 50	175	400
Rock Blaster, sonic blaster with tripod, backpack generator, face shield, 1972, No. 7312 10	20	35
Rocket Pack Set, 1972, No. 7315 10	20	75
Rocket Pack Set, reissue, 1974, No. 7315 10	20	50
Sample Analyzer Set, 1972, No. 7319-3 10	20	45
Search for the Abominable Snowman Set, Sears, white suit, belt, goggles, gloves, rifle, skis and poles, show shoes, sled, rope, net, supply chest, binoculars, Abominable Snowman, comic book, 1973, No. 7439.16 110	175	350
Secret Agent Set, 1971, No. 7375 30	55	175
Secret Courier, 1975, No. 7328-1 45	65	135
Secret Mission Set, deluxe set, 1975, No. 8030 65	95	200
Secret Mission Set, 1973, No. 7309-1 45	65	135
Secret Mission to Spy Island Set, comic, inflatable raft with oar, binoculars, signal light, flare gun, TNT and detonator, wire roll, boots, pants, sweater, black cap, camera, radio with earphones, .45 submachine gun, 1970, No. 7411 75	125	250
Secret Rendezvous Set, parka, pants, flare gun, 1973, No. 7308-4 10	20	35
Seismograph Set, 1972, No. 7319-6 10	20	35
Shocking Escape, escape slide, chest pack climber, jumpsuit with gloves and belt, high voltage sign, instructions and comic, 1975, No. 7338-3 25	65	125
Signal Flasher Set, large back pack type signal flash unit, 1971, No. 7362 15	30	50
Sky Dive to Danger, super deluxe set, 1975, No. 7440 90	150	325
Solar Communicator Set, 1972, No. 7314 10	20	35
Solar Communicator Set, reissue, 1974, No. 7314 10	20	95
Sonic Rock Blaster Set, reissue, 1974, No. 7312 10	20	35
Sonic Rock Blaster Set, 1972, No. 7312 10	20	35
Special Assignment, deluxe set, 1975, No. 8028-3 30	55	135
Thermal Terrain Scanner Set, 1972, No. 7319-4 25	35	50
Three-in-One Super Adventure Set, cold of the Arctic, Heat of the Desert and Danger of the Jungle, 1971, No. 7480 250	400	750

G.I. Joe High Voltage Escape Set, Adventure Team, 1971

	GOOD	EX	MIP
Three-in-One Super Adventure Set, Danger of the Depths, Secret Mission to Spy Island and Flying Space Adventure Packs, 1971, No. 7480 550		975	1250
Thrust into Danger, deluxe set, 1975, No. 7328-2 45		55	175
Trouble at Vulture Pass, Sears exclusive, super deluxe set, 1975, No. 59289 75		125	325
Turbo Copter Set, strap-on one man helicopter, 1971, No. 7363 15		35	65
Undercover Agent Set, trenchcoat and belt, walkie-talkie, 1973, No. 7309-6 15		30	35
Underwater Demolition Set, hand-held propulsion device, breathing apparatus, dynamite, 1972, No. 7310 15		20	40
Underwater Demolition Set, reissue, 1974, No. 7310 10		20	75
Underwater Explorer Set, self propelled underwater device, 1971, No. 7354 15		30	60
Volcano Jumper Set, jumpsuit with hood, belt, nylon rope, chest pack, TNT pack, 1971, No. 7344 45		80	250
White Tiger Hunt Set, hunter's jacket and pants, hat, rifle, tent, cage, chain, campfire, white tiger, comic, 1970, No. 7436 80		125	275
Windboat Set, back pack, sled with wheels, sail, 1971, No. 7353 10		25	55

	GOOD	EX	MIP
Winter Rescue Set, Replaced Photo Reconnaissance Set, 1973, No. 7309-4 40		75	150
Vehicle Sets			
Action Sea Sled, J.C. Penney, 13", Adventure Pack, 1973 25		40	85
Adventure Team Vehicle Set, 1970, No. 7005 50		75	225
All Terrain Vehicle, 14" vehicle, 1973, No. 23528 50		75	125
Amphicat, Irwin, scaled to fit two figures, 1973, No. 59158 35		55	125
Avenger Pursuit Craft, Sears exclusive, 1976 100		175	275
Big Trapper, without action figure, 1976, No. 7498 75		105	325
Big Trapper Adventure with Intruder, with action figure, 1976, No. 7494 100		150	425
Capture Copter, without action figure, 1976, No. 7480 80		175	325
Capture Copter Adventure with Intruder, with action figure, 1976, No. 7481 110		200	350
Chopper Cycle, 15" vehicle, J.C. Penney's, 1973, No. 59114 30		50	100
Combat Action Jeep, 18" vehicle, J.C. Penney's, 1973, No. 59751 50		65	125
Combat Jeep and Trailer, 1976, No. 7000 80		135	550

G.I. Joe Sky Dive to Danger, Adventure Team, 1975

G.I. JOE – VINTAGE

	GOOD	EX	MIP
Devil of the Deep, 1974, No. 7439 80	135	325
Fantastic Sea Wolf Submarine, 1975, No. 7460 60	100	175
Fate of the Troubleshooter, 1974, No. 7450 50	125	225
Giant Air-Sea Helicopter, 28" vehicle, J.C. Penney's, 1973, No. 59189 50	125	225
Helicopter, 14", yellow, with working winch, 1973, No. 7380 50	90	150
Helicopter, 1976, No. 7380 50	90	300
Mobile Support Vehicle Set, 1972, No. 7499 85	150	325
Recovery of the Lost Mummy Adventure Set, Sears exclusive, 1971 125	250	425
Sandstorm Survival Adventure, 1974, No. 7493 125	200	300
Search for the Stolen Idol Set, 1971, No. 7418 120	225	350
Secret of the Mummy's Tomb Set, with Land Adventurer figure, shirt, pants, boots, insignia, pith helmet, pick, shovel, Mummy's tomb, net, gems, vehicle with winch, comic, 1970, No. 7441 175	300	600
Sharks Surprise Set with Sea Adventurer, 1970, No. 7442 175	325	550
Signal All Terrain Vehicle, J.C. Penney's, 12" vehicle, 1973 30	65	125
Sky Hawk, 5-3/4-foot wingspan, 1975, No. 7470 65	100	175
Spacewalk Mystery Set with Astronaut, 1970, No. 7445 225	300	550
Trapped in the Coils of Doom, J.C. Penney's exclusive, 1974, No. 79-59301 250	300	550

Adventures of G.I. Joe

Figure Sets

	GOOD	EX	MIP
Aquanaut, 1969, No. 7910 175	550	3000
Challenge at Hawk River, Recreations of Adventure Team series, 1999 5	10	20
Negro Adventurer, Sears exclusive, includes painted hair figure, blue jeans, pullover sweater, shoulder holster and pistol, plus product letter from Sears, 1969, No. 7905 450	750	2750
Peril of the Raging Inferno, 1999 5	10	20
Save the Tiger, 1999 5	10	20
Sharks Surprise Set with Frogman, with figure, orange scuba suit, blue sea sled, air tanks, harpoon, face mask, treasure chest, shark, instructions and comic, 1969, No. 7980 125	300	750
Talking Astronaut, hard-hand figure with white coveralls with insignias, white boots, dog tags, 1969, No. 7615 85	275	1000

Uniform/Equipment Sets

	GOOD	EX	MIP
Adventure Locker, Footlocker, 1969, No. 7940 80	165	350
Aqua Locker, Footlocker, 1969, No. 7941 90	180	375
Astro Locker, Footlocker, 1969, No. 7942 90	180	375
Danger of the Depths Underwater Diver Set, 1969, No. 7920 140	275	500
Eight Ropes of Danger Set, diving suit, treasure chest, octopus, 1969, No. 7950 110	225	525
Fantastic Freefall Set, includes figure with parachute and pack, blinker light, air vest, flash light, crash helmet with visor and oxygen mask, dog tags, orange jump suit, black boots, 1969, No. 7951 150	325	675
Flight for Survival Set without Polar Explorer, reissue, 1969, No. 7982.83 150	300	500
Hidden Missile Discovery Set, 1969, No. 7952 70	135	400
Mouth of Doom Set, 1969, No. 7953 125	250	550
Mysterious Explosion Set, basic, 1969, No. 7921 60	125	425
Perilous Rescue Set, basic, 1969, No. 7923 150	300	500
Secret Mission to Spy Island Set, basic, 1969, No. 7922 110	225	450

Vehicle Sets

	GOOD	EX	MIP
Sharks Surprise Set with Frogman, 1969, No. 7980 175	325	650
Sharks Surprise Set without Frogman, 1969, No. 7980.83 150	300	550
Spacewalk Mystery Set with Spaceman, 1969, No. 7981 150	375	650
Spacewalk Mystery Set without Spaceman, reissue, 1969, No. 7981.83 125	275	550

GI Joe Action Series, Army, Navy, Marine and Air Force

Uniform/Equipment Sets

	GOOD	EX	MIP
Basic Footlocker, 1965, No. 8000 50	75	175
Footlocker Adventure Pack, fifteen pieces, 1968, No. 8002.83 65	135	450
Footlocker Adventure Pack, sixteen pieces, 1968, No. 8000.83 65	135	450
Footlocker Adventure Pack, fifteen pieces, 1968, No. 8001.83 65	135	450
Footlocker Adventure Pack, twenty-two pieces, 1968, No. 8002.83 70	145	450

Super Joe

Figure Sets

	GOOD	EX	MIP
Gor, 1977, No. 7510 40	70	130
Luminos, 1977, No. 7506 45	70	130

G.I. JOE - VINTAGE

	GOOD	EX	MIP
Super Joe, 1977, No. 7503 20		35	70
Super Joe (Black), 1977, No. 7504 35		50	100
Super Joe Commander, 1977, No. 7501 25		45	75
The Shield, 1977, No. 7505 40		65	125

Uniform/Equipment Sets

	GOOD	EX	MIP
Aqua Laser, 1977, No. 7528-1 10		20	30
Edge of Adventure, 1977, No. 7518-2 10		20	35
Emergency Rescue, 1977, No. 7518-3 10		20	30
Fusion Bazooka, 1977, No. 7528-3 10		20	30
Helipak, 1977, No. 7538-2 10		20	30
Invisible Danger, 1977, No. 7518-1 10		20	35
Magna Tools, 1977, No. 7538-1 10		20	30
Path of Danger, 1977, No. 7518-4 10		20	30
Sonic Scanner, 1977, No. 7538-3 10		20	30
Treacherous Dive, 1977, No. 7528-2 10		20	30

Vehicle Sets

	GOOD	EX	MIP
Rocket Command Center, 1977, No. 7570 50		100	200
Rocket Command Center, Super Adventure Set including Gor, 1977, No. 7571 60		115	225

3-3/4" Figures (1980s)

Series #1, Cobra

Figure Sets

	GOOD	EX	MIP
Cobra, Infantry Soldier, 1982, No. 6423 25		55	110
Cobra Commander, mail order; Commanding Leader, 1982 25		55	110
Cobra Officer, Infantry Officer, 1982, No. 6424 25		55	110
Major Bludd, mail order; Mercenary with card, 1982, No. 6426 10		25	50

Vehicle Sets

	GOOD	EX	MIP
C.A.T., Motorized Crimson Attack Tank, 1982 15		25	55

Series #1, GI Joe

Figure Sets

	GOOD	EX	MIP
Breaker, Communications Officer, 1982, No. 6403 20		35	75
Flash, Laser Rifle Trooper, 1982, No. 6406 20		35	75
Grunt, Infantry Trooper, 1982, No. 6409 20		35	75
Rock 'n Roll, Machine Gunner, 1982, No. 6408 20		35	75
Scarlett, Counter Intelligence, 1982, No. 6407 40		85	175
Short Fuse, Mortar Soldier, 1982, No. 6402 20		35	75
Snake Eyes, Commando, 1982, No. 6404 40		85	175
Stalker, Ranger, 1982, No. 6401 25		35	100

	GOOD	EX	MIP
Zap, Bazooka Soldier, 1982, No. 6405 20		35	75

Uniform/Equipment Sets

	GOOD	EX	MIP
F.L.A.K., Attack Cannon, 1982, No. 6075 20		45	90
H.A.L., Heavy Artillery Laser with Grand Slam, 1982, No. 6052 20		45	90
J.U.M.P., Jet Pack with Platform, 1982, No. 6071 20		45	90
M.M.S., Mobile Missile System with Hawk, 1982, No. 6054 20		45	90

Vehicle Sets

	GOOD	EX	MIP
M.O.B.A.T., Motorized Battle Tank with Steeler, 1982, No. 6000 30		65	125
R.A.M., Rapid Fire Motorcycle, 1982, No. 6073 15		25	55
V.A.M.P., Multi-Purpose Attack Vehicle with Clutch, 1982, No. 6050 20		35	70

G.I. Joe Spacewalk Mystery Set with Spaceman, Adventures of G.I. Joe

G.I. JOE – 3-3/4"

*G.I. Joe
Magna Tools,
Super Joe,
1977*

Series #2, Cobra

Figure Sets

	GOOD	EX	MIP
Cobra, Reissue, 1983, No. 6423	25	50	100
Cobra Commander, Reissue, 1983, No. 6425	25	50	100
Cobra Officer, Reissue, 1983, No. 6424	25	50	100
Destro, Enemy Weapons Supplier, 1983, No. 6427	25	50	75
Major Bludd, 1983, No. 6426	15	30	65

Uniform/Equipment Sets

Headquarters Missile-Command Center, with three figures, 1983, No. 6200	65	125	250
S.N.A.K.E., One-Man Battle Armor, 1983, No. 6083	10	25	50

Vehicle Sets

Cobra Glider, Attack Glider with Viper, 1983, No. 6097	35	75	150
F.A.N.G., Fully Armed Negator Gyro Copter, 1983, No. 6077	10	20	45
H.I.S.S., High Speed Sentry Tank with H.I.S.S., 1983, No. 6051	25	50	100

Series #2, GI Joe

Figure Sets

Airborne, Helicopter Assault Trooper, 1983, No. 6411	15	35	75

	GOOD	EX	MIP
Breaker, Reissue, 1983, No. 6403	15	30	65
Doc, Medic, 1983, No. 6415	10	20	45
Duke, mail order; Master Sergeant, 1983	10	25	40
Flash, Reissue, 1983, No. 6406	15	30	65
Grunt, Reissue, 1983, No. 6409	15	30	65
Gung-Ho, Marine, 1983, No. 6414	12	30	65
Rock 'n Roll, Reissue, 1983, No. 6408	15	30	65
Scarlett, 1983, No. 6407	30	80	165
Short Fuse, Reissue, 1983, No. 6402	15	30	65
Snake Eyes, Reissue, 1983, No. 6404	40	80	165
Snow Job, Arctic Trooper, 1983, No. 6412	15	25	50
Stalker, Reissue, 1983, No. 6401	25	45	90
Torpedo, Navy S.E.A.L., 1983, No. 6413	12	30	65
Tripwire, Mine Detector, 1983, No. 6410	15	30	65
Zap, Reissue, 1983, No. 6405	15	30	60

Uniform/Equipment Sets

Battle Gear Accessory Pack #1, 1983, No. 6088	10	20	40
Headquarters Command Center, 1983, No. 6020	40	85	175
Jump, Jet Pack and Platform with Grand Slam, 1983, No. 6065	25	50	100

	GOOD	EX	MIP
Pac/Rats Flamethrower, Remote Control Weapon, 1983, No. 6086-1	10	25	50
Pac/Rats Machine Gun, Remote Control Weapon, 1983, No. 6086-2	10	25	50
Pac/Rats Missile Launcher, Remote Control Weapon, 1983, No. 6086-3	10	25	50
Whirlwind, Twin Battle Gun, 1983, No. 6074	10	25	45

Vehicle Sets

	GOOD	EX	MIP
A.P.C., Amphibious Personnel Carrier, 1983, No. 6093	15	25	50
Dragon Fly XH-1, Assault Copter with Wild Bill, 1983, No. 4025	25	50	100
Falcon, Attack Glider with Grunt, 1983, No. 6097	30	75	150
Polar Battle Bear, Sky Mobile, 1983, No. 6072	15	25	50
Sky Striker XP-14F, F-14 Jet and Parachute with Ace, 1983, No. 6010	35	75	150
Wolverine, Armored Missile Vehicle with Cover Girl, 1983, No. 6048	25	50	100

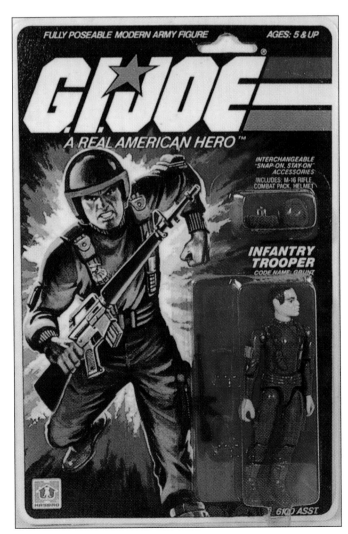

G.I. Joe Grunt, Series #1, 3-3/4" Figures, 1982

Series #3, Cobra
Figure Sets

	GOOD	EX	MIP
Baroness, Intelligence Officer, 1983-84, No. 6428	40	85	175
Cobra Commander, mail order; Enemy Leader with Hood, 1983-84, No. 6425	10	20	40
Fire Fly, Saboteur, 1983-84, No. 6432	40	85	175
Scrap Iron, Anti-Armor Specialist, 1983-84, No. 6431	15	30	60
Storm Shadow, Ninja, 1983-84, No. 6429	35	75	150

Uniform/Equipment Sets

	GOOD	EX	MIP
A.S.P., Assault System Pod, 1983, No. 6070	15	30	60
C.L.A.W., Cobra Covert Light Aerial Weapons, 1983, No. 6081-1	15	30	60
S.N.A.K.E., One-Man Armored Suit (white), 1983, No. 6081-2	10	25	50

Vehicle Sets

	GOOD	EX	MIP
Rattler, Ground Attack Jet with Wild Weasel, 1983-84, No. 6027	25	50	100
Stinger, Night Attack Jeep with Cobra Officer, 1983-84, No. 6055	20	40	80
Swamp Skier, Chameleon Vehicle with Zartan, 1983-84, No. 6064	30	55	125
Water Moccasin, Swamp Boat with Copperhead, 1983-84, No. 6058	20	40	80

Series #3, GI Joe
Figure Sets

	GOOD	EX	MIP
Blow Torch, Flamethrower, 1983-84, No. 6421	10	20	40
Duke, First Sergeant, 1983-84, No. 6422	15	25	50
Mutt, Dog Handler with Dog, 1983-84, No. 6416	10	25	50
Recondo, Jungle Trooper, 1983-84, No. 6420	15	25	50
Rip-Cord, H.A.L.O. Jumper, 1983-84, No. 6418	10	25	50
Road Block, Heavy Machine Gunner, 1983-84, No. 6419	15	25	50
Spirit, Tracker with Eagle, 1983-84, No. 6417	15	25	50

Uniform/Equipment Sets

	GOOD	EX	MIP
Battle Gear Accessory Pack #2, 1983, No. 6092	10	20	40
Bivouac, Battle Station, 1983, No. 6125-1	10	25	35
Machine Gun Defense Unit, 1983, No. 6129-2	10	20	40
Manta, mail order; Marine Assault Nautical Air Driven Transport, 1983	10	20	35
Missile Defense Unit, 1983, No. 6129-1	10	15	25
Mortar Defense Unit, 1983, No. 6129-3	10	15	25

	GOOD	EX	MIP
Mountain Howitzer, 1983, No. 6125-3 10	15	25
Parachute, mail order; Parachute Pack with Working Parachute, 1983 5	10	20
Watchtower, 1983, No. 6125-2 10	15	25

Vehicle Sets

	GOOD	EX	MIP
Attack Cannon (FLAK), 1983, No. 7444-3 5	10	15
Attack Vehicle (VAMP), 1983, No. 7444-1 ...15	35	70
Battle Tank (MOBAT), 1983, No. 7444-4 15	25	50
Heavy Artillery Laser (HAL), 1983, No. 7444-2 10	15	25
Killer W.H.A.L.E., Armored Hovercraft with Cutter, 1983, No. 6005 30	65	125
Mobile Missile System (MMS), 1983, No. 7444-5 10	15	30
RAM, HAL & VAMP, three-piece, die-cast set, 1983, No. 74450 10	20	40
Rapid-Fire Motorcycle (RAM), 1983, No. 7444-6 15	20	30
S.H.A.R.C., Submersible High-Speed Attack & Recon Craft with Deep Six, 1983, No. 6049 25	50	100
Sky Hawk, V.T.O.L. Jet, 1983, No. 6079 10	15	30
Slugger, Self-Propelled Cannon with Thunder, 1983, No. 6056 15	25	50
Vamp Jeep with H.A.L., Attack Vehicle with Heavy Artillery Laser Cannon, 1983, No. 6680 20	35	75

	GOOD	EX	MIP
Vamp Mark II, Desert Jeep with Clutch, 1983, No. 6055 25	40	80

Series #4, Cobra

Figure Sets

	GOOD	EX	MIP
Buzzer, Mercenary, 1984, No. 6433 10	25	50
Crimson Guard, Elite Trooper, 1984, No. 6450 15	30	60
Eel, Frogman, 1984, No. 6448 15	30	60
Ripper, Mercenary, 1984, No. 6434 15	30	60
Snow Serpent, Polar Assault Trooper, 1984, No. 6449 15	30	60
Tele-Viper, Communications Trooper, 1984, No. 6447 15	30	60
Tomax, Crimson Guard Commander with Xamot, 1984, No. 6063 30	65	125
Torch, Mercenary, 1984, No. 6435 15	30	60

Uniform/Equipment Sets

	GOOD	EX	MIP
Cobra Bunker, 1984, No. 6125 5	15	25
Flight Pod, One-Man Bubble Pod, 1984, No. 6081 5	15	25
Night Landing, Mini Battlefield Vehicles Assortment, 1984, No. 6085 5	15	25
Rifle Range, 1984, No. 6129 5	15	25

Vehicle Sets

	GOOD	EX	MIP
Ferret, All-Terrain Vehicle, 1984, No. 6069 10	15	30

G.I. Joe Killer W.H.A.L.E., Series #3, 3-3/4" Figures, 1983

	GOOD	EX	MIP
Moray, Hydrofoil with Lamprey, 1984, No. 6024 15		25	50
Motorized Crimson Attack Tank, MOBAT Tank, 1984, No. 6687 30		60	125
Sentry and Missile System, Sears, with H.I.S.S. Tank, Cobra Commander, Officer and Soldier, 1984, No. 6686 75		150	250

Series #4, GI Joe
Figure Sets

	GOOD	EX	MIP
Air Tight, Hostile Environment Trooper, 1984, No. 6439 20		40	85
Alpine, Mountain Trooper, 1984, No. 6443 ..15		25	50
Barbecue, Fire Fighter, 1984, No. 6445 10		25	50
Bazooka, Missile Specialist, 1984, No. 6438 10		25	50
Dusty, Desert Trooper, 1984, No. 6442 10		25	50
Flint, Warrant Officer, 1984, No. 6436 10		25	50
Footloose, Infantry Trooper, 1984, No. 6444 10		25	50
Lady Jaye, Covert Operations Officer, 1984, No. 6440 25		50	100
Quick Kick, Silent Weapons Martial Artist, 1984, No. 6441 20		40	85
Shipwreck, Sailor and Parrot, 1984, No. 6446 15		25	50
Snake Eyes, Commando and Wolf, 1984, No. 6437 30		60	125
Tripwire, Mine Detector, 1984, No. 6102 20		35	75

Uniform/Equipment Sets

	GOOD	EX	MIP
Air Defense, 1984, No. 6125-2 10		15	25
Ammo Dump, 1984, No. 6129-1 10		15	25
Battle Gear Accessory Pack #3, 1984, No. 6092 5		10	15
Bomb Disposal, 1984, No. 6085-2 10		15	25
Check Point, 1984, No. 6125-1 10		15	25
Forward Observer, 1984, No. 6129-2 10		15	25
Tactical Battle Platform, 1984, No. 6021 10		20	40
Weapon Transport, Battlefield, 1984, No. 6085-1 10		15	25

Vehicle Sets

	GOOD	EX	MIP
A.W.E. Striker, All-Weather Environment Jeep with Crankcase, 1984, No. 6053 15		25	50
Armadillo, One-Man Mini-Tank, 1984, No. 6078 10		15	35
Bridge Layer, Bridge Laying Trank with Toll Booth, 1984, No. 6023 15		25	50
Mauler, Motorized Tank with Heavy Metal, 1984, No. 6015 15		25	50
Silver Mirage, Motorcycle with Sidecar, 1984, No. 6076 10		15	35
Snowcat, Snow Half-Track Vehicle with Frost-Bite, 1984, No. 6057 15		25	50

	GOOD	EX	MIP
U.S.S. Flagg, Aircraft Carrier with Admiral Keel Haul, 1984, No. 6001 125		250	500

Series #5, Cobra
Figure Sets

	GOOD	EX	MIP
B.A.T., Battle Android Trooper, 1985, No. 6456 10		15	35
Dr. Mindbender, Master of Mind Control, 1985, No. 6461 10		15	35
Monkey Wrench, Mercenary, 1985, No. 6460 10		15	35
Viper, Infantry Trooper, 1985, No. 6473 10		15	35
Zandar, Zartan's Brother Mercenary, 1985, No. 6457 10		15	35
Zarana, Reissue with earrings, 1985, No. 6472 30		65	125
Zarana, Zartan's Sister Mercenary, 1985, No. 6472 10		15	35

Uniform/Equipment Sets

	GOOD	EX	MIP
Battle Gear Accessory Pack #4, 1985, No. 6096 5		10	15
Surveillance Port Playset, 1985, No. 6130 15		30	75
Terror Drome, Armored Headquarters with Fireball Jet and A.V.A.C., 1985, No. 6003 75		150	300

Vehicle Sets

	GOOD	EX	MIP
Air Assault, Air Vehicle, 1985 10		15	25
Air Chariot, Vehicle with Serpentor "Cobra Emperor", 1985, No. 6062 15		20	55
Ground Assault, Land Vehicle, 1985 10		20	25
Hydro Sled, 1985, No. 6099-2 10		15	25
Jet Pack, One-Man Jet Set, 1985, No. 6099j-1 10		15	25
Night Raven S-3P, Surveillance Jet with Drone Pod and Strato Viper, 1985, No. 6014 20		35	70

G.I. Joe Tactical Battle Platform, Series #4, 3-3/4" Figures, 1984

G.I. JOE – 3-3/4"

G.I. JOE – 3-3/4"

	GOOD	EX	MIP
Stun, Split Attack Vehicle with Motor Viper, 1985, No. 6041 10		20	35
Swamp Fire, Air/Swamp Transforming Vehicle with Color-Change, 1985, No. 6068 10		15	30
Thunder Machine, Compilation Vehicle of Spare Parts with Thrasher, 1985, No. 6042 10		20	35

Series #5, GI Joe
Figure Sets

	GOOD	EX	MIP
Beach Head, Ranger, 1985, No. 6463 10		15	30
Dial Tone, Communications Expert, 1985, No. 6471 10		15	30
Hawk, Commander, 1985, No. 6468 10		15	30
Ice Berg, Snow Trooper, 1985, No. 6466 10		15	30
Leather Neck, Marine Gunner, 1985, No. 6458 10		15	30
Life Line, Rescue Trooper, 1985, No. 6465 ..10		15	30
Low-Light, Night Spotter, 1985, No. 6459 10		15	30
Main Frame, Computer Specialist, 1985, No. 6462 10		15	30
Road Block, Heavy Machine Gunner, 1985, No. 6467 10		15	30
Sci-Fi, Laser Trooper, 1985, No. 6469 10		15	30
Sgt. Slaughter, Mail order; Drill Instructor, 1985 10		15	30
Wet-Suit, Navy S.E.A.L., 1985, No. 6470 15		20	40

Uniform/Equipment Sets

	GOOD	EX	MIP
Outpost Defender Mini Playset, 1985, No. 6130 5		10	15

Vehicle Sets

	GOOD	EX	MIP
Conquest X-30, Super-Sonic Jet with Slip Stream, 1985, No. 6031 15		30	65
Devil Fish, High-Speed Attack Boat, 1985, No. 6066 10		15	30
H.A.V.O.C., Heavy Artillery Vehicle Ordinance Carrier with Cross-Country, 1985, No. 6030 10		15	35
L.V.C. Recon Sled, Low-Crawl Vehicle Cycle, 1985, No. 6067 10		15	30
Tomahawk, Troop Transit Helicopter with Lift Ticket, 1985, No. 6022 15		30	65
Triple T, One-Man Tank with Sgt. Slaughter, 1985, No. 6061 10		25	50

Series #6, Cobra
Figure Sets

	GOOD	EX	MIP
Big Boa, Troop Trainer, 1986-87, No. 6484 5		10	20
Cobra Commander, Cobra Leader with Battle Armor, 1986-87, No. 6474 10		15	30
Cobra-La Team, three-figure set, 1986-87, No. 6154 20		40	75
Crocmaster, Reptile Trainer, 1986-87, No. 6487 10		15	30

	GOOD	EX	MIP
Crystal Ball, Hypnotist, 1986-87, No. 6479 5		10	20
Raptor, Falconer, 1986-87, No. 6485 5		10	20
Techno-Viper, Battlefield Technician, 1986-87, No. 6490 5		10	20

Uniform/Equipment Sets

	GOOD	EX	MIP
Earth Borer, 1986, No. 6133-3 5		10	15
Mountain Climber, 1986, No. 6133-7 5		10	15
Pom-Pom Gun Pack, 1986, No. 6133-8 5		10	15
Rope Crosser, 1986, No. 6133-5 5		10	15

Vehicle Sets

	GOOD	EX	MIP
Buzz Boar, Underground Attack Vehicle, 1986-87, No. 6087-3 5		10	15
Dreadnok Air Skiff, Mini-set with Zanzibar, 1986-87, No. 6070 10		20	30
Dreadnok Cycle, Compilation Cycle with Gunner Station, 1986-87, No. 6171 5		10	20
Maggot, three-in-one tank vehicle with W.O.R.M.S. driver, 1986-87, No. 6029 10		15	35
Mamba, Attack Copter with removable pods with Gyro-Viper, 1986-87, No. 6026 10		15	30
Pogo, Ballistic Battle Ball, 1986-87, No. 6170 5		10	20
Sea Ray, Combination Submarine/Jet with Sea Slug, 1986-87, No. 6040 10		20	40
Wolf, Arctic Terrain Vehicle with Ice Viper, 1986-87, No. 6039 10		20	45

Series #6, GI Joe
Figure Sets

	GOOD	EX	MIP
Chuckles, Undercover M.P., 1986-87, No. 6482 3		5	10
Crazy Legs, Air Assault Trooper, 1986-87, No. 6475 10		15	30
Falcon, Green Beret, 1986-87, No. 6476 10		15	30
Fast Draw, Mobile Missile Specialist, 1986-87, No. 6488 10		15	25
Gung-Ho, Marine in Dress Blues, 1986-87, No. 6486 10		15	25
Jinx, Ninja Intelligence Officer, 1986-87, No. 6480 10		15	25
Law & Order, M.P. with Dog, 1986-87, No. 6478 10		15	25
Outback, Survivalist, 1986-87, No. 6483 5		10	20
Psych-Out, Deceptive Warfare Trooper, 1986-87, No. 6477 5		10	20
Secret Mission: Brazil, Toys R Us set with four figures, 1986-87 75		150	300
Sgt. Slaughter Set, Three-figure set, 1986-87, No. 6153 10		25	50
Sneak Peek, Advanced Recon Trooper, 1986-87, No. 6491 10		15	30

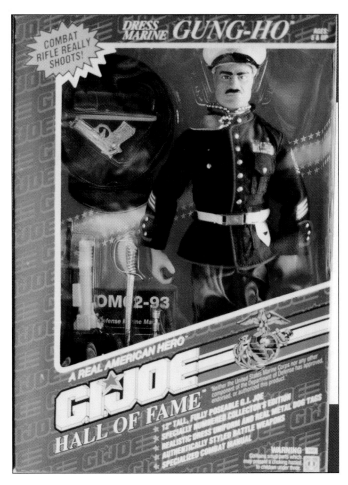

G.I. Joe Gung-Ho, Dress Marine, 12" Hall of Fame Figures, 1993,

	GOOD	EX	MIP
Tunnel Rat, Underground Explosive Expert, 1986-87, No. 6481 5		10	20

Uniform/Equipment Sets

	GOOD	EX	MIP
Antiaircraft Gun, 1986, No. 6133-1 5		10	15
Battle Gear Accessory Pack #5, 1986, No. 6677 5		10	15
Helicopter Pack, 1986, No. 6133-2 5		10	15
Mobile Command Center Play Set, 1986, No. 6006 25		50	100
Rope Walker, 1986, No. 6133-4 5		10	15
S.L.A.M., Strategic Long-Range Artillery Machine, 1986, No. 6172 10		15	30
Vehicle Gear Accessory Pack #1, 1986, No. 6098 5		10	15

Vehicle Sets

	GOOD	EX	MIP
Coastal Defender, Mini-Vehicle with accessories, 1986-87, No. 6087-2 5		10	15
Crossfire-Alfa, Radio Control Vehicle with Rumbler, 1986-87, No. 6004-1 25		50	100
Crossfire-Delta, Radio Control Vehicle with Rumbler, 1986-87, No. 6004-2 25		50	100
Defiant Space Shuttle Complex, Space shuttle, space station, crawler, 1986-87, No. 6002 75		350	525

	GOOD	EX	MIP
Persuader, Laser Tank with Backstop, 1986-87, No. 6038 10		15	35
Radar Station, 1986-87, No. 6133-3 5		10	15
Road Toad, Tow Vehicle with accessories, 1986-87, No. 6087-1 5		10	15

Collector Editions (1990s)

12" Hall of Fame Figures

	GOOD	EX	MIP
Ace, Fighter Pilot, 1993, No. 6837 10		15	25
Cobra Commander, Cobra Leader, 1992, No. 6827 15		20	35
Destro, Weapons Manufacturer, 1993, No. 6839 10		15	25
Duke, Combat Camo, 1994, No. 6044 10		12	15
Duke, Master Sergeant, 1991, No. 6019 15		30	45
Duke, Master Sergeant, 1992, No. 6826 15		25	35
Flint, Battle Bazooka, 1994, No. 6127 10		12	30
Grunt, Infantry Squad Leader, 1993, No. 6111 10		20	25
Gung-Ho, Dress Marine, 1993, No. 6849 10		20	25
Heavy Duty, Heavy Ordinance Specialist, 1993, No. 6114 10		20	35
Major Budd, Battle-Pack, 1994, No. 6159 10		15	30
Rapid Fire, Commando, 1993, No. 6924 20		50	60
Roadblock, Combat Camo, 1994, No. 6049 10		12	20
Rock 'n Roll, Heavy Weapons Gunner, 1993, No. 6128 10		20	25
Rock n Roll, Gatlin' Blastin', 1994, No. 6128 10		25	30
Snake Eyes, Commando, 1992, No. 6828 15		30	35
Snake-Eyes, Karate Choppin', 1994, No. 6089 10		25	30
Stalker, Ranger, 1992, No. 6829 15		30	35
Storm Shadow, Ninja, 1993, No. 6848 10		20	25
Talking Duke, Talking Battle Commander, 1993, No. 6117 15		35	50

Classic Collection

30th Salute Series

	GOOD	EX	MIP
30th Salute Black Action Soldier, 1994, No. 81271 55		100	150
35th Anniversary Gift Set, Then and Now, 1964 figure, 1999 figure, set of two, 1999 25		50	75
Action Marine, 1994, No. 81047 45		60	80
Action Pilot, 1994, No. 81046 50		75	125
Action Sailor, 1994, No. 81048 60		80	100
Action Soldier, 1994, No. 81045 25		50	95
Green Beret Lt. Joseph Colton, mail order, 1994 75		125	175

G.I. Joe Action Marine, Classic Collection, 1994

G.I. Joe Action Pilot, Classic Collection, 1994

Action Assortment

	GOOD	EX	MIP
Adventures of G.I. Joe: Peril of the Raging River, 1999 7		15	30
Delta Force, 1999 7		15	30
Salute to the Millennium Marine, 1999 7		15	30

Alpha Assortment

	GOOD	EX	MIP
Navy Seal, 2000 7		15	30

Armed Forces Assortment

	GOOD	EX	MIP
Army National Guard, 1998 10		20	30
U.S. Air Force Crew Chief, 1998 10		20	30
U.S. Marine Corps Korean Soldier, 1998 10		20	30
U.S. Marine Corps Recruit, 1998 10		20	30
U.S. Navy Serviceman, 1998 10		20	30

Armed Forces Service Collection

	GOOD	EX	MIP
Police Officer, 1999 5		10	20
U.S. Army Infantry Desert Soldier, 1999 5		10	20
U.S. Army Pacific Forces, 1999 5		10	20
U.S. Army Vietnam Soldiers, 1998 5		10	20
U.S. Navy SEAL, 1999 5		10	20
USAF Fighter Pilot: Korean War, 1999 5		10	20
Vietnam Marine, 1999 5		10	20

Astronaut Assortment

	GOOD	EX	MIP
Mercury Astronaut, 1997 15		30	40
Space Shuttle Astronaut, 1997 15		30	40

Bravo Assortment

	GOOD	EX	MIP
Vietnam Jungle Recon Soldier, 2000 7		15	30

G.I. Joe Navy SEAL, Classic Collection, 2000. Photo Courtesy Hasbro

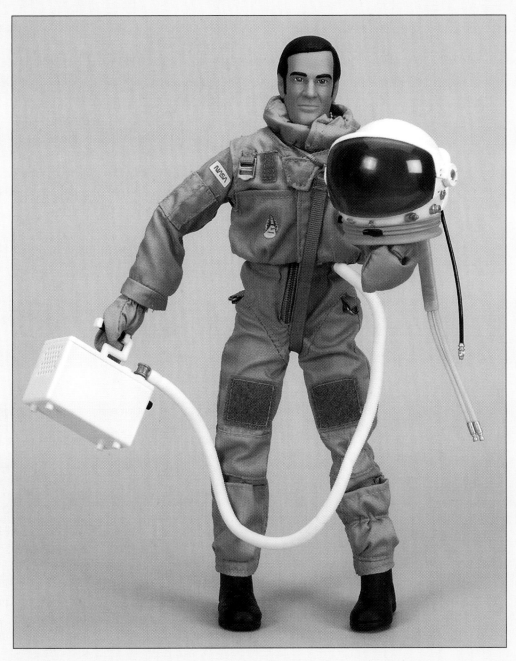

G.I. Joe Space Shuttle Astronaut, Classic Collection, 1997. Photo Courtesy Hasbro

G.I. JOE – COLLECTOR EDITIONS

G.I. Joe Action Sailor, Classic Collection, 1994

G.I. Joe British SAS, Classic Collection, 1996

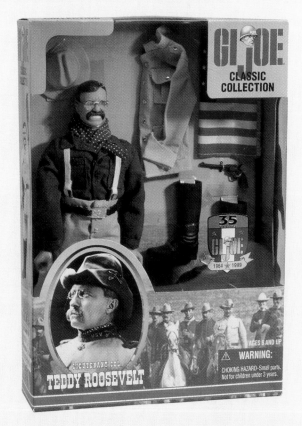

G.I. Joe Lt. Colonel Theodore Roosevelt, Classic Collection, 1999

G.I. Joe Vietnam Jungle Recon Soldier, Classic Collection, 2000. Photo Courtesy Hasbro

G.I. Joe George Washington, Classic Collection, 1998. Photo Courtesy Hasbro

Core Figure Assortment

	GOOD	EX	MIP
Adventures of G.I. Joe: Save the Tiger, 1999 10		20	40
G.I. Joe: Challenge at Hawk River, 1999 10		20	40
U.S. Army Nurse, Vietnam, 1999 5		10	20
U.S. Coast Guard Boarding Party, 1999 5		10	20

Delta Assortment

	GOOD	EX	MIP
Navajo Code Talker, 2000 7		15	30
U.S. Marine Dog Unit, 2000 7		15	30

Echo Assortment

	GOOD	EX	MIP
WWI Doughboy, 2000 7		15	30
WWII U.S. Army Airborne Normandy, 2000 7		15	30

Fourth of July Edition

	GOOD	EX	MIP
D-Day Salute, 1997 15		30	40

Greatest Heroes

	GOOD	EX	MIP
Buzz Aldrin, 1999 10		20	30
Lt. Colonel Theodore Roosevelt, 1999 10		20	30
Ted Williams, 1999 10		20	30
WWII Flame Thrower Soldier, 1999 10		20	30

Historical Commanders Assortment

	GOOD	EX	MIP
Colin Powell, 1998 20		45	60
Dwight Eisenhower, 1997 20		35	50

G.I. Joe U.S. Marine Corp Force Recon, Classic Collection, 1998. Photo Courtesy Hasbro

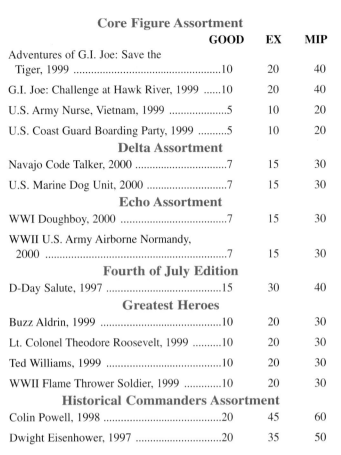

G.I. Joe U.S. Navy Blue Angel, Classic Collection, 1998. Photo Courtesy Hasbro

G.I. JOE – COLLECTOR EDITIONS

G.I. Joe Navajo Code Talker, Classic Collection, 2000. Photo Courtesy Hasbro

G.I. Joe U.S. Marine Dog Unit, Classic Collection, 2000. Photo Courtesy Hasbro

G.I. Joe 442nd Americans of Japanese Descent Combat So, Classic Collection, 1998. Photo Courtesy Hasbro

G.I. Joe Congressional Medal of Honor, Sgt. Francis S. Currey, Classic Collection, 1997. Photo Courtesy Hasbro

G.I. JOE – COLLECTOR EDITIONS

*G.I. Joe U.S. Air Force B-17 Bomber
Crewman, Classic Collection, 1998.
Photo Courtesy Hasbro*

*G.I. Joe U.S. Navy PT-Boat
Commander, Classic Collection, 1998.
Photo Courtesy Hasbro*

G.I. Joe WWI Doughboy, Classic Collection, 2000. Photo Courtesy Hasbro

G.I. Joe WWII U.S. Army Airborne Normandy, Classic Collection, 2000. Photo Courtesy Hasbro

G.I. JOE – COLLECTOR EDITIONS

Classic Collection G.I. Joes from 1995. Left to Right: Action Sailor; Action Soldier; Action Pilot; Action Marine. Photo Courtesy Hasbro

	GOOD	EX	MIP
General Patton, 1997	20	35	50
Omar Bradley, 1998	20	45	60
Holiday Salute			
George Washington, 1998	20	45	60
Hollywood Heroes			
Bob Hope, 1998	15	25	35
Military Sports Assortment			
Army Football, 1998	10	20	30
Navy Football, 1998	10	20	30
Modern Forces Assortment			
82nd Airborne Division, female, 1998	15	25	35
Australian O.D.F., 1996	7	15	30
Battle of the Bulge, Toys R Us exlcusive, 1996	10	20	40
Belgium Para Commando, 1997	15	40	45
British SAS, 1996	10	20	40
Dress Marine, Toys R Us exclusive, 1996	10	20	40
French Foreign Legion Legionnaire, 1997	15	30	40
U.S. Airborne Ranger HALO Parachutist, 1996	7	15	30
U.S. Army Coldweather Soldier, 1998	10	20	30
U.S. Army Drill Sergeant, 1997	10	20	30
U.S. Army Helicopter Pilot, female, 1997	15	30	55
U.S. Army Infantry Soldier, 1996	7	15	30

	GOOD	EX	MIP
U.S. Army M-1 Tank Commander, 1997	10	20	30
U.S. Marine Corp Force Recon, 1998	10	20	30
U.S. Marine Corps Sniper, 1996	10	20	35
U.S. Navy Blue Angel, 1998	15	30	40
U.S. Navy Flight Deck Fuel Handler, 1997	10	20	30
WWII Commemorative Figures, Target Exclusive			
Action Marine, 1995	10	20	40
Action Pilot, 1995	10	20	40
Action Sailor, 1995	10	20	40
Action Soldier, 1995	10	20	40
WWII Forces Assortment			
442nd Americans of Japanese Descent Combat So, 1998	10	20	30
Congressional Medal of Honor, Platoon Sgt. Mitchell Paige, 1998	10	20	40
Congressional Medal of Honor, Sgt. Francis S. Currey, 1997	10	20	40
Tuskegee B-25 Bomber Pilot, African American, 1997	7	15	30
Tuskegee Fighter Pilot, African American, 1997	7	15	30
U.S. Air Force B-17 Bomber Crewman, 1998	15	25	35
U.S. Navy PT-Boat Commander, 1998	15	25	35

Gargoyles—Bronx, Kenner

Gargoyles—Claw Climber Goliath, Kenner

Gargoyles (Kenner, 1995)
Accessories

	MNP	MIP
Gargoyle Castle	20	40
Night Striker	10	20
Rippin' Rider Cycle	7	12

Figures

Battle Goliath	3	15
Broadway	3	15
Bronx	3	15
Brooklyn	4	15
Claw Climber Goliath	3	15
Demona	4	15
Lexington	3	15
Mighty Roar Goliath	5	15
Power Wing Goliath	5	15
Quick Strike Goliath	3	15
Steel Clan Robot	3	15
Stone Armor Goliath	5	15
Strike Hammer Macbeth	3	15
Xanatos	3	15

Generation X (Toy Biz, 1995-96)
Freshman, 5" Figures

	MNP	MIP
Chamber	2	6
Emplate	2	6
Jubilee	2	6
Penance	2	6
Phalanx	2	6
Skin	2	7

Sophomore, 5" Figures

Banshee	3	8
Marrow	3	8
Mondo	3	8
Protector, The	3	8
White Queen	3	8

Ghost Rider (Toy Boz, 1995)
10" Figures

Blaze	4	8
Ghost Rider	4	8
Vengence	4	8

5" Figures

Blackout	2	4

Generation X—Emplate, Toy Biz

Generation X—Jubilee, Toy Biz

Generation X—Penance, Toy Biz

Generation X—Phalanx, Toy Biz

Generation X—Skin, Toy Biz

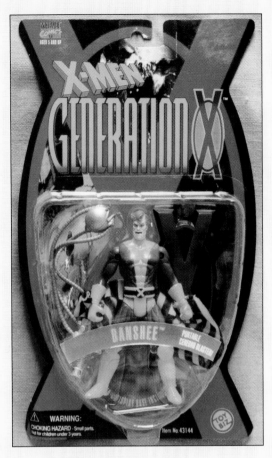

Generation X—Banshee, Toy Biz

Generation X—Marrow, Toy Biz

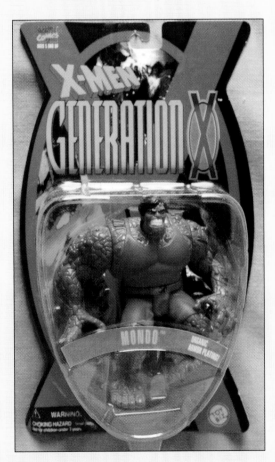

Generation X—Mondo, Toy Biz

Generation X—White Queen, Toy Biz

Generation X—Protector, The, Toy Biz

*Ghost Rider—
Blaze, Toy Biz*

*Ghost Rider—Ghost Rider,
Toy Biz*

	MNP	MIP
Blaze 2		4
Ghost Rider 2		4
Skinner 2		4
Vengence 2		4
Zarathos 2		4

Flamin' Stunt Cycles with molded-on figures

	MNP	MIP
Blaze 4		8
Ghost Rider 4		8
Vengeance 4		8

Play Sets

	MNP	MIP
Ghost Rider Play Set 8		20

Spirit of Vengeance Motorcycles and Figures

	MNP	MIP
Blaze 4		8
Ghost Rider 4		8
Vengeance 4		8

Ghostbusters (Kenner, 1986-91)

1986

	MNP	MIP
Bad to the Bone Ghost 5		15
Banshee Bomber Gooper Ghost with Ecto-Plazm 5		15
Bug-Eye Ghost 5		15
Ecto-1 35		80
Egon Spengler & Gulper Ghost 6		15
Firehouse Headquarters 25		50
Ghost Pooper 5		10
Ghost Zapper 5		15
Gooper Ghost Sludge Bucket 5		15

	MNP	MIP
Gooper Ghost Squisher with Ecto-Plazm 5		15
H2 Ghost 5		15
Peter Venkman & Grabber Ghost 6		15
Proton Pack 20		40
Ray Stantz & Wrapper Ghost 6		15
Slimer Plush Figure, 13" 20		35
Slimer with Pizza 20		40
Stay-Puft Marshmallow Man Plush, 13" 15		30
Winston Zeddmore & Chomper Ghost 7		18

1988

	MNP	MIP
Brain Blaster Ghost Haunted Human 5		15
Ecto-2 Helicopter 5		15
Fright Feature Egon 5		15
Fright Feature Janine Melnitz 5		15
Fright Feature Peter 5		15
Fright Feature Ray 5		15
Fright Feature Winston 5		15
Gooper Ghost Slimer 12		25
Granny Gross Haunted Human 5		15
Hard Hat Horror Haunted Human 5		15
Highway Haunter 10		20
Mail Fraud Haunted Human 5		15
Mini Ghost Mini-Gooper 5		10
Mini Ghost Mini-Shooter 5		10
Mini Ghost Mini-Trap 5		10
Pull Speed Ahead Ghost 5		15
Terror Trash Haunted Human 5		15

Ghostbusters—Ray Stantz & Wrapper Ghost, Kenner

Ghostbusters—Peter Venkman & Grabber Ghost, Kenner

Ghostbusters, Filmation—Fangster, Schaper

	MNP	MIP
Tombstone Tackle Haunted Human	5	15
X-Cop Haunted Human	5	15

1989

	MNP	MIP
Dracula	5	15
Ecto-3	5	15
Fearsome Flush	5	10
Frankenstein	3	15
Hunchback	3	15
Mummy	3	15
Screaming Hero Egon	5	15
Screaming Hero Janine Melnitz	5	15
Screaming Hero Peter	5	15
Screaming Hero Ray	5	15
Screaming Hero Winston	5	15
Slimer with Proton Pack, red or blue	15	35
Super Fright Egon with Slimy Spider	5	15
Super Fright Janine with Boo Fish Ghost	5	15
Super Fright Peter Venkman & Snake Head	5	15
Super Fright Ray	5	15
Super Fright Winston Zeddmore & Meanie Wienie	5	15
Wolfman	5	15
Zombie	5	15

1990

	MNP	MIP
Ecto Bomber with Bomber Ghost	5	15
Ecto-1A with Ambulance Ghost	20	40
Ghost Sweeper	5	15
Gobblin' Goblin Nasty Neck	6	15
Gobblin' Goblin Terrible Teeth	6	15

	MNP	MIP
Gobblin' Goblin Terror Tongue	6	15
Slimed Hero Egon	5	15
Slimed Hero Louis Tully & Four Eyed Ghost	5	15
Slimed Hero Peter Venkman & Tooth Ghost	5	15
Slimed Hero Ray Stantz & Vapor Ghost	5	15
Slimed Hero Winston	5	15

1991

	MNP	MIP
Ecto-Glow Egon	10	30
Ecto-Glow Louis Tully	10	30
Ecto-Glow Peter	10	30
Ecto-Glow Ray	10	30
Ecto-Glow Winston Zeddmore	10	30

Ghostbusters, Filmation (Schaper, 1986)

	MNP	MIP
Time Hopper Vehicle	10	15
Tracy	10	15

Figures

	MNP	MIP
Belfry and Brat-A-Rat	10	15
Bone Troller	10	15
Eddie	10	15
Fangster	10	15
Fib Face	10	15
Futura	10	15
Ghost Popper Ghost Buggy	20	40
Haunter	10	15
Jake	10	15
Jessica	10	15

Ghostbusters, Filmation—Scared Stiff, Schaper

GHOSTBUSTERS

	MNP	MIP
Mysteria	10	15
Prime Evil	10	15
Scare Scooter Vehicle	10	20
Scared Stiff	6	15

Godzilla (Trendmasters, 1998-present)
Figures

	MNP	MIP
Baby X Baby Godzilla	3	8
Capture Net Phillipe	2	8
Claw Slashing Baby Godzilla	3	6
Combat Claw Godzilla	8	16
Double Blast O'Neil	3	7
Fang Bite Godzilla	3	7
Grapple Gear Nick	3	7
Hammer Tail Baby Godzilla Hatchling	3	7
Living Godzilla	10	25
Monster Claw Baby Godzilla Hatching	3	7
Nuclear Strike Godzilla vs. Hornet Jet	3	7
Power Shield Jean-Luc	3	7
Razor Bite Godzilla	10	25
Razor Fang Baby Godzilla	3	7
Shatter Blast Godzilla vs. Rocket Launcher	3	7
Shatter Tail Godzilla	7	15
Spike Jaw Baby Godzilla Hatchling	3	7
Supreme Godzilla	15	30
Tail Thrasher Baby Godzilla	3	7
Thunder Tail Godzilla	7	15
Ultimate Godzilla	12	30
Ultra Attack Animal	3	7

Vehicles

	MNP	MIP
All-Terrain Vehicle with figure	7	15
Apache Attack Copter	10	20
Battle Bike with figure	7	15
Battle Blaster with figure	7	15
Combat Cannon with figure	7	15
Thunderblast Tank	7	15

Godzilla Wars (Trendmasters, 1996)
Figures

	MNP	MIP
Battra	4	8
Biollante	4	8
Gigan	4	8
Moguera	5	10
Space Godzilla	5	10
Supercharged Godzilla	4	8

Godzilla: King of the Monsters
10" Figures

	MNP	MIP
Ghidorah	4	10
Ghidorah, walking	6	12
Godzilla	4	10
Godzilla, walking	7	15
Mecha-Ghidora	6	12
Mecha-Godzilla	6	12
Mothra	8	16
Rodan	4	10

Figures

	MNP	MIP
Battra	4	8
Biollante	4	8
Ghidorah, boxed	4	8
Ghidorah, carded	5	10
Gigan	5	10

	MNP	MIP
Godzilla, boxed	4	8
Mecha-Ghidorah, boxed	4	8
Mecha-Ghidorah, carded	3	6
Mecha-Godzilla, boxed	4	8
Mecha-Godzilla, carded	3	6
Moguera	4	10
Mothra, boxed	5	10
Mothra, carded	4	8
Rodan, boxed	4	8
Rodan, carded	3	6

Greatest American Hero, The (Mego, 1981)
Vehicles

	MNP	MIP
Convertible Bug with Ralph and Bill figures	150	450

Happy Days (Mego, 1978)
Figures

	MNP	MIP
Fonzie, boxed	30	100
Fonzie, carded	30	75
Potsie, carded	30	75
Ralph, carded	30	75
Richie, carded	30	75

Play Sets

	MNP	MIP
Fonzie's Garage Play Set, 1978	60	150

Vehicles

	MNP	MIP
Fonzie's Jalopy, 1978	40	80
Fonzie's Motorcycle, 1978	40	80

He-Man (Mattel, 1989-91)
Figures

	MNP	MIP
Artilla	7	15
Battle Blade Skelator	7	15
Battle Punch He-Man	7	15
Brakk	6	12
Butthead	7	15
Disks of Doom Skeletor	6	14
Flipshot	6	12
Flogg	6	12
He-Man	6	12
He-Man with Flogg	7	18
He-Man with Skeletor	7	20
He-Man with Slush Head	7	20
Hoove	8	22
Hydron	6	12
Kalamarr	6	12
Karatti	6	12
Kayo	6	12
Lizorr	6	14
Nocturna	6	14
Optikk	6	14
Quakke	6	14
Skelator	6	12
Slush Head	6	12
Spin-Fist Hydron	6	14
Spinwit	6	14
Staghorn	6	14
Thunder Punch He-Man	8	20
Too-Tall hoove	15	35
Tuskador	6	14
Vizar	6	14

Vehicles

	MNP	MIP
AstroSub	6	14

	MNP	MIP
Battle Bird	4	12
Bolajet	4	12
Doomcopter	4	12
Sagitar	6	14
Shuttle Pod	4	12
Starship Eterna	25	65
Terroclaw	6	14
Terrotread	6	14

Hercules: The Legend Continues
(Toy Biz, 1995-97)

Deluxe 10" Figures

	MNP	MIP
Hercules and Xena	20	40

Figures

	MNP	MIP
Ares, Detachable Weapons of War	3	5
Centaur, Bug Horse Kick	3	5
Hercules I, Iron Spiked Spinning Mace	3	5
Hercules II, Archery Combat Set	3	5
Hercules III, Herculean Assault Blades	3	6
Hercules with Chain Breaking Strength	3	5
Hercules, Swash Buckling	3	5
Iolaus, Catapult Battle Gear	3	5
Minotaur, Immobilizing Sludge Mask	3	6
Mole-Man, Exploding Body	3	5
She-Demon, Stone Strike Tail	4	8
Xena, Warrior Princess Weaponry	5	25

Monsters

	MNP	MIP
Cerberus	4	10
Echidna	4	10

Honey West—Karate Outfit, Gilbert

Honey West—Honey West Doll, Gilbert

	MNP	MIP
Graegus	4	10
Hydra	4	10
Labyrinth Snake	4	10
Stymphalian Bird	4	10

Play Sets

	MNP	MIP
Hercules Tower of Power Play Set	4	10

Hercules: The Legendary Journeys
(Toy Biz, 1995-97)

Deluxe 10" Figures

	MNP	MIP
Hercules with bladed shield and sword dagger	8	20
Xena with two sets of body armor	8	20

Legendary Warrior Twin Packs, 5" Figures

	MNP	MIP
Hercules and Iolaus	8	20
Hercules and Xena	8	20
Xena and Gabrielle	10	40

Legendary Warriors, 5" Figures

	MNP	MIP
Hercules, Mace Hurling Hercules	3	8
Iolaus, Catapult Back-pack Iolaus	4	12
Nessus, Leg Kicking Centaur	3	8
Xena, Temptress Costume Xena	4	12

Monsters, 6" Figures

	MNP	MIP
Cerberus	3	10
Graegus	3	10
Hydra	3	10

Mt. Olympus Games, 5" Figures

	MNP	MIP
Atlanta, Spear Shooting Weaponry Rack	4	12
Hercules, Discus Launcher	3	8

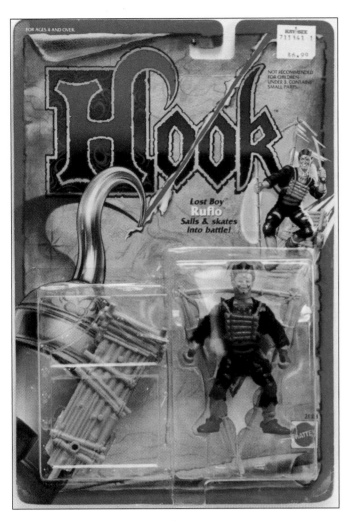

Hook—Lost Boy Ruffio, Mattel

	MNP	MIP
Mesomorph, Shield Attack Action	3	8
Salmoneus, Light-up Olympic Torch	3	8

Honey West (Gilbert, 1965)
Accessories

	MNP	MIP
Formal Outfit	55	110
Honey West Accessory Set: cap-firing pistol, binoculars, shoes and glasses	45	85
Honey West Accessory Set: telephone purse, lipstick, handcuffs and telescope lens necklace	45	85
Karate Outfit	50	100
Pet Set with Ocelot	60	100
Secret Agent Outfit	50	95

Figures

	MNP	MIP
Honey West Doll, 12" tall with black leotards, belt, shoes, binoculars and gun	175	325

Hook (Mattel, 1991-92)
Deluxe Figures

	MNP	MIP
Captain Hook, Skull Armor	10	25
Lost Boy Attack Croc	8	18
Pete Pan, Learn to Fly	10	25

Figures

	MNP	MIP
Captain Hook, Multi-blade	4	10
Captain Hook, Swiss Army	8	18
Captain Hook, Tall Terror	4	10

	MNP	MIP
Lost Boy Ace	3	10
Lost Boy Ruffio	3	10
Lost Boy Thud Bud	8	18
Peter Pan, Air Attack	4	10
Peter Pan, Battle Swing	5	15
Peter Pan, Food Fighting	5	15
Peter Pan, Swashbuckling	4	10
Pirate Bill Jukes	4	10
Pirate Smee	5	12

Vehicles

	MNP	MIP
Lost Boy Attack Raft	8	20
Lost Boy Strike Tank	8	20

Incredible Hulk, The (Toy Biz, 1996-97)
6" Figures

	MNP	MIP
Abomination, Toxic Blaster	5	12
Gray Hulk Battle Damaged	4	10
Leader, Anti-Hulk Armor	4	10
Savage Hulk, Transforming Action	4	10
She Hulk, Gamma Cross Bow	5	12

Outcasts, 5" Figures

	MNP	MIP
Battle Hulk, Mutant Outcast	2	6
Chainsaw, Gamma Outcast Bat	3	7
Leader-Hulk Metamorphosized, Gargoyle Sidekick	3	7

Independence Day—Alien Shock Trooper, Trendmasters

Independence Day—Alien Attacker Pilot,
Trendmasters

Independence Day—Alien Science Officer,
Trendmasters

Independence Day—Alien Supreme Commander, Trendmasters

	MNP	MIP
Two-Head, Gamma Outcast Kangaroo-Rat........................3		7
Wendingo, Gamma Outcast Rattlesnake 3		7

Play Sets

Gamma Ray Trap..3		10
Steel Body Trap 3		10

Smash and Crash, 5" Figures

Battle-Damaged Hulk with Restraints and Smash Out Action 3		8
Doc Samson, Omega with Missile Firing Action 3		8
Incredible Hulk, Crash out Action 3		8
Leader, Evil Robot Drone with Missile Firing Action........3		8
Zzzax with Energy Trap 3		8

Indiana Jones and The Temple of Doom—Indiana Jones, LJN

Transformations, 6" Figures

	MNP	MIP
Absorbing Man, Breakaway Safe and Wrecking Ball 3		8
Hulk 2099, Futuristic Clip-on Weapons 3		8
Maestro, Fallen Hero Armor 3		8
Smart Hulk, Gamma Blaster Backpack..............................3		8

Independence Day (Trendmasters, 1996)
Figures

	MNP	MIP
Alien Attacker Pilot 5		10
Alien in Bio Chamber 8		12
Alien Science Officer 5		10
Alien Shock Trooper 5		10
Alien Supreme Commander 15		25
David Levinson...5		10
President Thomas Whitmore 5		10
Steve Hiller...5		10
Ultimate Alien Commander...20		35
Weapons Expert...10		20
Zero Gravity 8		15

Indiana Jones (Toys McCoy, 1999)
12" Figures

	MNP	MIP
Arabian Horse...150		450
Indiana Jones 250		750

Indiana Jones and The Temple of Doom (LJN, 1984)
Figures

	MNP	MIP
Giant Tungee 45		75

Indiana Jones and The Temple of Doom—Indiana Jones, LJN

The Adventures of Indiana Jones—Cairo Swordsman, Kenner

The Adventures of Indiana Jones—Indiana Jones with whip, Kenner

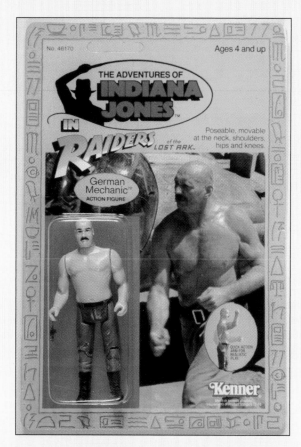

The Adventures of Indiana Jones—German Mechanic, Kenner

The Adventures of Indiana Jones—Indiana Jones in German Uniform, Kenner

The Adventures of Indiana Jones—Sallah, Kenner

The Adventures of Indiana Jones—Indiana Jones, 12", Kenner

	MNP	MIP
Indiana Jones	65	150
Mola Ram	55	80

Indiana Jones, The Adventures of
(Kenner, 1982-83)
Figures

Belloq	25	65
Belloq in Ceremonial Robe, mail away	20	45
Belloq in Ceremonial Robe Carded	20	500
Cairo Swordsman	15	40
German Mechanic	25	75
Indiana Jones in German Uniform	25	90
Indiana Jones with whip	50	250
Indiana Jones, 12"	150	450
Marion Ravenwood	100	350
Sallah	30	90
Toht	15	40

Play Sets

Map Room Play Set	35	90
Streets of Cairo Play Set	35	90
Well of Souls Play Set	50	125

Vehicles and Accessories

Arabian Horse	75	250
Convoy Truck	35	80

*The Adventures of Indiana Jones—Marion
Ravenwood, Kenner*

Iron Man—Iron Man Hologram, Toy Biz

INDIANA JONES

Iron Man—Iron Man Space Armor, Power-lift Space Pack, Toy Biz

Iron Man—Iron Man Stealth Armor, Toy Biz

Inspector Gadget (Galoob, 1984)

12" Figure

	MNP	MIP
Inspector Gadget	55	110

Inspector Gadget (Tiger Toys, 1992)

Figures

	MNP	MIP
Dr. Claw	8	20
Inspector Gadget that Falls Apart	5	15
Inspector Gadget that Squirts Water	5	15
Inspector Gadget with Expanding Arms	4	12
Inspector Gadget with Expanding Legs	5	15
Inspector Gadget with Snap Open Hat	5	15
Inspector Gadget with Telescopic Neck	5	15
MAD Agent with Bazooka	8	20
Penny and Brain	8	20

Vehicles

	MNP	MIP
Gadgetmoile	10	30

Iron Man (Toy Biz, 1995-96)

5" Figures, 1995

	MNP	MIP
Backlash, Nunchaku and Whip-cracking Action	3	8
Blizzard, Ice-Fist Punch	7	15
Century, Cape and Battle Staff	3	8

	MNP	MIP
Dreadknight, Firing Lance Action	3	8
Grey Gargoyle, Stone Hurling Action	3	8
Hawkeye, Bow and Arrow	7	15
Hulkbuster Iron Man, Removable Armor	3	8
Iron Man Arctic Armor, Removable Armor and Launching Claw Action	3	8
Iron Man Hologram	3	8
Iron Man Space Armor, Power-lift Space Pack	3	8
Iron Man Stealth Armor	3	8
Iron Man, Hydro Armor	4	10
Iron Man, Plasma Cannon Missile Launcher	3	8
Mandarin, Light-up Power Rigs	3	8
Modok, Energy Brain Blasts	3	8
Spider-Woman, Psisonic Web Hurling Action	7	15
Titanium Man, Retractable Blade Action	5	12
Tony Stark, Armor Carrying Suitcase	3	8
US Agent, Firing Shield Action	15	35
War Machine, Shoulder-Mount Cannons	3	8
Whirlwind, Whirling Battle Action	5	12

5" Figures, 1996

	MNP	MIP
Crimson Dynamo	3	8
Iron Man Inferno Armor	3	8
Iron Man Lava Armor	3	8

Iron Man—Modok, Energy Brain Blasts, Toy Biz

	MNP	MIP
Iron Man Magnetic Armor	3	8
Iron Man Radiation Armor	3	8
Iron Man Samurai Armor	3	8
Iron Man Subterranean Armor	3	8
War Machine 2	4	10

Deluxe 10" Figures

Iron Man	4	12
Mandarin	4	12
War Machine	4	12

Deluxe Dragons

Argent	7	15
Aureus	7	15
FinFang Foom	7	15

James Bond: Moonraker (Mego, 1979)

12" Figures

Drax	150	200
Holly	150	200
James Bond	125	150
James Bond, deluxe version	350	500
Jaws	300	500

Figures

Drax	45	100
Holly Goodhead	45	100
James Bond	45	100
Jaws	200	525

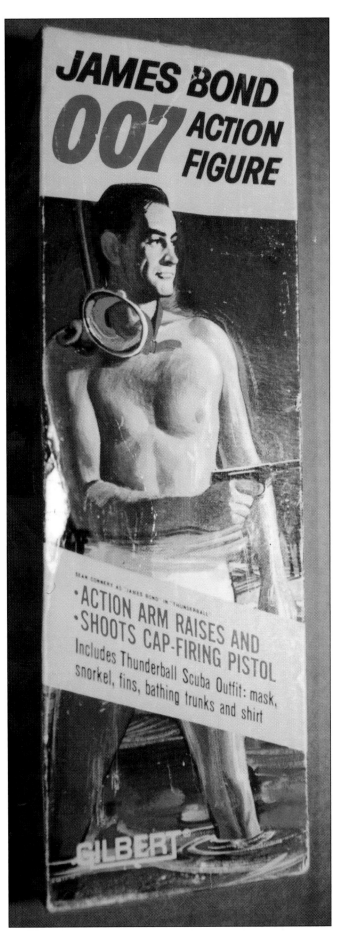

James Bond: Secret Agent 007, Gilbert

James Bond: Secret Agent 007
(Gilbert, 1965-66)
Figures

	MNP	MIP
James Bond	190	400
Oddjob	200	550

Johnny Hero (Rosko, 1965-68)
13" Figures

Johnny Hero	65	100
Johnny Hero, Olympic Hero	65	100

Jonny Quest (Galoob, 1996)
Accessories

Cyber Copter	5	15
Quest Porpoise with Deep Sea Jonny	5	15
Quest Rover	5	15

Quest World Figures

Cyber Cycle Jonny Quest	5	10
Cyber Jet Race	5	10
Cyber Suit Hadji	5	10
Cyber Trax Surd	5	10

Real World Figures

Deep Sea Race Bannon & Hadji	4	8
Jungle Commando Dr. Quest & Ezekiel Rage	4	8
Night Stryker Jonny Quest & Jessie	5	10
Shuttle Pilot Jonny Quest & Race Bannon	4	8
X-Treme Action Jonny Quest & Hadji	4	8

KISS (McFarlane, 1997)
6" Figures

Ace Frehley with album	7	15

KISS, Paul Stanley—Mego

	MNP	MIP
Ace Frehley with letter stand	5	10
Gene Simmons with album	7	15
Gene Simmons with letter base	5	10
Paul Stanley with album	7	15
Paul Stanley with letter stand	5	10

KISS—Ace Frehley with album, McFarlane Toys. Photo Courtesy McFarlane Toys

KISS—Peter Criss with album, McFarlane Toys. Photo Courtesy McFarlane Toys

KISS: Psycho Circus Tour—Ace Frehley, McFarlane Toys. Photo Courtesy McFarlane Toys

KISS: Psycho Circus Tour—Gene Simmons, McFarlane Toys. Photo Courtesy McFarlane Toys

KISS: Psycho Circus Tour—Paul Stanley, McFarlane Toys. Photo Courtesy McFarlane Toys

KISS: Psycho Circus Tour—Peter Criss, McFarlane Toys. Photo Courtesy McFarlane Toys

KISS

KISS

KISS—Gene Simmons, Mego

KISS: Psycho Circus—Ace Frehley with Stiltman, McFarlane Toys. Photo Courtesy McFarlane Toys

	MNP	MIP
Peter Criss with album	7	15
Peter Criss with letter stand	5	10

KISS (Mego, 1978)
12" Boxed Figures

Ace Frehley	100	260
Gene Simmons	110	260

KISS: Psycho Circus—Gene Simmons with Ring Master, McFarlane Toys. Photo Courtesy McFarlane Toys

KISS: Psycho Circus—Peter Criss with Animal Wrangler, McFarlane Toys. Photo Courtesy McFarlane Toys

	MNP	MIP
Paul Stanley	100	260
Peter Criss	100	260

KISS: Psycho Circus (McFarlane, 1998)
Figures

Ace Frehley with Stiltman	5	10
Gene Simmons with Ring Master	5	10
Paul Stanley with The Jester	5	10
Peter Criss with Animal Wrangler	5	10

KISS: Psycho Circus Tour (McFarlane, 1999)
Figures

Ace Frehley	4	8
Gene Simmons	4	8
Paul Stanley	4	8
Peter Criss	4	8

Laverne and Shirley (Mego, 1978)
12" Boxed Figures

Laverne and Shirley	60	150
Lenny and Squiggy	90	150

Legends of Batman (Kenner, 1994)
Figures

Catwoman	8	15
Crusader Batman	4	15

KISS: Psycho Circus—Paul Stanley with The Jester, McFarlane Toys. Photo Courtesy McFarlane Toys

	MNP	MIP
Crusader Robin	4	10
Cyborg Batman	4	10
Dark Rider Batman with horse	10	25
Dark Warrior Batman	4	10
Desert Knight Batman	5	10
Flightpak Batman	5	10
Future Batman	5	10
Joker	10	15
Knightquest Batman	5	10
Knightsend Batman	4	10
Long Bow Batman	4	10
Nightwing Robin	5	10
Power Guardian Batman	5	10
Riddler	10	15
Samurai Batman	4	10

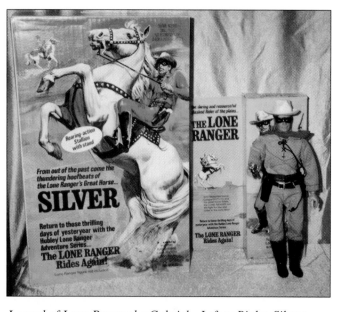

*Legend of Lone Ranger by Gabriel—Left to Right: Silver;
Lone Ranger*

*Legend of Lone Ranger by Gabriel—Left to Right: Scout;
Tonto*

*Legend of Lone Ranger by Gabriel—Left to Right: Smoke,
Cavendish*

	MNP	MIP
Silver Knight Batman	5	10
Viking Batman	4	10

Vehicles

Batcycle	10	20
Batmobile	10	30

Lone Ranger Rides Again (Gabriel, 1979)
Figures

Butch Cavendish	40	75
Dan Reid	25	60
Little Bear with Hawk	25	60
Lone Ranger	20	60
Red Sleeves	25	60
Tonto	20	60

Lone Ranger, Legend of (Gabriel, 1982)
Figures

Buffalo Bill Cody	10	25
Butch Cavendish	10	20
General Custer	10	20
Lone Ranger	15	30
Lone Ranger with Silver	25	50
Scout	10	20
Silver	15	30
Smoke	10	25
Tonto	7	15
Tonto with Scout	25	50

Lord of the Rings (Toy Vault, 1998-99)
Figures

Balrog	7	13
Frodo in Lorien	7	13
Frodo in the Barrow	8	18
Gandalf the Wizard	7	13
Gimli in Battle	7	13
Gimli of the Fellowship	8	18
Gimli in Lorien	7	13
Gollum	7	13
Gollum the Fisherman	7	13

Lord of the Rings—Ugluk at War, Toy Vault

Lord of the Rings—Frodo in Lorien, Toy Vault

Lord of the Rings—Gandalf the Wizard, Toy Vault

Lord of the Rings—Ugluk on the Hunt, Toy Vault

	MNP	MIP
Ugluk at War	7	13
Ugluk on the Hunt	7	13

Lost in Space (Trendmasters, 1998)
Figures

Battle Armor Don West	4	8
Cryo Chamber Judy Robinson	4	8
Cryo Chamber Judy Robinson	4	8
Cryo Chamber Will Robinson	4	8
Cyclops	25	60
Dr. Smith	7	15
Judy Robinson	7	15
Proteus Armor Dr. Smith	4	8
Proteus Armor John Robinson	4	8
Tybo the Carrot Man	20	45
Will Robinson	7	15

Play Sets

Jupiter 2 play set	25	75

Lost World of The Warlord (Remco, 1983)
Accessories and Teams

Warpult	30	60
Warteam with Arak	50	150
Warteam with Deimos	50	150
Warteam with Manchitse	50	150
Warteam with Mikola	50	150

Figures

Arak	25	60
Deimos	30	75
Hercules	25	60
Manchitse	30	75
Mikola	30	75
Warlord	15	50

Love Boat (Mego, 1981)
4" Figures

Captain Stubing	10	20
Doc	10	20
Gopher	10	20
Isaac	10	20
Julie	10	25
Vicki	10	25

M*A*S*H (Tristar, 1982)
3-3/4" Figures and Vehicles

B.J.	5	15
Colonel Potter	5	15
Father Mulcahy	5	15
Hawkeye	5	15
Hawkeye with Ambulance	15	35
Hawkeye with Helicopter	8	35
Hawkeye with Jeep	10	35
Hot Lips	10	20
Klinger	5	15
Klinger in Drag	15	35
M*A*S*H Figures Collectors Set	26	65
Winchester	5	15

8" Figures

B.J.	35	75
Hawkeye	20	50
Hot Lips	20	50

M.A.S.K. (Kenner, 1985-87)
Figure Sets

	MNP	MIP
Coast Patrol	8	20
Jungle Challenge	8	20
Rescue Mission	8	20
T-Bob	8	20
Venom's Revenge	8	20

M.A.S.K. Vehicles

Billboard Blast with Dusty Hayes	10	30
Bulldog with Boris Bushkin	15	45
Bullet with Ali Bombay	15	45

Mad Monster Series—The Monster Frankenstein, Mego

	MNP	MIP
Buzzard with Miles Mayhem and Maximus Mayhem	15	45
Condor with Brad Turner	10	30
Firecracker with Hondo Mac Lean	10	30
Firefly with Julio Lopez	10	30
Gator with Dirty Hayes	10	30
Goliath	15	45
Hurricane with Hondo Mac Lean	10	30
Iguana with Lester Sludge	10	30
Manta with Vanessa Warfield	15	45
Meteor with Ace Riker	10	25
Pit Stop Catapult with Sly Rax	10	30
Raven with Calhoun Burns	10	30
Razorback with Brad Turner	10	30
Rhino with Bruce Sato and Matt tracker	15	45
Slingshot with Ace Riker	10	30
Thunder Hawk with Matt Tracker	15	45
Volcano with Matt Tracker and Jacques LaFleur	15	45
Wildcat with Clutch Hawks	10	35

Play Sets

	MNP	MIP
Boulder Play Set	40	120

Split Seconds M.A.S.K. Vehicles

	MNP	MIP
Afterburner with Dusty Hanes	20	55
Detonator	10	30
Dynamo with Bruce Sato	15	55
Fireforce	10	30

Split Seconds V.E.N.O.M. Vehicles

	MNP	MIP
Barracuda with Bruno Shepherd	15	55
Vandal with Floyd Malloy	10	30

V.E.N.O.M. Vehicles

	MNP	MIP
Jackhammer with Cliffhanger	10	30
Outlaw with Miles Mayhem and Nash Gorey	15	50
Piranha with Sly Rax	10	25
Stinger with Bruno Shepherd	10	35
Switchblade with Miles Mayhem	15	50
Vampire with Floyd Malloy	10	30

Mad Monster Series (Mego, 1974)

8" Figures

	MNP	MIP
The Dreadful Dracula	80	160
The Horrible Mummy	50	100
The Human Wolfman	75	150
The Monster Frankenstein	45	90

Accessories

	MNP	MIP
Mad Monster Castle, vinyl	300	600

Major Matt Mason (Mattel, 1967-70)

Figures

	MNP	MIP
Callisto, 6"	100	250
Captain Lazer, 12"	125	300
Doug Davis, 6"	100	300
Jeff Long, 6"	150	550
Major Matt Mason, 6"	75	225
Mission Team Four-Pack	350	625
Scorpio, 7"	350	850
Sergeant Storm, 6"	100	400

Major Matt Mason by Mattel—Back row, left to right: Callisto; Doug Davis. Front row, left to right: Scorpio; Major Matt Mason

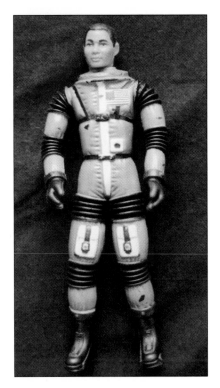

Major Matt Mason—Jeff Long,
Mattel. Photo Courtesy Corey
LeChat

Major Matt Mason—Doug Davis,
Mattel. Photo Courtesy Corey
LeChat

Major Matt Mason—Sergeant
Storm, Mattel. Photo Courtesy
Corey LeChat

Vehicles and Accessories

	MNP	MIP
Astro-Trak	50	150
Firebolt Space Cannon	45	125
Gamma Ray Guard	30	100
Moon Suit Pak	35	100
Reconojet Pak	25	75
Rocket Launch	25	75
Satellite Launch Pak	25	75
Satellite Locker	30	80
Space Power Suit	30	110
Space Probe Pak	25	75
Space Shelter Pak	25	75
Space Station Set	150	350
Star Seeker	85	180
Supernaut Power Limbs	30	110
Uni-Tred & Space Bubble	95	175
XRG-1 Reentry Glider	150	395

Man from U.N.C.L.E. (Gilbert, 1965)

Accessories

Action Figure Apparel Set: bullet proof vest, three
targets, three shells, binoculars, and bazooka............100   200
Action Figure Armament Set: jacket, cap firing pistol
with barrel extension, bipod stand, telescopic sight,
grenade belt, binoculars, accessory pouch and beret...90   180
Action Figure Arsenal Set #1: tommy gun, bazooka,
three shells, cap firing pistol and attachments, in
shallow window box 80   175
Action Figure Arsenal Set #2: cap firing THRUSH
rifle with telescopic sight, grenade belt and four
grenades, on wrapped header card..............................80   175

	MNP	MIP
Action Figure Jumpsuit Set: jumpsuit with boots, helmet with chin strap, 28" parachute and pack, cap firing tommy gun with scope, instructions	100	225
Action Figure Pistol Conversion Kit: binoculars and pistol with attachments, for 12" figures, on wrapped header card	45	90
Action Figure Scuba Set: swim trunks, air tanks, tank bracket, tubes, scuba jacket and knife	130	260

Figures

Illya Kuryakin Doll: black sweater, pants and shoes,
spring loaded arm for firing cap pistol, folding
badge, ID card and instruction sheet, in photo box...200   400
Napoleon Solo Doll: plastic, white shirt, black pants
and shoes, spring loaded arm for firing cap pistol,
folding badge, ID card and instruction sheet.............145   325

Mars Attacks! (Trendmasters, 1997)

Figures

Martian Ambassador	6	12
Martian Leader	6	12
Martian Spy Girl	45	65
Martian Spy Girl	35	70
Martian Trooper	8	15

Marvel Famous Covers (Toy Biz, 1997-98)

8" Figures

Aunt May	15	40
Captain America	8	20
Cyclops	5	15
Dark Phoenix	4	12
Dr. Doom	4	12
Green Goblin	15	45

Marvel Famous Covers—Black Widow, box closed, Toy Biz

Marvel Famous Covers—Black Widow, box open, Toy Biz

Marvel Famous Covers—Daredevil, box closed, Toy Biz

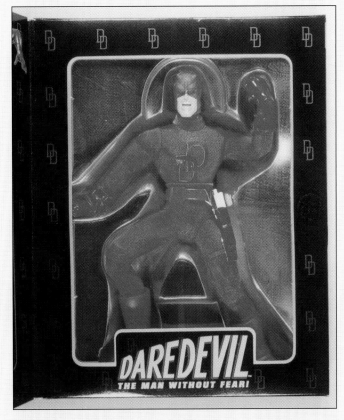

Marvel Famous Covers—Daredevil, box open, Toy Biz

MARVEL FAMOUS COVERS

Marvel Famous Covers—The Falcon, box closed, Toy Biz

Marvel Famous Covers—The Falcon, box open, Toy Biz

Marvel Famous Covers—Mister Sinister, box closed, Toy Biz

Marvel Famous Covers—Mister Sinister, box open, Toy Biz

	MNP	MIP
Magneto	5	15
Nightcrawler	5	15
Rogue	5	15
Spider-Man, red and black costume	15	50
Storm	12	35
Thor	4	12
Wolverine	10	35

Marvel Milestone, 8" Figures

Black Widow	3	8
Daredevil	3	8
Falcon	3	8
Mr. Sinister	3	8

Marvel Famous Covers Avengers Assemble (Toy Biz, 1999)
8" Figures

Hawkeye	5	15
Hulk	5	15
Iron man	5	15
Vision	5	15

Marvel Gold (Toy Biz, 1998)
Figures

Black Panther	8	16
Captain Marvel	8	16
Iron Fist	10	20
Marvel Girl	8	16
Moon Knight	8	16
Power Man	8	16
Vision	8	16

Marvel Shape Shifters (Toy Biz, 1999)
7" Figures

Hulk forms into Dino Beast	3	7
Rhino forms into Racing Rhino	3	7
Sabretooth forms into Sabretooth Tiger	3	7
Spider Sense Spider-Man forms into Spider-Bat	3	7

Marvel Shape Shifters II (Toy Biz, 1999)
7" Figures

Captain America forms into American Eagle	3	7
Colossus forms into Cyborg Gorilla	3	7
Kraven forms into Mighty Lion	3	7
Thor forms into Winged Stallion	3	7

Marvel Shape Shifters Weapons (Toy Biz, 1999)
Deluxe Figures

Apocalypse forms into Gattling Gun	3	7
Iron Man forms into Battle Axe	3	7
Punisher forms into Power Pistol	3	7
Spider-Man forms into Wrist Blaster	3	7

Marvel Special Edition Series (Toy Biz, 1998)
12" Figures

Dr. Octopus	3	7
Punisher	3	7
Spider-Woman	3	7

Marvel Super Heroes (Toy Biz, 1990-92)
Series 1, 1990

Captain America	10	20
Daredevil	15	40
Doctor Doom	10	25

Marvel Famous Covers—Aunt May, Toy Biz

	MNP	MIP
Doctor Octopus	10	25
Hulk	5	15
Punisher (cap firing)	5	15
Silver Surfer	10	30
Spider-Man (suction cups)	5	20

Series 2, 1991

Green Goblin (back lever)	15	40
Green Goblin (no lever)	10	25
Iron Man	10	25
Punisher (machine gun sound)	5	15
Spider-Man (web climbing)	15	35
Spider-Man (web shooting)	10	30
Thor (back lever)	15	40
Thor (no lever)	10	25
Venom	10	20

Series 3, 1992

Annihilus	5	15
Deathlok	5	15
Human Torch	5	15
Invisible Woman, catapult	5	15
Invisible Woman, vanishing	75	150
Mister Fantastic	5	15
Silver Surfer (chrome)	5	15
Spider-Man (ball joints)	5	15
Spider-Man (web tracer)	5	15
Thing	5	15
Venom (tongue flicking)	15	20

*Marvel Super Heroes Secret Wars—
Baron Zemo, Mattel*

*Marvel Super Heroes Secret Wars—
Captain America, Mattel*

*Marvel Super Heroes Secret Wars—
Daredevil, Mattel*

*Marvel Super Heroes Secret Wars—
Doctor Doom, Mattel*

*Marvel Super Heroes Secret Wars—
Doctor Octopus, Mattel*

*Marvel Super Heroes Secret Wars—
Hobgoblin, Mattel*

Marvel Super Heroes Secret Wars—Iron Man, Mattel

Marvel Super Heroes Secret Wars—Kang, Mattel

Marvel Super Heroes Secret Wars—Magneto, Mattel

Marvel Super Heroes Secret Wars—Spider-Man (black outfit), Mattel

Marvel Super Heroes Secret Wars—Spider-Man, Mattel

Marvel Super Heroes Secret Wars—Three-Figure Set, Mattel

MARVEL SUPER HEROES SECRET WARS

Talking Heroes

	MNP	MIP
Cyclops	10	20
Hulk	10	20
Magneto	10	20
Punisher	10	20
Spider-Man	10	20
Venom	10	25
Wolverine	10	20

Marvel Super Heroes Cosmic Defenders
(Toy Biz, 1992-93)
Figures

	MNP	MIP
Annihilus	5	15
Deathlok	5	15
Human Torch	5	15
Invisible Woman, vanishing color action	50	150
Mr. Fantastic	8	20
Silver Surfer	4	12

	MNP	MIP
Spider-Man, enemy tracking tracer	8	20
Spider-Man, multi-jointed	5	15

Marvel Super Heroes Secret Wars
(Mattel, 1984-85)
4" Figures

	MNP	MIP
Baron Zemo	15	35
Captain America	10	25
Constrictor (foreign release)	30	75
Daredevil	15	35
Doctor Doom	10	20
Doctor Octopus	10	20
Electro (foreign release)	30	75
Falcon	20	40
Hobgoblin	30	60
Ice Man (foreign release)	30	75
Iron Man	20	35
Kang	10	20

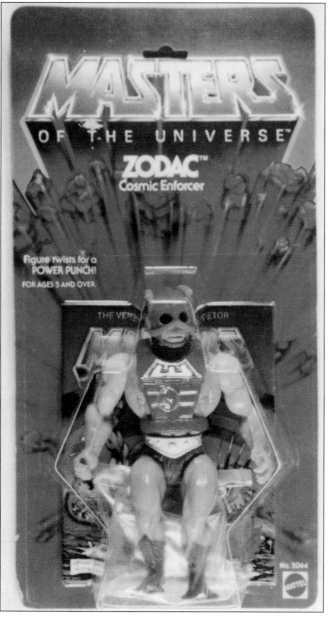

Masters of The Universe—Zodac, Mattel

Masters of The Universe—Stratos, blue wings, Mattel

	MNP	MIP
Magneto	10	20
Spider-Man, black outfit	25	50
Spider-Man, red and blue outfit	20	40
Three-Figure Set	40	90
Two-Figure Set	25	50
Wolverine, black claws	25	75
Wolverine, silver claws	25	40

Accessories

	MNP	MIP
Secret Messages Pack	1	5
Tower of Doom	20	35

Vehicles

	MNP	MIP
Doom Copter	10	35
Doom Copter with Doctor Doom	15	55
Doom Cycle	6	20
Doom Cycle with Doctor Doom	10	40
Doom Roller	10	20
Doom Star Glider with Kang	15	30
Freedom Fighter	10	30

	MNP	MIP
Star Dart with Spider-Man (black outfit)	25	50
Turbo Copter	10	40
Turbo Cycle	5	20

Marvel's Most Wanted (Toy Biz, 1998)
6" Figures

	MNP	MIP
Blink	3	7
Spat and Grovel	3	7
X-Man	3	7

Masters of The Universe (Mattel, 1981-1990)
12" Figures (Italian)

	MNP	MIP
Megator	300	1000
Tytus	400	1200

Accessories

	MNP	MIP
Battle Bones Carrying Case	10	20
Battle Cat	15	50
Battle Cat with Battle Armor He-Man	50	125

Masters of The Universe—Man-At-Arms, Mattel

Masters of The Universe—Faker, Mattel

MASTERS OF THE UNIVERSE

	MNP	MIP
Battle Cat with He-Man	50	150
Beam Blaster and Artillery	25	60
Jet Sled	5	15
Mantisaur	15	25
Megalaser	5	15
Monstroid Creature	30	75
Night Stalker	15	30
Night Stalker with Jitsu	40	75
Panthor	25	50
Panthor with Battle Armor Skeletor	35	125
Panthor with Skeletor	40	150
Screech	15	40
Screech with Skeletor	40	70
Stilt Stalkers	5	20
Stridor Armored Horse	10	30
Stridor with Fisto	30	75
Weapons Pak	5	15
Zoar	15	30
Zoar with Teela	40	120

Fifth Anniversary Figures

	MNP	MIP
Dragon Blaster Skeletor	25	75
Flying Fists He-Man	25	75
Hurricane Hordak	15	60
Terror Claws Skeletor	25	75
Thunder Punch He-man	25	60

Figures

	MNP	MIP
Battle Armor He-Man	15	40
Battle Armor Skeletor	15	40
Beast Man	25	70
Blade	25	70
Blast-Attack	20	40
Buzz-Off	25	40
Buzz-Saw Hordak	15	40
Clamp Champ	15	45
Clawful	20	45
Dragstor	15	40
Evil-Lyn	25	50
Extendar	15	35
Faker	30	120
Faker II	20	70
Fisto	10	40
Grizzlor	15	40
Grizzlor, black	75	150
Gwildor	15	75
He-Man, original	40	130
Hordak	20	40
Horde Trooper	20	40
Jitsu	20	45
King Hiss	20	45
King Randor	30	75
Kobra Kahn	10	35
Leech	10	35
Man-At-Arms	20	40
Man-E-Faces	25	50
Man-E-Faces, five extra weapons	75	175
Mantenna	25	40
Mekaneck	20	40
Mer-Man	25	50
Modulok	15	35
Mosquitor	25	45
Moss Man	10	40
Multi-Bot	20	40

	MNP	MIP
Ninjor	35	80
Orko	20	50
Prince Adam	20	60
Ram Man	20	60
Rattlor	10	35
Rattlor, red neck	10	30
Rio Blast	25	40
Roboto	15	35
Rokkon	15	35
Rotar	35	70
Saurod	30	70
Scare Glow	35	75
Skeletor, original	35	110
Snake Face	25	45
Snout Spout	15	40
Sorceress	25	70
Spikor	15	40
Sssqueeze	25	45
Stinkor	15	35
Stonedar	15	35
Stratos, blue wings	25	75
Stratos, red wings	25	75
Sy-klone	20	40
Teela	25	65
Trap Jaw	30	85
Tri-Klops	30	40
Tung Lashor	10	45
Twistoid	30	75
Two-Bad	10	30
Webstor	10	30
Whiplash	10	25
Zodiac	25	50

Grayskull Dinosaur Series

	MNP	MIP
Bionatops	35	75
Turbodaltyl	25	50
Tyrantisaurus Rex	75	125

Laser Figures

	MNP	MIP
Laser Light Skeletor	75	250
Laser Power He-Man	75	250

Mail Away Figures

	MNP	MIP
Savage He-Man (Wonder Bread exclusive)	n/a	500

Meteorbs

	MNP	MIP
Astro lion	15	30
Comet Cat	15	30
Cometroid	15	30
Crocobite	15	30
Dinosorb	15	30
Gore-illa	15	30
Orbear	15	30
Rhinorb	15	30
Tuskor	15	30
Ty-Gyr	15	30

Overseas Accessories

	MNP	MIP
Cliff Climber	25	75
Scubattack	25	75
Tower Tools	25	75

Play Sets

	MNP	MIP
Castle Grayskull	75	165
Eternia	350	700

	MNP	MIP
Fright Zone	45	125
Slime Pit	25	75
Snake Mountain	50	150

Vehicles

	MNP	MIP
Attack Trak	25	75
Bashasaurus	25	50
Battle Ram	30	75
Blasterhawk	25	60
Dragon Walker	20	45
Fright Fighter	15	45
Land Shark	15	35
Laser Bolt	15	40
Point Dread	25	75
Road Ripper	10	30
Roton	10	30
Spydor	25	50
Wind Raider	15	60

Metal Gear Solid (McFarlane, 1998)
Figures

	MNP	MIP
Liquid Snake	4	8
Meryl Silverburgh	4	8
Ninja	4	8
Psycho Mantis	4	8
Revolver Ocelot	4	8
Sniper Wolf	4	8
Solid Snake	4	8
Vulcan Raven	4	8

Metal Gear—Solid Sniper Wolf, McFarlane Toys

Micronauts (Mego, 1976-80)
Alien Invaders Carded

	MNP	MIP
Antron, 1979	15	30
Centaurus, 1980	35	70
Karrio, 1979	10	20
Kronos, 1980	35	70
Lobros, 1980	35	70
Membros, 1979	15	30
Repto, 1979	13	25

Alien Invaders Play Sets

	MNP	MIP
Rocket Tubes, 1978	23	50

Alien Invaders Vehicles

	MNP	MIP
Alphatron	5	10
Aquatron, 1977	10	20
Betatron	5	10
Gammatron	5	10
Hornetroid, 1979	20	40
Hydra, 1976	7	15
Mobile Exploration Lab, 1976	17	35
Solarion, 1978	15	30
Star Searcher, 1978	15	40
Taurion, 1978	11	22
Terraphant, 1979	20	40

Boxed Figures

	MNP	MIP
Andromeda, 1977	10	25
Baron Karza, 1977	15	30
Biotron, 1976	10	25
Force Commander, 1977	10	25
Giant Acroyear, 1977	10	25
Megas, 1981	10	25
Microtron, 1976	5	20
Nemesis Robot, 1978	7	15
Oberon, 1977	10	25
Phobos Robot, 1978	12	25

Carded Figures

	MNP	MIP
Acroyear II, 1977, red, blue, orange	7	15
Acroyear, 1976, red, blue, orange	10	20
Galactic Defender, 1978, white, yellow	7	15
Galactic Warriors, 1976, red, blue, orange	4	10
Pharoid with Time Chamber, 1977, blue, red, gray	10	20
Space Glider, 1976, blue, green, orange	5	10
Time Traveler, 1976, clear plastic, yellow, orange	3	10
Time Traveler, 1976, solid plastic, yellow, orange	5	15

Micropolis Play Sets

	MNP	MIP
Galactic Command Center, 1978	20	40
Interplanetary Headquarters, 1978	20	40
Mega City, 1978	20	30
Microrail City, 1978	20	40

Play Sets

	MNP	MIP
Astro Station, 1976	10	20
Stratstation, 1976	15	30

Vehicles

	MNP	MIP
Battle Cruiser, 1977	30	60
Crater Cruncher with figure, 1976	5	15
Galactic Cruiser, 1976	7	17
Hydro Copter, 1976	10	25
Neon Orbiter, 1977	6	20
Photon Sled with figure, 1976	5	15

MICRONAUTS

MIGHTY MORPHIN POWER RANGERS

*Mighty Morphin Power Rangers—Putty Patrol,
Bandai*

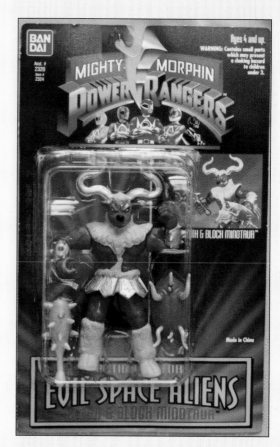

*Mighty Morphin Power Rangers—Minotar,
Bandai*

*Mighty Morphin Power Rangers—Snizard Lips,
Bandai*

*Mighty Morphin Power Rangers—Black Ranger,
Bandai*

	MNP	MIP
Rhodium Orbiter, 1977......................6	20
Thorium Orbiter, 1977......................6	20
Ultronic Scooter with figure, 1976......5	15
Warp Racer with figure, 1976............5	15

Mighty Morphin Power Rangers
(Bandai, 1993-95)
3" Figures

	MNP	MIP
Black Ranger 5	15
Blue Ranger 5	15
Pink Ranger 5	15
Red Ranger 5	15
Yellow Ranger 5	15

5" Figures with Thunder Bikes

	MNP	MIP
Black Ranger 6	15
Blue Ranger 6	15
Pink Ranger 6	15
Red Ranger 6	15
Yellow Ranger 6	15

8" Aliens, 1993

	MNP	MIP
Baboo.......................................10	20
Bones 10	20
Finster 10	20

Mighty Morphin Power Rangers—Goldar, Bandai

	MNP	MIP
Goldar 10	20
King Sphinx 10	20
Putty Patrol 10	20
Squatt 10	20

8" Figures, 1993

	MNP	MIP
Black Ranger 7	20
Blue Ranger 7	20
Pink Ranger 10	20
Red Ranger 5	20
Yellow Ranger 10	20

8" Movie Figures, 1995

	MNP	MIP
Black Ranger 6	15
Blue Ranger 6	15
Pink Ranger 6	15
Red Ranger 6	15
White Ranger 6	15
Yellow Ranger 6	15

Action Feature Evil Space Aliens, 5-1/2" Figures, 1994

	MNP	MIP
Dark Knight................................6	15
Eye Guy 6	15
Minotar 6	15
Mutaytus 6	15
Pudgy Pig 6	15
Rita Repulsa 6	15
Snizard Lips 6	15
Spidertron 6	15

Auto-Morphin Power Rangers, 5-1/2" Figures, 1994

	MNP	MIP
Black Ranger 3	15
Blue Ranger 3	15
Green Ranger 3	15
Pink Ranger 3	15
Red Ranger 2	15
Yellow Ranger 3	15

Deluxe Evil Space Aliens, 8" Figures, 1994

	MNP	MIP
Evil Eye 7	15
Goo Fish 7	15
Guitardo 7	15
Lord Zedd 8	18
Pirantus Head..............................7	15
Pudgy Pig 7	15
Putty Patrol 7	15
Rhino Blaster 7	15
Socaddillo 7	15

Karate Action Figures, 1994

	MNP	MIP
Black Ranger 6	12
Blue Ranger 6	12
Pink Ranger 8	16
Red Ranger 5	10
Yellow Ranger 8	16

Power Rangers for Girls

	MNP	MIP
Kimberly 10	20
Kimberly/Trini Set........................20	40
Trini 10	20

Zords, 1993

	MNP	MIP
Dragon Dagger 20	50
Dragon Zord with Green Ranger.........25	55

Mighty Morphin Power Rangers—Blue Ranger, Bandai

Mighty Morphin Power Rangers—Green Ranger, Bandai

Mighty Morphin Power Rangers—Red Ranger, Bandai

Mighty Morphin Power Rangers—Yellow Ranger, Bandai

Monsters—The Mummy, McFarlane Toys. Photo Courtesy McFarlane Toys

	MNP	MIP
MegaZord	15	30
MegaZord Deluxe	20	40
Titanus the Carrier Zord	35	75

Zords, 1994

	MNP	MIP
MegaZord, black/gold, limit. ed.	50	100
Power Cannon	15	35
Power Dome Morphin Set	25	55
Red Dragon Thunder Zord	25	45
Saba (White Sword)	15	30

	MNP	MIP
Thunder Zord Assault Team	25	45
TOR the Shuttle Zord	30	60
Ultra Thunder Zord	35	70
White Tiger Zord with White Ranger	25	50

Monsters (McFarlane, 1998)

Series 1, Play Sets with 4" Figures

	MNP	MIP
Dracula and Bat	5	15
Frankenstein and Igor	8	20
Hunchback, Quasimodo and Gargoyle	5	15

Monsters—Dracula and Bat, McFarlane Toys. Photo Courtesy McFarlane Toys

MONSTERS

Monsters—Werewolf and Victim, McFarlane Toys.
Photo Courtesy McFarlane Toys

Monsters—The Phantom of the Opera, McFarlane
Toys. Photo Courtesy McFarlane Toys

	MNP	MIP
Werewolf and Victim 5		15

Series 2, Play Sets with 4" Figures

	MNP	MIP
Dr. Frankenstein 6		12
The Mummy 6		12
The Phantom of the Opera 6		12
The Sea Creature 6		12

Mork and Mindy (Mattel, 1980)
Figures

	MNP	MIP
Mindy...20		45
Mork from Ork with egg 20		45
Mork with Talking Spacepack, upside down 20		50

Movie Maniacs (McFarlane, 1998-99)
Series 1

	MNP	MIP
Eve, *Species II* 4		8
Freddy Krueger, *Nightmare on Elm Street* 5		15
Freddy Krueger, gorey, *Nightmare on Elmstreet* 5		15
Jason, *Friday the 13th* 4		8
Jason, gorey, *Friday the 13th* 10		30
Leatherface, *The Texas Chainsaw Massacre* 15		25

Mork and Mindy—Mork with Talking Spacepack, Mattel

Movie Maniacs—Michael Myers from Halloween, *McFarlane Toys*

Movie Maniacs—Eric Draven from The Crow, *McFarlane Toys*

Movie Maniacs—Pumkinhead from Pumpkinhead, *McFarlane Toys*

Movie Maniacs—Ghostface from Scream, *McFarlane Toys*

	MNP	MIP
Leatherface, gorey, *The Texas Chainsaw Massacre*	25	45
Patrick, *Species II*	4	8

Series 2

	MNP	MIP
Chucky and Tiffany, *Bride of Chucky*	8	20
Chucky, *Child's Play*	5	15
Eric Draven, *The Crow*	5	15
Ghostface, *Scream*	5	15
Michael Myers, *Halloween*	5	15
Norman Bates, *Psycho*	5	15
Pumkinhead, *Pumpkinhead*	5	15

MOVIE MANIACS

Nightmare Before Christmas—Jack Skellington,
Hasbro

Nightmare Before Christmas—Behemouth, Hasbro

Nightmare Before Christmas—Jack Skellington as
Santa, Hasbro

Nightmare Before Christmas—Mayor, Hasbro

NIGHTMARE BEFORE CHRISTMAS

Nightmare Before Christmas—Sally, Hasbro

Nightmare Before Christmas—Werewolf, Hasbro

Nightmare Before Christmas—Oogie Boogie, Hasbro

Nightmare Before Christmas
(Hasbro, 1993)
Figures

	MNP	MIP
Behemouth	35	80
Evil Scientist	50	150
Jack Skellington	40	100
Jack Skellington as Santa	35	80
Lock, Shock and Barrel	75	250
Mayor	45	125
Oogie Boogie	75	250
Sally	40	100
Santa	75	250
Werewolf	40	100

Noble Knights
(Marx, 1968)

Bravo Armor Horse	75	150

Figures

Black Knight	250	550
Gold Knight	75	150
Silver Knight	75	150
Valiant Armor Horse	200	400
Valor Armor Horse	75	150
Victor Armor Horse	75	150

NOBLE KNIGHTS

Noble Knights—Gold Knight, Marx

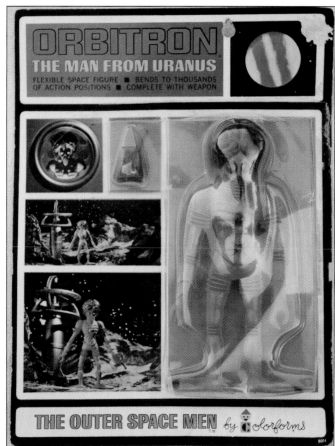

Outer Space Men—Orbitron / Man from Uranus, Colorforms

One Million Years, B.C. (Mego, 1976)
Figures

	MNP	MIP
Dimetrodon, 1976, boxed	75	150
Grok, 1976, carded	25	50
Hairy Rhino, 1976, boxed	75	150
Mada, 1976, carded	25	50
Orm, 1976, carded	25	50
Trag, 1976, carded	25	50
Tribal Lair Gift Set (five figures), 1976	70	180
Tribal Lair, 1976	60	120
Tyrannosaur, 1976, boxed	75	150
Zon, 1976, carded	25	50

Outer Space Men (Colorforms, 1968)
Figures

Alpha 7 / Man from Mars	150	450
Astro-Nautilus / Man from Neptune	300	750
Colossus Rex / Man from Jupiter	300	800
Commander Comet / Man from Venus	200	500

Outer Space Men—Electron / Man from Pluto, Colorforms

Planet of the Apes by Mego—Left to Right: Cornelius, carded; Galen, carded; Soldier Ape, carded

	MNP	MIP
Electron / Man from Pluto	200	500
Orbitron / Man from Uranus	200	600
Xodiac / Man from Saturn	200	500

Ozzy Osbourne (McFarlane, 1999)
Figures

	MNP	MIP
Ozzie Osbourne	5	15

Pee-Wee's Playhouse
5" Figures

	MNP	MIP
Chairry	12	30
Conky	15	40
Cowboy Curtis	12	30
Globey and Randy	12	30
Jambi and Puppetland Band	15	35
King of Cartoons	10	25
Magic Screen	8	20
Miss Yvonne	20	40
Pee-Wee Herman	8	20
Pee-Wee Herman with Scooter	12	30
Pterri	10	25
Reba	15	35
Ricardo	10	25

Play Sets

	MNP	MIP
Pee-Wee's Playhouse	50	175

Planet of the Apes (Hasbro, 1998)
Figures

	MNP	MIP
Cornelius	8	20
Dr. Zaius	8	20
General Ursus	8	20

Planet of the Apes (Mego, 1973-75)
8" Figures

	MNP	MIP
Astronaut Burke, 1975, boxed	50	250
Astronaut Burke, 1975, carded	50	100
Astronaut Verdon, 1975, boxed	50	250
Astronaut Verdon, 1975, carded	50	125
Astronaut, 1973, boxed	50	250
Astronaut, 1975, carded	50	100
Cornelius, 1973, boxed	40	200

	MNP	MIP
Cornelius, 1975, carded	40	100
Dr. Zaius, 1973, boxed	40	200
Dr. Zaius, 1975, carded	40	100
Galen, 1975, boxed	40	200
Galen, 1975, carded	40	100
General Urko, 1975, boxed	50	250
General Urko, 1975, carded	50	100
General Ursus, 1975, boxed	50	250
General Ursus, 1975, carded	50	100
Soldier Ape, 1973, boxed	50	250
Soldier Ape, 1975, carded	50	100
Zira, 1973, boxed	30	200
Zira, 1975, carded	30	100

Accessories

	MNP	MIP
Action Stallion, brown motorized, 1975, boxed	50	100
Battering Ram, 1975, boxed	20	40
Dr. Zaius' Throne, 1975, boxed	20	40
Jail, 1975, boxed	20	40

Play Sets

	MNP	MIP
Forbidden Zone Trap, 1975	90	200
Fortress, 1975	85	200
Treehouse, 1975	75	200
Village, 1975	85	200

Vehicles

	MNP	MIP
Catapult and Wagon, 1975, boxed	75	150

Pocket Super Heroes (Mego, 1976-79)
3-3/4" Figures

	MNP	MIP
Aquaman, 1976, white card	50	100
Batman, 1976, red card	20	40
Batman, 1976, white card	20	40
Captain America, 1976, white card	50	100
General Zod, 1979, red card	5	15
Green Goblin, 1976, white card	50	100
Hulk, 1976, white card	15	40
Hulk, 1979, red card	15	30
Jor-El (Superman), 1979, red card	10	20
Lex Luthor (Superman), 1979, red card	10	20
Robin, 1976, white card	20	40
Robin, 1979, red card	20	40

	MNP	MIP
Spider-Man, 1976, white card	15	40
Spider-Man, 1979, red card	15	30
Superman, 1976, white card	15	30
Superman, 1979, red card	15	30
Wonder Woman, 1979, white card	20	45

Accessories

	MNP	MIP
Batcave, 1981	120	300

Vehicles

	MNP	MIP
Batmachine, 1979	40	100
Batmobile, 1979, with Batman and Robin	80	200
Spider-Car, 1979, with Spider-Man and Hulk	30	75
Spider-Machine, 1979	40	100

Power Rangers in Space (Bandai, 1998)
Action Zords, 5" Figures

	MNP	MIP
Astro Megaship	2	6
Astro Megazord	2	6
Delta Megazord	2	6
Mega Tank	2	6
Mega Winger	2	6

Astro Ranger, 5" Figures

	MNP	MIP
Black Ranger	2	6
Pink Ranger	2	6
Red Ranger	2	6
Red Ranger	2	6
Silver Ranger	2	6
Yellow Ranger	2	6

Battlized Power Rangers, 5" Figures

	MNP	MIP
Black Ranger	2	6
Blue Ranger	2	6
Red ranger	2	6
Silver	2	6

Evil Space Aliens, 5" Figures

	MNP	MIP
Craterite	2	6
Ecliptor	2	6

Star Power Rangers in Space, 5" Figures

	MNP	MIP
Blue Ranger	2	6
Green Ranger	2	6
Pink Ranger	2	6
Red Ranger	2	6
Yellow Ranger	2	6

Power Rangers Turbo (Bandai, 1997)
Evil Space Aliens, 5" Figures

	MNP	MIP
Amphibitor	2	6
Chromite	2	6
Divatox	2	6
Elgar	2	6
Griller	2	6
Hammeron	2	6
Rygog	2	6
Visceron	2	6

Repeat Turbo Rangers, 5" Figures

	MNP	MIP
Blue Ranger	2	6
Green Ranger	2	6
Pink Ranger	2	6
Red Ranger	2	6
Yellow Ranger	2	6

Turbo Carts with 4" Figure

	MNP	MIP
Cart with Blue Turbo Ranger	3	8
Cart with Green Turbo Ranger	3	8
Cart with Pink Turbo Ranger	3	8
Cart with Red Turbo Ranger	3	8
Cart with Yellow Turbo Ranger	3	8

Turbo Rangers, 5" Figures, each activated with key

	MNP	MIP
Blue Turbo Ranger	2	6
Green Turbo Ranger	2	6
Pink Turbo Ranger	2	6
Red Turbo Ranger	2	6
Yellow Turbo Ranger	2	6

Turbo Shifter, 5" Figures

	MNP	MIP
Blue Ranger	2	6
Green Ranger	2	6
Pink Ranger	2	6
Red Ranger	2	6
Yellow Ranger	2	6

Power Rangers Zeo (Bandai, 1996)
Auto Morphin, 5-1/2" Figures

	MNP	MIP
Blue	2	6
Gold Warrior	2	6
Green	2	6
Pink	2	6
Red	2	6
Yellow	2	6

Evil Space Aliens, 5-1/2" Figures

	MNP	MIP
Cogs	2	6
Drill Master	2	6
Mechanizer	2	6
Quadfighter	2	6
Silo	2	6

Zeo Jet Cycles with Figure

	MNP	MIP
Cycle with Blue Zeo Ranger III	2	6
Cycle with Gold Zeo Ranger	2	6
Cycle with Green Zeo Ranger IV	2	6
Cycle with Pink Zeo Ranger I	2	6
Cycle with Red Zeo Ranger V	2	6
Cycle with Yellow Zeo Ranger II	2	6

Zeo Power Zords, 5-1/2" Figures

	MNP	MIP
1-2 Punching Action Red Battlezord	2	6
Auric the Conqueror Zord	2	6
Power Sword Action Zeo Megazord	2	6
Pyramidas	2	6
Super Zeo Megazord	2	6
Warrior Wheel	2	6

Zeo Rangers, 5-1/2" Figures

	MNP	MIP
Blue Zeo Ranger III	2	6
Gold Zeo Ranger	2	6
Green Zeo Ranger IV	2	6
Pink Zeo Ranger I	2	6
Red Zeo Ranger V	2	6
Yellow Zeo Ranger II	2	6

Zeo Rangers, 8" Figures

	MNP	MIP
Blue Zeo Ranger III	3	8
Gold Zeo Ranger	3	8
Green Zeo Ranger IV	3	8
Pink Zeo Ranger I	3	8
Red Zeo Ranger V	3	8
Yellow Zeo Ranger II	3	8

Puppet Master—Blade, Full Moon Toys. Photo Courtesy Full Moon Toys

Puppet Master—Leech Woman, Full Moon Toys. Photo Courtesy Full Moon Toys

Puppet Master—Pinhead, Full Moon Toys. Photo Courtesy Full Moon Toys

Puppet Master—Six Shooter, Full Moon Toys. Photo Courtesy Full Moon Toys

PUPPET MASTER

PUPPET MASTER

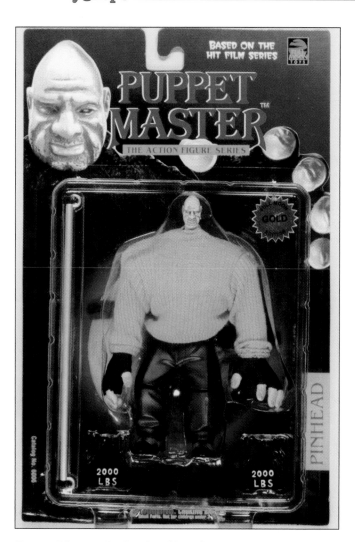

Puppet Master—Pinhead, gold, Full Moon Toys. Photo
Courtesy Full Moon Toys

Puppet Master—Leech Woman, gold, Full Moon Toys. Photo
Courtesy Full Moon Toys

Puppetmaster (Full Moon Toys, 1997-present)
Figures

	MNP	MIP
Blade	8	20
Blade, blood splattered	25	85
Blade, bullet-eyed (Troll & Joad)	15	40
Blade, gold	8	20
Blade, red Japanese exclusive	15	40
Jester	3	12
Jester, gold	8	20
Jester, Japanese exclusive, Carse of Jester	3	12
Jester, Previews exclusive	8	20
Leech Woman	3	12
Leech Woman, gold	8	20
Leech Woman, Japanese exclusive, Geisha Leech Woman	3	12
Leech Woman, Previews exclusive	8	20
Mephisto	3	12
Mephisto, clear	5	15
Mephisto, Japanese exclusive, death Mephisto	8	20
Mephisto, Previews exclusive	8	20
Pinhead	3	12
Pinhead, gold	8	20
Pinhead, Halloween 1999	8	20
Pinhead, Japanese exclusive, Pinhead in the Dark	8	25

	MNP	MIP
Pinhead, Previews exclusive	8	20
Sixshooter	8	20
Sixshooter	8	20
Sixshooter, Japanese exclusive, DOA Sixshooter	10	30
Sixshooter, Troll & Joad edition	10	30
Torch	3	12
Torch, gold	8	20
Torch, Japanese Exclusive, Camouflage Torch	8	20
Torch, Previews Exclusive	8	20
Totem	3	12
Totem, 1998 San Diego Comicon	15	45
Totem, gold	5	15
Totem, Japanese exclusive, Evil Spirit Totem	10	35
Totem, Preview exclusive	8	20
Tunneler	3	12
Tunneler, Australian exclusive	15	45
Tunneler, gold	8	20
Tunneler, Japanese exclusive, Cruel Sgt. Tunneler	15	45
Tunneler, Previews exclusive	8	20

Rambo (Coleco, 1985)
Figures

	MNP	MIP
Black Dragon	8	20
Chief	15	30
Colonel Troutman	7	15

	MNP	MIP
Dr. Hyde	20	45
General Warhawk	8	20
Gripper	8	20
K.A.T.	10	20
Mad Dog	8	20
Nomad	15	25
Rambo	10	25
Rambo with Fire Power	10	25
Sergeant Havoc	8	20
Turbo	8	20
White Dragon	8	20

Resident Evil (Toy Biz, 1998)
5" Figures

	MNP	MIP
Chris Redfield and Cerberus	5	15
Hunter and Chimera	3	8
Jill Valentine and Web Spinner	3	8
Maggot Zombie and Forrest Speyer	3	8
Tyrant	3	8

Robin Hood and His Merry Men (Mego, 1974)
8" Figures

	MNP	MIP
Friar Tuck	25	75
Little John	45	100
Robin Hood	75	150
Will Scarlett	75	150

Figures

	MNP	MIP
Friar Tuck	25	60
Little John	65	150
Robin Hood	90	300
Will Scarlett	75	275

Robin Hood Prince of Thieves (Kenner, 1991)
Accessories

	MNP	MIP
Battle Wagon	15	30
Bola Bomber	5	10
Net Launcher	5	10
Sherwood Forest Play Set	30	60

Figures

	MNP	MIP
Azeem	7	15
Friar Tuck	15	30
Little John	7	15
Robin Hood, Crossbow	5	18
Robin Hood, Crossbow, Costner Head	7	20
Robin Hood, Long Bow	8	17
Robin Hood, Long Bow, Costner Head	10	20
Sheriff of Nottingham	5	15
The Dark Warrior	8	20
Will Scarlett	8	20

RoboCop and the Ultra Police (Kenner, 1989-90)
Figures

	MNP	MIP
Ace Jackson	5	15
Anne Lewis	5	15
Birdman Barnes	8	15
Chainsaw	5	15
Claw Callahan	7	15
Dr. McNamara	5	15
Ed-260	10	25

	MNP	MIP
Headhunter	5	15
Nitro	5	15
RoboCop	9	20
RoboCop Night Fighter	6	20
RoboCop, Gatlin' Gun	15	30
Scorcher	6	15
Sgt. Reed	6	15
Toxic Waster	10	20
Wheels Wilson	6	15

Vehicles

	MNP	MIP
Robo-1	10	25
Robo-Command with figure	10	30
Robo-Copter	15	35
Robo-Cycle	5	10
Robo-Hawk	10	35
Robo-Jailer	15	40
Robo-Tank	10	35
Skull-Hog	5	10
Vandal-1	5	20

Robotech (Matchbox, 1986)
11-1/2" Figures

	MNP	MIP
Dana Sterling	20	50
Lisa Heyes	20	50
Lynn Minemei	20	50
Rink Hunter	20	50

3-3/4" Figures

	MNP	MIP
Bioroid Terminator	5	15
Corg	8	20
Dana Sterling	12	30
Lisa Hayes	8	20
Lunk	8	20
Max Sterling	8	20
Miriya, black	25	65
Miriya, red	8	20
Rand	5	12
Rick Hunter	10	25

Robotech by Matchbox—Left to Right: Roy Fokker; Lisa Hayes

	MNP	MIP
Robotech Master	5	12
Rook Bartley	20	50
Roy Fokker	12	30
Scott Bernard	12	37

8" Figures

	MNP	MIP
Armoured Zentraedi Warrior	8	20
Breetai	8	20
Dolza	5	15
Exedore	8	20
Khryon	8	20
Miriya	8	20

Vehicles and Accessories

	MNP	MIP
Armoured Cyclone	8	20
Bioroid Hover Craft	10	25
Dana's Hover Cycle	12	35
Invid Scout Ship	12	30
Tactical Battle Pod	12	30
Veritech Fighter	15	40
Veritech Hover Tank	15	40
Zentraedi Officer's Battle pod	12	35

Shogun Warriors
(Mattel, 1979)
24" Figures

	MNP	MIP
Daimos	75	150

Figures

	MNP	MIP
Dragun	75	175
Dragun (2nd figure)	75	150
Gaiking	75	150
Godzilla	100	200
Godzilla (2nd figure)	150	200
Mazinga	85	175
Mazinga (2nd figure)	75	150
Raydeen	75	150
Rodan	150	300

Silver Surfer
(Toy Biz, 1997-98)
Cosmic Power Alien Fighters

	MNP	MIP
Adam Warlock with Cosmic Skull Space Racer	3	8
Cosmic Silver Surfer and Pip the Troll	3	8
Galactus with Silver Surfer in Cosmic Orb, 8" figure	3	8
Ivar and Ant Warrior with Alien Annihilator	3	8
Molten Lava Silver Surfer with Eyeball Alien Space Racer	3	8
Ronan the Accussor with Tree Root Space Racer	3	8
Solar Silver Surfer & Draconian Warrior	3	8
Super Nova with Flaming Bird	3	8

Figures

	MNP	MIP
Beta Ray Bull, Thunder Hammer	3	10
Classic Silver Surfer with Cosmetic Surf Board	3	10
Meegan Alien, Galactic Weapon Seeker	3	10
Nova, Poseable Flaming Hair	3	10

Infinity Gauntlet Series, 10" Figure

	MNP	MIP
Silver Surfer	5	15

Simpsons
(Mattel, 1990)
Figures

	MNP	MIP
Bart	10	30
Bartman	10	30

Simpsons—Bartman, Mattel

	MNP	MIP
Homer	10	35
Lisa	15	40
Maggie	15	40
Marge	10	30
Nelson	10	30
Sofa Set	10	40

Simpsons (Playmates, 2000)
Accessories

	MNP	MIP
Kwiki Mart with Apu, interactive	8	20
Living Room with Marge and Maggie, interactive	10	25
Nuclear Power Plant with Homer, interactive	10	25

Figures

	MNP	MIP
Bart	3	8
C. Montgomery Burns	5	15
Grandpa	5	15
Homer	4	12
Krusty the Clown	5	15
Lisa	5	15

Sin City
(McFarlane, 1999-Present)
Figures

	MNP	MIP
Death Row Marv	5	15
Marv	3	10

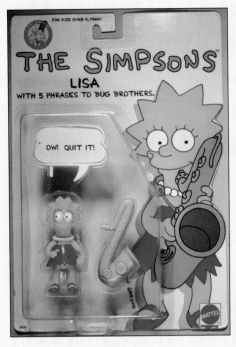

Simpsons—Lisa, Mattel

Simpsons—Marge, Mattel

Simpsons—Homer, Mattel

Simpsons—Maggie, Mattel

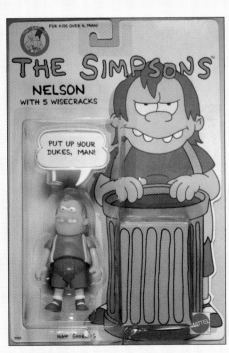

Simpsons—Nelson, Mattel

THE SIMPSONS

Sin City—Death Row Marv, McFarlane Toys

Six Million—Dollar Man Maskatron, Kenner

Six Million Dollar Man—Oscar Goldman, Kenner

Six Million Dollar Man (Kenner, 1975-78)
Accessories

	MNP	MIP
Backpack Radio	10	25
Bionic Cycle	10	20
Bionic Mission Vehicle	25	25
Bionic Transport	10	45
Bionic Video Center	35	100
Critical Assignment Arms	15	45
Critical Assignment Legs	15	45
Dual Launch Drag Set with 4" Steve Austin Bionic Bigfoot figure	45	80
Flight Suit	15	30
Mission Control Center	25	75
Mission to Mars Space Suit	15	30
OSI Headquarters	30	70
OSI Undercover Blue Denims	15	30
Porta-Communicator	20	50
Tower & Cycle Set	25	50
Venus Space Probe	125	275

Figures

Bionic Bigfoot	75	175
Maskatron	40	150
Oscar Goldman	50	100
Steve Austin	50	100
Steve Austin with biosonic arm	75	300
Steve Austin with engine block	50	150
Steve Austin with girder	60	200

Sleepy Hollow—Headless Horseman, McFarlane Toys. Photo Courtesy McFarlane Toys

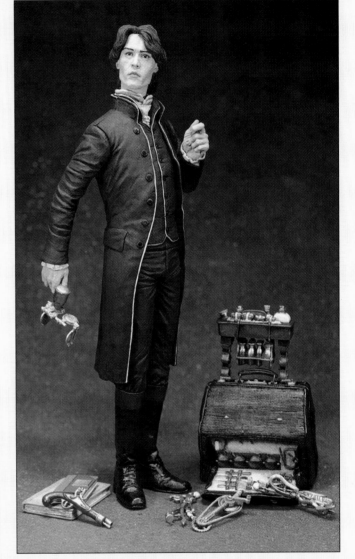

Sleepy Hollow—Ichabod Crane, McFarlane Toys. Photo Courtesy McFarlane Toys

Sleepy Hollow—Headless Horseman and Horse, McFarlane Toys. Photo Courtesy McFarlane Toys

SLEEPY HOLLOW

Slap Shot—Jack Hanson, McFarlane Toys

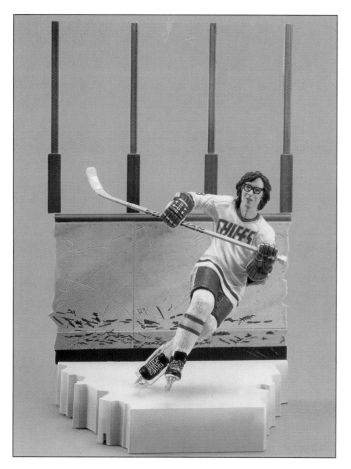

Slap Shot—Jeff Hanson, McFarlane Toys

Slap Shot—Steve Hanson, McFarlane Toys

Slap Shot (McFarlane, 2000)
Figures

	MNP	MIP
Jack Hanson	5	15
Jeff Hanson	5	15
Steve Hanson	5	15

Sleepy Hollow (McFarlane, 1999)
Figures

Crone	3	10
Headless Horseman	3	10
Headless Rider and Horse box set	8	20
Ichabod Crane	3	10

Space: 1999 (Mattel, 1976)
Figures

Commander Koenig	30	60
Dr. Russell	30	60
Professor Bergman	30	60
Zython Alien	75	200

Play Set

Eagle Playset with three 3" figures	150	300
Moonbase Alpha Deluxe Playset with three figures	75	200
Moonbase Alpha Playset	35	80

Space: 1999 (Palitoy, 1975)
Figures

Alan Carter	200	425
Captain Koenig	150	250
Captain Zantor	75	160
Mysterious Alien	75	160
Paul Morrow	175	300

Space: 1999—Commander Koenig, Mattel, Photo Courtesy Corey LeChat

Space: 1999—Dr. Russell, Mattel, Photo Courtesy Corey LeChat

Space: 1999—Professor Bergman, Mattel, Photo Courtesy Corey LeChat

SPACE: 1999

Space: 1999—Eagle Playset with three 3" figures, Mattel, Photo Courtesy Corey LeChat

Space: 1999— Moonbase Alpha Playset, Mattel. Photo Courtesy Corey LeChat

Inside view of Space: 1999 Moonbase Alpha Deluxe Playset. Photo Courtesy Corey LeChat

Space: 1999— Moonbase Alpha Deluxe Playset with three figures, Mattel. Photo Courtesy Corey LeChat

Space: 1999—Alan Carter, Palitoy. Photo Courtesy Corey LeChat

Space: 1999—Captain Koenig, Palitoy. Photo Courtesy Corey LeChat

Space: 1999—Mysterious Alien, Palitoy. Photo Courtesy Corey LeChat

Space: 1999—Paul Morrow, Palitoy. Photo Courtesy Corey LeChat

White and blond hair variations of Space: 1999 *Captain Zantor. Photo Courtesy Corey LeChat*

Space: 1999—Captain Zantor, Palitoy. Photo Courtesy Corey LeChat

Spawn (McFarlane, 1994-present)

13" Figures

	MNP	MIP
Angela	10	25
Medieval Spawn, Kay Bee exclusive	10	25
Spawn	10	25

Accessories

Spawn Alley Play Set	15	50
Spawnmobile	12	40
Violator Monster Rig	12	45

Series 1, 1994 (Todd Toys Packaging)

Clown, clown head	6	20
Clown, Kay Bee exclusive	3	10
Clown, monster head	6	10
Medieval Spawn, black armor	5	25
Medieval Spawn, Kay Bee exclusive	5	15
Medieval Spawn, blue armor	5	20
Overtkill, dark green	5	15
Overtkill, Kay Bee exclusive	3	12
Overtkill, turquoise	7	20
Spawn, Club exclusive, blue body	8	20
Spawn, Club exclusive, green body	8	20
Spawn, Diamond Exclusive	45	120
Spawn, full mask	5	25
Spawn, Kay Bee Exclusive	10	30
Spawn, Spawn No. 50 premium (Worm Head)	50	150
Spawn, unmasked (Hamburger Head), first card	15	40
Tremor, dark green costume	5	15
Tremor, Kay Bee exclusive	3	12
Tremor, orange skin	8	15
Violator	5	20
Violator, chrome card	8	20
Violator, club version	8	20
Violator, green card	5	15
Violator, Kay Bee exclusive	4	12
Violator, mail-order	20	75
Violator, red card	5	15

Manga Spawn (Series 10)—Samurai Spawn, McFarlane Toys

SPAWN

SPAWN

Dark Ages Spawn (Series 11)—The Horrid, McFarlane Toys

Dark Ages Spawn (Series 11)—The Ogre, McFarlane Toys

Dark Ages Spawn (Series 11)—The Raider, McFarlane Toys

Dark Ages Spawn (Series 11)—The Skull Queen, McFarlane Toys

Series 10, Manga, 1998

	MNP	MIP
Beast	4	15
Cyber Violator	4	8
Dead Spawn	4	8
Freak	4	8
Overkill	4	8
Samurai Spawn	4	8

Series 11, Dark Ages, 1998

	MNP	MIP
Horrid, The	3	8
Ogre, The	5	15
Raider, The	3	8

	MNP	MIP
Skull Queen, The	4	12
Spawn-The Black Knight	5	15
Spellcaster, The	4	15

Series 12, 1998

	MNP	MIP
Bottom Line	5	15
Creech, The	5	20
Cy-Gor	5	25
Heap, The	5	15
Reanimated Spawn	5	15
Spawn IV	5	15
Top Gun	5	15

Dark Ages Spawn (Series 11)—The Spellcaster, McFarlane Toys

Dark Ages Spawn (Series 14)—Necromancer, McFarlane Toys

Dark Ages Spawn (Series 14)—Iguantus and Tuskadon, McFarlane Toys

Dark Ages Spawn (Series 14)— The Scarlet Edge, McFarlane Toys

SPAWN

SPAWN

Dark Ages Spawn (Series 14)—Spawn: The Black Heart, McFarlane Toys

Dark Ages Spawn (Series 14)—Tormentor, McFarlane Toys

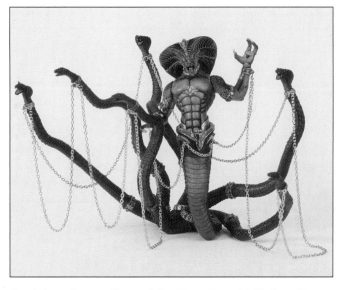

Dark Ages Spawn (Series 14)—Viper King, McFarlane Toys,

Series 14, Dark Ages, 1999

	MNP	MIP
Iguantus and Tuskadon	5	15
Necromancer	5	15
Scarlet Edge, The	5	15
Spawn: The Black Heart	5	15
Tormentor	5	15
Viper King	5	15

Series 15, Techno Spawn, 1999

Code Red	5	15
Cyber Spawn	5	15
Gray thunder	3	10
Iron Express	3	10
Steel Trap	3	10
Warzone	3	10

Series 16, Spawn Nitroriders, 2000

After Burner	3	10
Eclipse 5000	3	10
Flash point	3	10
Green Vapor, The	3	10

Series 2, 1995

Angela	5	25

	MNP	MIP
Angela, Club exclusive, blue	8	20
Angela, Club exclusive, pewter	8	20
Angela, gold headpiece with gold and purple costume	20	50
Angela, Kay Bee exclusive	3	12
Angela, McFarlane Toy Collector's Club exclusive	12	35
Angela, silver headpiece with silver and blue costume	10	25
Badrock, blue	10	25
Badrock, red pants	3	12
Chapel, blue/black pants	6	20
Chapel, green khaki pants	3	12
Commando Spawn	7	20
Malebolgia	40	80
Pilot Spawn, black costume	8	20
Pilot Spawn, Kay Bee Toys	3	12
Pilot Spawn, white "Astronaut Spawn"	5	16

Series 3, 1995

	MNP	MIP
Cosmic Angela	5	15
Cosmic Angela, McFarlane Collector's Club exclusive	5	15
Cosmic Angela, No. 62 Spawn and No. 9 Curse of Spawn, Diamond Exclusive	25	100
Curse, The	5	15
Curse, The, McFarlane Collector's Club exclusive	5	15
Ninja Spawn	7	15
Ninja Spawn, McFarlane Collector's Club exclusive	5	15
Redeemer	5	15
Redeemer, McFarlane Collector's Club exclusive	5	15
Spawn II	10	15
Spawn II, McFarlane Collector's Club exclusive	5	15
Vertebreaker	10	25
Vertebreaker, gray or black body, exclusive available through various stores	5	15
Vertebreaker, McFarlane Collector's Club exclusive	5	15
Violator II	10	20
Violator II, McFarlane Collector's Club exclusive	5	15

Series 4, 1996

	MNP	MIP
Clown II, black guns	6	20
Clown II, neon orange guns	3	12
Cy-Gor, gold trim	4	15
Cy-Gor, purple trim	4	15
Cy-Gor, Target exclusive	5	15
Exo-Skeleton Spawn, black and gray exo-skeleton	5	20
Exo-Skeleton Spawn, Target exclusive	5	15
Exo-Skeleton Spawn, white and light gray bones and white costume	8	20
Future Spawn, red trimmed	10	15
Maxx, The, FAO Schwarz exclusive	15	40
Maxx, The, with black Isz	15	40
Maxx, The, with white Isz	10	35
Shadowhawk, black with silver trim	4	15
Shadowhawk, gold with gray trim	3	10
She-Spawn, black mask	5	20
She-Spawn, red face mask	5	20

Series 5, 1996

	MNP	MIP
Nuclear Spawn, green skin	3	10
Nuclear Spawn, orange skin	4	15
Overtkill II, flesh colored with gray trim	5	15
Overtkill II, silver with gold trim	5	15
Tremor II, orange with red blood	3	10
Tremor II, purple with green bloob	3	10
Vandalizer, FAO Schwarz exclusive	10	25
Vandalizer, gray skinned with black trim	3	10

	MNP	MIP
Vandalizer, tan skinned with brown trim	3	10
Viking Spawn	5	25
Widow Maker, black and red with flesh-colored body	5	15
Widow Maker, purple and rose outfit, gray body	8	20

Series 6, 1996

	MNP	MIP
Alien Spawn, black with white	5	15
Alien Spawn, white with black	3	10
Battleclad Spawn, black costume	5	20

Spawn (Series 7)—Sam and Twitch, McFarlane Toys. Photo Courtesy McFarlane Toys

Spawn (Series 7)—Scourge, McFarlane Toys. Photo Courtesy McFarlane Toys

SPAWN

Spawn: The Movie—Burnt Spawn, McFarlane Toys

Spawn: The Movie—Jessica Priest, McFarlane Toys

	MNP	MIP
Battleclad Spawn, tan sections	4	12
Freak, The, purplish flesh with brown and silver weapons	3	10
Freak, The, tan flesh	5	15
Sansker, black and yellow	3	10
Sansker, brown and tan	5	15
Sansker, human arms and head with blond hair, exclusive available through various stores	5	15
Superpatriot, metallic blue arms and legs	3	10
Superpatriot, silver arms and legs	3	10
Tiffany the Amazon, green trim	5	15
Tiffany the Amazon, McFarlane Collector's Club exclusive	8	25
Tiffany the Amazon, red trim	5	15

Series 7, 1997

	MNP	MIP
Crutch, green goatee	5	15
Crutch, purple goatee	3	10
Mangler, The	5	15
No-Body	5	15
Sam and Twitch	5	15
Scourge	5	15
Spawn III, with owl and bat	8	25
Spawn III, with wolf and bat	8	25
Zombie Spawn, tan skin with red tunic	3	10

Series 8, 1997

	MNP	MIP
Curse of the Spawn	5	15

	MNP	MIP
Gate keeper	4	12
Grave Digger	4	12
Renegade, tan flesh	4	12
Rotarr	4	12
Sabre	4	12

Series 9, 1997

	MNP	MIP
Goddess, The	4	12
Manga Clown	4	12
Manga Curse	4	12
Manga Ninja Spawn	4	12
Manga Spawn	5	15
Manga Violator	4	12

Store Exclusives

	MNP	MIP
Manga Spawn, Toy R Us	15	30
Spiked Spawn, Target Exclusive	15	30

Spawn: The Movie
(McFarlane, 1997)

Deluxe Figures

	MNP	MIP
Attack Spawn	10	30
Malebolgia	10	30
Violator	10	30

Figures

	MNP	MIP
Al Simmons	4	10
Burnt Spawn	4	10

SPAWN

Spawn: The Movie—Jason Wynn, McFarlane Toys

	MNP	MIP
Clown	4	10
Jason Wynn	4	10
Jessica Priest	4	10

Play Sets

Final Battle	10	20
Graveyard	10	20
Spawn Alley	10	20

Spider-Man Electro-Spark (Toy Biz, 1997)

5" Figures

Captain America	5	15
Electro	3	8
Electro-Shock Spidey	3	8
Electro-Spark Spider-Man	3	8
Steel-Shock Spider-Man	3	8

Spider-Man Sneak Attack (Toy Biz, 1998)

Bug Busters, 5" Figures

Jack O'Lantern and Bug Eye Blaster	3	8
Silver Sable and Beetle Basher	3	8
Spider-Man and Spider Stinger	3	8
Vulture and Jaw Breaker	3	8

Shape Shifters, 7" Figures

Lizard forms into Mutant Alligator	2	6
Spider-Man forms into Monster Spider	2	6
Venom forms into 3-Headed Serpent	2	6

Street Warriors, 5" Figures

	MNP	MIP
Scarecrow with Pitchfork Projectile	2	6
Spider-Sense Peter Parker	2	6
Street War Spider-Man	2	6
Vermin with Rat-firing Fire Hydrant	2	6

Web Flyers, 5" Figures

Carnage	2	6
Copter Spider-Man	2	6
Hobgoblin	2	6
Spider-Man	2	6

Spider-Man Special Edition Series (Toy Biz, 1998)

12" Figures

Black Cat	10	30
Spider-Man	8	25
Venom	8	25

Spider-Man Spider Force (Toy Biz, 1997)

5" Figures

Beetle with Transforming Beetle Armor	2	6
Cybersect Spider-Man with Transforming Cyber Spider	2	6
Swarm with Transforming Bee Action	2	6
Tarantula with Transforming Tarantula Armor	2	6
Wasp with Transforming Wasp Armor	2	6

Spider-Man Venom—Venom the Madness, Surprise Attack Heads, Toy Biz

Spider-Man Spider Power (Toy Biz, 1999)

Series I, 5" Figures

	MNP	MIP
Slime Shaker Venom	2	6
Spider Sense Spider-Man	2	6
Street Warrior Spider-Man	2	6
Triple Threat Spider-Man	2	6

Series II, 5" Figures

Doctor Octopus	2	6
Flip and Swing Spider-man	2	6
J. Jonah Jameson	2	6
Spider Sense Peter Parker	2	6

Spider-Man Vampire Wars (Toy Biz, 1996)

5" Figures

Air-Attack Spider-Man	3	8
Anti-Vampire Spider-Man	3	8
Blade-The Vampire Hunter	3	10
Morbius Unbound	3	10
Vampire Spider-Man	3	8

Spider-Man Venom (Toy Biz, 1996-97)

Along Came a Spider, 6" Figures

Bride of Venom and Vile the Spider	3	10
Phage and Pincer the Spider	3	8
Spider-Carnage and Spit the Spider	3	8
Venom the Symbiote and Riper the Spider	3	8

Planet of the Symbiotes, 6" Figures

	MNP	MIP
Hybrid, pincer Wing Action	3	8
Lasher, Tentacle Whipping Action	3	8
Riot, Launching Attack Arms	3	8
Venom the Madness, Surprise Attack Heads	3	8

Planet of the Symbiotes, Deluxe 6" Figures

Hybrid, Pincer Wing Action	3	8
Lasher, Tentacle Whipping Action	3	8
Riot, Launcing Attack Arms	3	8
Scream, Living Tendril Hair	3	8
Venom the Madness, Surprise Attack Heads	3	8

Spider-Man Web Force (Toy Biz, 1997)

5" Figures

Daredevil, Transforming Web Tank Armor	2	6
Lizard, Transforming Swamp Rider	2	6
Vulture, Transforming Vuture-Bot	2	6
Web Commando Spidey, Transforming Web Copter	2	6
Web Swamp Spidey, Transforming Web Swamp Seeker Armor	2	6

Spider-Man Web Traps (Toy Biz, 1997)

5" Figures

Future Spider-Man with Snapping Cacoon Trap	2	6
Monster Spider-Man with Grappling Spider Sidekick	2	6

Spider-Man: The Animated Series—Alien Spider Slayer, Toy Biz

Spider-Man: The Animated Series—Cameleon, Toy Biz

Spider-Man: The Animated Series by Toy Biz—Left to Right: Battle-Ravaged Spider-Man; Spider-Man Six Arm

Spider-Man: The Animated Series by Toy Biz—Left to Right: Hobgoblin; Spider-Man with Web Racer

Spider-Man: The Animated Series by Toy Biz—Left to Right: Morbius; Spider-Sense Spider-Man

SPIDER-MAN: THE ANIMATED SERIES

Spider-Man: The Animated Series—Prowler, Toy Biz

Spider-Man: The Animated Series—Spider-Man in Black Costume, Toy Biz

Spider-Man: The Animated Series—Spider-Man with Web Shooter

Spider-Man: The Animated Series—Vulture, Toy Biz

Spider-Man: The Animated Series—Kingpin, Toy Biz

	MNP	MIP
Rhino with Rotating Web Snare	2	6
Scorpion with Whipping Tail Attacker trap	3	8
Spider-Man with Pull-string Web Trap	2	6

Spider-Man: The Animated Series (Toy Biz, 1994-96)
15" Talking Figures

	MNP	MIP
Spider-Man	12	25
Venom	12	25

2-1/2" Die-Cast Figures

Spider-Man vs. Carnage	2	4
Spider-Man vs. Dr. Octopus	2	4
Spider-Man vs. Hobgoblin	2	4
Spider-Man vs. Venom	2	4

5" Figures

Alien Spider Slayer	3	8
Battle-Ravaged Spider-Man	3	10
Cameleon	4	12
Carnage	5	15
Carnage II	4	12
Dr. Octopus	4	12
Green Goblin	5	15
Hobgoblin	4	12
Kingpin	5	15
Kraven	4	12
Lizard	5	15
Morbius	4	12
Mysterio	3	12
Nick Fury	3	12
Peter Parker	5	15

	MNP	MIP
Prowler	3	12
Punisher	3	12
Rhino	6	25
Scorpion	5	15
Shocker	4	15
Smythe	5	12
Spider-Man in Black Costume	3	12
Spider-Man Six Arm	3	12
Spider-Man with Parachute Web	3	12
Spider-Man with Spider Armor	3	15
Spider-Man with Web Parachute	8	15
Spider-Man with Web Racer	5	15
Spider-Man with Web Shooter	5	15
Spider-Man, multi-jointed	3	15
Spider-Sense Spider-Man	3	12
Symbiotic Venom Attack	3	12
Venom	4	15
Venom II	3	12
Vulture	5	15

Accessories

Daily Bugle Play Set	10	15

Deluxe 10" Figures

Carnage	8	20
Dr. Octopus	7	15
Hobgoblin	7	15
Kraven	7	15
Lizard	7	15
Spider-Man Spider Sense	7	15
Spider-Man with suction cups	7	15
Spider-Man, wall hanging	7	15
Venom	7	15
Vulture	10	20

Projectors

Hobgoblin	5	15
Lizard	5	15
Spider-Man	5	15
Venom	5	15

Vehicles

Hobgoblin Wing Bomber	10	25
Smythe Battle Chair Attack Vehicle	15	40
Spider-Man Wheelie Cycle	7	15
Spider-Man's Cycle (radio-controlled)	15	30
Tri-Spider Slayer	10	25

Star Trek (Mego, 1974-80)
8" Carded Figures

Andorian, 1976	300	650
Captain Kirk, 1974	25	50
Cheron, 1975	85	175
Dr. McCoy, 1974	35	75
Gorn, 1975	80	180
Klingon, 1974	25	50
Lt. Uhura, 1974	50	135
Mr. Spock, 1974	25	50
Mugato, 1976	275	500
Neptunian, 1975	100	225
Romulan, 1976	600	1000
Scotty, 1974	35	80
Talos, 1976	275	500
The Keeper, 1975	75	175

Play Sets

	MNP	MIP
Mission to Gamma VI	700	1200
U.S.S. Enterprise Bridge	100	275

Star Trek Alien Combat (Playmates, 1999)
Figures

	MNP	MIP
Borg Drone	15	25
Klingon Warrior	15	25

Star Trek Collector Assortment (Playmates, 1999)
Figures

	MNP	MIP
Andorian Ambassador	5	10
Captain Janeway	5	10
Counselor Troi	5	10
Dr. McCoy	5	10

Star Trek—Cheron, 1975, Mego. Photo Courtesy Corey LeChat

Star Trek—Gorn, 1975, Mego. Photo Courtesy Corey LeChat

Star Trek—Dr. McCoy, 1974, Mego

Star Trek—Klingon, 1974, Mego. Photo Courtesy Corey LeChat

	MNP	MIP
Ensign Chekov	5	10
Geordi LaForge	5	10
Gorn Captain	5	10
Khan	5	10
Lieutenant Sulu	5	10
Lieutenant Uhura	5	10
Locutus of Borg	5	10
Mr. Spock	5	10
Mugatu	5	10
Q	5	10
Scotty	5	10
Seven of Nine	5	10

Star Trek Collector Series
(Playmates, 1994-95)
9-1/2" Boxed Figures

	MNP	MIP
Borg	10	25
Captain Benjamin Sisko (Command Edition)	10	25
Captain Jean-Luc Picard (Command Edition)	10	25
Captain Jean-Luc Picard (Movie Edition)	10	25
Captain Kirk (Command Edition)	10	25
Captain Kirk (Movie Edition)	10	25
Commander Riker	10	25
Data (Movie Edition)	10	25
Dr. Beverly Crusher	10	25
Geordi La Forge (Movie Edition)	10	25

Star Trek Electronic Display Assortment
(Playmates, 1999)
Figures

	MNP	MIP
Captain Kirk	20	40
Captain Picard	20	40
Commander Riker	20	40

Back of card from 1976 Star Trek from Mego. Photo Courtesy Corey LeChat

Star Trek by Mego—Left to Right: Neptunian; The Keeper. Photo Courtesy Corey LeChat

	MNP	MIP
Lieutenant Commander Data	20	40
Lieutenant Worf	20	40
Mr. Spock	20	40

Star Trek Millennium Collector's Set
(Playmates, 1999)
Figures

	MNP	MIP
Captain Janeway/Commander Chakotay	15	40
Captain Kirk/Mr. Spock	15	40
Captain Picard/Commander Riker	15	40
Captain Sisko/Commander Riker	15	40

Star Trek V (Galoob, 1989)
Boxed Figures

	MNP	MIP
Captain Kirk	15	75
Dr. McCoy	15	75
Klaa	15	75
Mr. Spock	15	75
Sybok	15	75

Star Trek: Babylon 5
(Exclusive Toy Products, 1997)
6" Figures

	MNP	MIP
Ambassador Juphar Trkider	3	7
Ambassador Kosh	3	7
Ambassador Londo Mollari	3	7
Ambassador She'Lah	3	7
Ambassador Vlur/Nhur	3	7
Captain Elizabeth Lochley	3	7
Chief Garabaldi	4	10
Delenn	3	7
Delenn with Minbari, Diamond Exclusive	5	15
G'Kar	3	7

STAR TREK

Star Trek: First Contact—Jean-Luc Picard in 21st century outfit, Playmates

Star Trek: First Contact—Jean-Luc Picard, Playmates

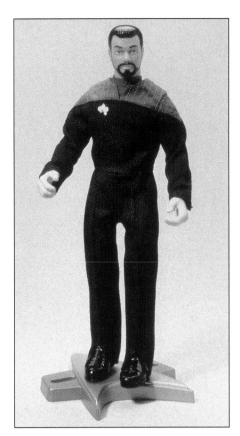

Star Trek: First Contact—William Riker, Playmates

	MNP	MIP
G'Kar, green outfit, Diamond Exclusive	5	15
John Sheridan	3	7
Lennier	4	10
Lyta Alexander	4	10
Marcus Cole	4	10
PSI Cop Bester	4	10
Shadow Sentient, Diamond Exclusive	10	50
Stephen Franklin	3	7
Susan Ivanova	4	10
Susan Ivanova, White's Collecting Figures Exclusive	5	20
Vir Cotto	3	7
Vorlon Visitor, Diamond Exclusive	5	20

9" Figures

Ambassador Delenn	5	20
Ambassador G'Kar	5	20
Ambassador G'Kar, Diamond Exclusive	5	30
Chief Michael Girabaldi	5	25
John Sheridan	5	25
Lennier, Diamond Exclusive	5	25
Londo	5	25
Marcus Cole	5	20
Michael Garibaldi	5	20
Susan Ivanova	5	25
Vir Cotto	5	20

Star Trek: First Contact (Playmates, 1996)

Figures

Borg, 5" figure	8	15
Data, 5" figure	5	10
Data, 9" figure	12	18
Deanna Troi, 5" figure	5	10

Star Trek: First Contact—Zefram Cochrane, Playmates

	MNP	MIP
Dr. Beverly Crusher, 5" figure	6	12
Geordi LaForge, 5" figure	5	10
Jean-Luc Picard in 21st century outfit, 9" figure	15	23
Jean-Luc Picard in space suit, 5" figure	6	12
Jean-Luc Picard, 5" figure	5	10
Jean-Luc Picard, 9" figure	12	18
Lily, 5" figure	8	15
William Riker, 5" figure	5	10
William Riker, 9" figure	12	18
Worf, 5" figure	5	10
Zefram Cochrane, 5" figure	5	10
Zefram Cochrane, 9" figure	18	25

Star Trek: Insurrection (Playmates, 1998)
Figures

	MNP	MIP
Counselor Troi	8	15
Data	8	15
Geordi LaForge	8	15
Jean-Luc Picard	8	15
Ru' Afo	8	15
Worf	8	15

Star Trek: Space Talk Series
(Playmates, 1995)
Space Talk Series

	MNP	MIP
Borg	5	20
Picard	5	10

Star Trek: Starfleet—Academy Cadet Jean-Luc Picard, Playmates

Star Trek: The Motion Picture—Acturian, Mego

	MNP	MIP
Q	5	20
Riker	5	10

Star Trek: Starfleet Academy
(Playmates, 1996)
Figures

	MNP	MIP
Cadet Geordi LaForge	8	15
Cadet Jean-Luc Picard	8	15
Cadet William Riker	8	15
Cadet Worf	8	15

Star Trek: The Motion Picture
(Mego, 1980-81)
12" Boxed Figures

	MNP	MIP
Arcturian, 1979	40	125
Captain Kirk, 1979	40	75
Decker, 1979	45	115
Ilia, 1979	40	75
Klingon, 1979	40	125
Mr. Spock, 1979	40	75

3-3/4" Carded Figures

	MNP	MIP
Acturian	75	150
Betelgeusian	75	150
Captain Kirk	12	35
Decker, 1979	12	35

STAR TREK

Star Trek: The Motion Picture—Dr. McCoy, Mego

Star Trek: The Motion Picture—Klingon, Mego

Star Trek: The Motion Picture—Mr. Spock, Mego

Star Trek: The Motion Picture by Mego—Left to Right: Scotty; Ilia; Captain Kirk

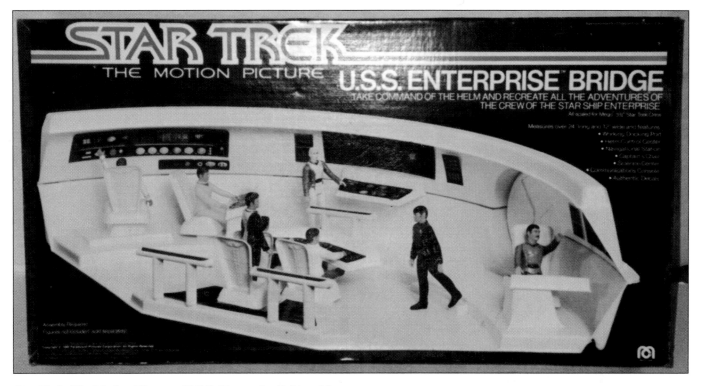

Star Trek: The Motion Picture—U.S.S. Enterprise Bridge, Mego

	MNP	MIP
Dr. McCoy	12	35
Ilia	10	20
Klingon	75	150
Megarite	75	150
Mr. Spock	12	35
Rigellian	75	150
Scotty	12	35
Zatanite	75	150

Play Sets

U.S.S. Enterprise Bridge	45	105

Star Trek: The Next Generation
(Galoob, 1988-89)

3-3/4" Figures, Series 1

Data, blue face	70	160
Data, brown face	30	60
Data, flesh face	15	30
Data, spotted face	15	30
Geordi La Forge	5	15
Jean-Luc Picard	5	15
Lt. Worf	5	15
Tasha Yar	10	25
William Riker	5	15

3-3/4" Figures, Series 2

Antican	35	100
Ferengi	35	100
Q	35	100
Selay	35	100

Accessories

Enterprise	10	35
Ferengi Fighter	15	50
Galileo Shuttle	15	50
Phaser	20	40

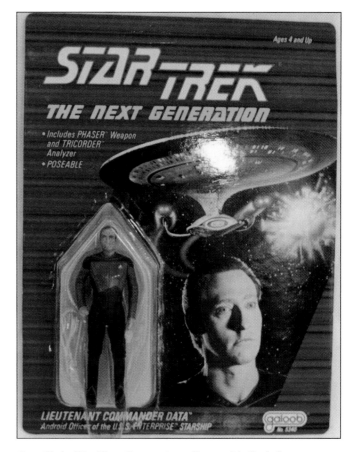

Star Trek: The Next Generation—Data with flesh face, Galoob

Star Trek: The Next Generation—Jean-Luc Picard, Galoob

Star Trek: The Next Generation (Playmates, 1992-96)

Series 1, 1992

	MNP	MIP
Borg	10	20
Commander Riker	10	18
Data	10	20
Deanna Troi	15	30
Ferengi	10	25
Geordi LaForge	10	25
Gowron the Klingon	12	25
Jean-Luc Picard	10	20
Romulan	15	30
Worf	10	20

Series 2, 1993

Admiral McCoy	5	12
Benzite	7	15
Borg	5	10
Captain Scott (Scotty)	5	10
Commander Riker	6	12
Commander Sela	6	12
Data	6	12
Dathon	7	15
Deanna Troi	6	12
Dr. Beverly Crusher	6	12

	MNP	MIP
Geordi LaForge	7	15
Guinan	7	15
Jean-Luc Picard	6	12
K'Ehleyr	6	12
Locutus	6	12
Lore	7	15
Q	6	12
Spock	6	12
Vorgon	10	20
Wesley Crusher	6	12
Worf	6	12

Series 3, 1994

Barclay	5	15
Beverly Crusher	5	15
Data as Romulan	5	15
Data, dress uniform	5	15
Data, Redemption outfit	75	300
Deanna Troi	3	15
Dr. Noonian Soong	5	15
Ensign Ro Laren	10	20
Esoqq	20	75
Geordi La Forge	5	15
Gowron	10	25
Guinan	5	15
Hugh Borg	5	15
Lore	3	15
Lwaxana Troi	3	15
Nausicaan	5	15
Picard as Dixon Hill	5	15
Picard as Romulan	3	15
Picard, red uniform	3	15
Q, judge's robes	5	15
Riker, Malcorian	3	15
Riker, red uniform	65	150
Sarek	5	15
Sela	5	15
Spock	5	15
Tasha Yar	5	15
Wesley Crusher	5	15
Worf	8	15

Star Trek: Voyager (Playmates, 1995-96)

5" Figures

B'Elanna Torres	15	25
Chakotay	5	10
Chakotay as a Maquis	8	15
Doctor	8	15
Harry Kim	8	15
Kathryn Janeway	15	25
Kazon	5	10
Kes the Ocampa	12	18
Neelix	5	10
Seska	5	10
Tom Paris	5	10
Tuvok	5	10

Action Figures, 3-3/4"

Star Wars

Series 1

	MNP	MIP
Boba Fett, 1978	25	970
C-3PO, 1977	10	195
Chewbacca, 1977	9	230
Darth Vader, 1977	11	280
Death Squad Commander, 1977	9	185
Death Star Droid, 1978	8	140
Early Bird Figures—Luke, Leia, R2-D2, Chewbacca, 1977	220	550
Greedo, 1978	7	150
Hammerhead, 1978	7	165
Han Solo, Large Head, 1977	20	510
Han Solo, Small Head, 1977	25	450
Jawa, Cloth Cape, 1977	10	200
Jawa, Vinyl Cape, 1977	230	2570
Luke Skywalker, 1977	25	400
Luke with Telescoping Saber, 1977	195	4850
Luke as X-Wing Pilot, 1978	8	140
Obi-Wan Kenobi, 1977	11	250
Power Droid, 1978	6	110
Princess Leia, 1977	30	330
R2-D2, 1977	9	165
R5-D4, 1978	8	110
Snaggletooth, Blue Body, Sears Exclusive, 1978	185	n/a
Snaggletooth, Red Body, 1978	7	160

Chewbacca, Star Wars, Series 1

Boba Fett, Star Wars, Series 1

Darth Vader, Star Wars, Series 1

STAR WARS – 3-3/4"

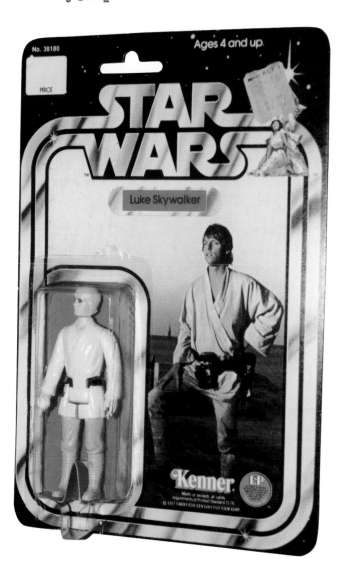

Luke with Telescoping Saber, Star Wars, Series 1

	MNP	MIP
Stormtrooper, 1977	12	200
Tusken Raider, 1977	9	220
Walrus Man, 1978	7	125

Empire Strikes Back

Series 2

	MNP	MIP
2-1B, 1980	7	85
4-LOM	9	105
AT-AT Commander, 1980	6	50
AT-AT Driver, 1981	8	65
Bespin Security Guard, black, 1980	8	55
Bespin Security Guard, white, 1980	8	60
Bossk, 1980	9	95
C-3PO with Removable Limbs, 1982	7	55
Cloud Car Pilot, 1982	12	70
Dengar, 1980	7	65
FX-7, 1980	6	60
Han in Bespin Outfit, 1981	10	105
Han in Hoth Gear, 1980	8	85
Hoth Rebel Soldier, 1980	6	55
IG-88, 1980	10	115
Imperial Commander, 1981	6	45
Imperial TIE Fighter Pilot, 1982	10	100

	MNP	MIP
Lando Calrissian	8	70
Leia in Bespin Gown, 1980	12	125
Leia in Hoth Gear, 1981	15	100
Lobot, 1981	5	50
Luke in Bespin Outfit, 1980	15	150
Luke in Hoth Gear, 1982	8	70
R2-D2 with Sensorscope	9	60
Rebel Commander, 1980	6	50
Snowtrooper, 1980	8	70
Ugnaught, 1981	6	55
Yoda, 1981	16	140
Zuckuss, 1982	7	85

Return of the Jedi

Series 3

	MNP	MIP
8D8, 1983	7	25
Admiral Ackbar, 1983	8	30
AT-ST Driver	9	25
B-Wing Pilot	7	25
Bib Fortuna	10	30
Biker Scout, 1983	10	45
Chief Chirpa, 1983	8	30
Emperor Palpatine, 1983	8	40
Emperor's Royal Guard	8	35
Gamorrean Guard, 1983	7	35
General Madine, 1983	7	30

R2-D2, Star Wars, Series 1

	MNP	MIP
Han in Trenchcoat, 1984	11	35
Klaatu, 1983	9	25
Klaatu in Skiff Guard Outfit, 1983	9	25
Lando Calrissian, Skiff Guard Outfit, 1983	9	35
Leia in Battle Poncho, 1984	20	45
Leia in Boushh Disguise, 1983	12	40
Logray, 1983	7	25
Luke as Jedi Knight, blue saber, 1983	35	145
Luke as Jedi Knight, green saber, 1983	25	90
Lumat, 1983	14	35
Nien Nunb, 1983	6	30
Nikto, 1984	10	30
Paploo	14	40
Pruneface, 1984	8	30
Rancor Keeper, 1984	9	25
Rebel Commando, 1983	8	25
Ree-Yees, 1983	7	25
Squid Head, 1983	8	35
Sy Snootles and the Rebo Band, 1984	25	150
Teebo, 1984	10	35
Weequay	10	30
Wicket, 1984	13	50

Episode I

Series 1

	MNP	MIP
Anakin Skywalker (Tatooine), 1999	3	8
Battle Droid (four versions), 1999	3	8
Darth Maul (Jedi Duel), 1999	3	9

Star Wars, Episode I, Series I. Left to Right: Obi-Wan Kenobi (Jedi Duel); Darth Maul (Jedi Duel)

	MNP	MIP
Jar Jar Binks, 1999	3	8
Obi-Wan Kenobi (Jedi Duel), 1999	3	8
Padme Naberrie, 1999	3	8
Queen Amidala (Naboo) with Blaster Pistols, 1999	3	8
Qui-Gon Jinn (Jedi Duel), 1999	3	8

Series 2

	MNP	MIP
C-3PO, 1999	3	8
Darth Sidious, 1999	3	8
Ric Olie, 1999	3	8
Senator Palpatine, 1999	3	8
Watto, 1999	3	9

Anakin Skywalker (Tatooine), Episode I, Series 1

Padme Naberrie, Episode I, Series 1

STAR WARS – 3-3/4"

STAR WARS – 3-3/4"

*Queen Amidala (Naboo) with Blaster Pistols,
Episode I, Series 1*

Darth Sidious, Episode I, Series 2

Senator Palpatine, Episode I, Series 2

Series 3

	MNP	MIP
Boss Nass, 1999	3	8
Chancellor Valorum, 1999	3	8
Gasgano, 1999	3	8
Ki-Adi-Mundi, 1999	3	8
Mace Windu, 1999	3	8

Series 4

Captain Tarpals, 1999	3	8
Ody Mandrell with Pit Droid, 1999	3	8
OOM-9, 1999	3	8

Series 5

Destroyer Droid, 1999	3	8
Yoda, 1999	3	8

Series 6

Darth Maul (Tatooine), 1999	3	8
Obi-Wan Kenobi (Naboo), 1999	3	8
Queen Amidala (Coruscant), 1999	3	10
Qui-Gon Jinn (Naboo), 1999	3	8

Series 7

Adi Gallia, 1999	3	8
Anakin Skywalker (Naboo), 1999	3	8

Series 8

Captain Panaka, 2000	3	9
Naboo Royal Security, 2000	3	9

Series 9

Darth Sidious (Holograph), 2000	3	8
Naboo Royal Guard, 2000	3	8

Chancellor Valorum, Episode I, Series 3

Gasgano, Episode I, Series 3

Series 10

	MNP	MIP
Anakin Skywalker (Naboo Pilot), 2000	3	8
Darth Maul (Sith Lord), 2000	3	8
Obi-Wan Kenobi (Jedi Knight), 2000	3	8

Series 11

R2-B1, 2000	3	8
TC-14, 2000	3	8

Series 12

Pit Droids, 2000	3	8
Queen Amidala (Battle), 2000	3	8
Sio Bibble, 2000	3	8

Series 13

Destroyer Droid (Battle Damaged), 2000	3	8
Jar Jar Binks (Swamp), 2000	3	8
Qui-Gon Jinn (Jedi Master), 2000	3	8

Cinema Scene 3-Packs

Mosespa Encounter—Sebulba, Jar Jar, Anakin, 1999	6	12
Tatooine Showdown—Darth Maul, Qui-Gon, Anakin, 1999	6	15
Watto's Box—Watto, Graxol Kelvyyn, Shakka, 2000	6	20

Deluxe

Darth Maul, 1999	3	10
Obi-Wan Kenobi, 1999	3	10
Qui-Gon Jinn, 1999	3	10

Droids

Series 5

A-Wing Pilot, 1985	25	170

	MNP	MIP
Boba Fett, 1985	17	670
C-3PO, 1985	45	125
Jann Tosh, 1985	8	20
Jord Dusat, 1985	8	20
Kea Moll, 1985	10	30
Kez-Iban, 1985	10	25
R2-D2, 1985	40	85
Sise Fromm, 1985	35	85
Thall Joben, 1985	8	20
Tig Fromm, 1985	30	75
Uncle Gundy, 1985	8	19

Ewoks

Series 5

Dulok Scout, 1985	8	18
Dulok Shaman, 1985	8	19
King Gornesh, 1985	8	18
Logray, 1985	10	20
Urgah, 1985	8	18
Wicket, 1985	11	35

Power of the Force

Series 4

A-Wing Pilot, with coin, 1985	45	80
Amanaman, with coin, 1985	105	230
Anakin Skywalker, with coin, 1985	20	2330
AT-AT Driver, with coin	4	550
AT-ST Driver, with coin	5	50
B-Wing Pilot, with coin, 1985	4	30
Barada, with coin, 1985	35	105
Biker Scout, with coin, 1985	6	90

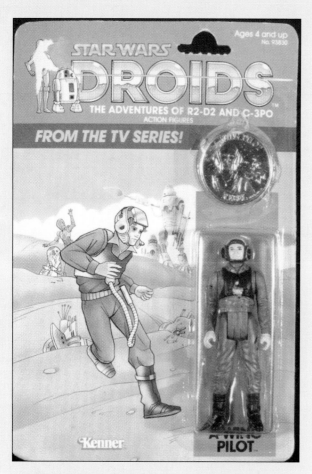

A-Wing Pilot, Droids, Series 5

Lando as General Pilot, with coin, Power of the Force, Series 4

Han in Carbonite, with coin, Power of the Force, Series 4

Luke in Stormtrooper Disguise, with coin, Power of the Force, Series 4

	MNP	MIP
C-3PO with Removable Limbs, with coin	4	70
Chewbacca, with coin	5	100
Darth Vader, with coin	6	115
Emperor Palpatine, with coin, 1985	5	60
EV-9D9, with coin, 1985	60	140
Gamorrean Guard, with coin	4	240
Han in Carbonite, with coin, 1985	80	195
Han in Trenchcoat, with coin	6	490
Imperial Dignitary, with coin, 1985	40	70
Imperial Gunner, with coin, 1985	60	130
Jawa, with coin, 1985	7	85
Lando as General Pilot, with coin, 1985	55	105
Leia in Battle Poncho	10	80
Luke as Jedi Knight with Green Saber, with coin	18	195
Luke as X-Wing Pilot, with coin, 1985	6	85
Luke in Battle Poncho, with coin	50	115
Luke in Stormtrooper Disguise, with coin, 1985	125	380
Lumat, with coin, 1985	8	45
Nikto, with coin	6	590
Obi-Wan Kenobi, with coin, 1985	7	95
Paploo, with coin, 1985	8	50
R2-D2 with pop-up Lightsaber, with coin, 1985	85	155
Romba, with coin, 1985	30	55
Stormtrooper, with coin	7	190
Teebo, with coin	6	135
Warok, with coin, 1985	30	65
Wicket, with coin, 1985	8	135
Yak Face, with coin, 1985	175	1500
Yoda, with coin	12	340

Power of the Force 2

Series 1

	MNP	MIP
C-3PO, 1995	3	10
Chewbacca, 1995	3	12
Darth Vader, 1995	4	13
Han Solo, 1995	3	12
Luke Skywalker, 1995	4	12
Obi-Wan Kenobi, 1995	4	12
Princess Leia, 1995	3	13
R2-D2, 1995	3	12
Stormtrooper, 1995	3	11

Series 2

	MNP	MIP
Boba Fett, 1996	4	15
Han in Hoth Gear, 1996	3	12
Lando Calrissian, 1996	3	10
Luke as X-Wing Pilot, 1996	3	14
TIE Fighter Pilot, 1996	3	11
Yoda, 1996	3	11

Series 3

	MNP	MIP
Death Star Gunner, 1996	3	18
Greedo, 1996	3	18
Luke in Dagobah Fatigues, 1996	3	12
Sandtrooper, 1996	3	12

Series 4

	MNP	MIP
Jawas, 1996	3	20
Luke in Stormtrooper Disguise, 1996	4	24
Momaw Nadon (Hammerhead), 1996	2	16
R5-D4, 1996	3	11
Tusken Raider, 1996	3	13

Series 5

	MNP	MIP
2-1B Medic Droid, 1997	2	8

Yoda, with coin, Power of the Force, Series 4

	MNP	MIP
AT-ST Driver, 1997	3	10
Bossk, 1997	3	10
Hoth Rebel Soldier, 1997	3	10
Luke in Hoth Gear, 1997	3	11

Series 6

	MNP	MIP
Bib Fortuna, 1997	3	10
Emperor Palpatine, 1997	3	10
Han in Endor Gear, 1997	3	12
Lando as Skiff Guard, 1997	3	10

Series 7

	MNP	MIP
4-LOM, 1997	3	10
Admiral Ackbar, 1997	3	10
ASP-7 Droid, 1997	3	8
Dengar, 1997	3	10
Garindan (Long Snoot), 1997	3	10
Grand Moff Tarkin, 1997	3	10
Ponda Baba, 1997	3	10
Rebel Fleet Trooper, 1997	3	11
Weequay Skiff Guard, 1997	3	10

Series 8

	MNP	MIP
Emperor's Royal Guard, 1997	3	12
Han in Bespin Outfit, 1997	3	10
Leia as Jabba's Prisoner, 1997	3	10
Snowtrooper, 1997	3	10

STAR WARS – 3-3/4"

Series 9

	MNP	MIP
EV-9D9, 1997	3	10
Gamorrean Guard, 1997	3	10
Malakili (Rancor Keeper), 1997	3	8
Nien Nunb, 1997	3	10
Saelt-Marae (Yak Face), 1997	3	10

Series 10

	MNP	MIP
Endor Rebel Soldier, 1998	3	14
Lando as General, 1998	3	14
Leia in Ewok Celebration Outfit, 1998	3	14
Luke in Bespin Outfit, 1998	3	16
Luke in Ceremonial Garb, 1997	3	12

Series 11

	MNP	MIP
Biggs Darklighter, 1998	3	14
Lak Sivrak, 1998	3	12
Wicket and Logray, 1998	3	10

Series 12

	MNP	MIP
Captain Piett, 1998	3	14
Darth Vader with Removable Helmet, 1998	4	24
Ishi Tib, 1998	3	14
Zuckuss, 1998	3	14

Series 13

	MNP	MIP
C-3PO with Removable Limbs and Backpack, 1998	3	16
Leia with All-New Likeness, 1998	3	16
Luke with Blast Shield Helmet, 1998	3	16
R2-D2 with Datalink and Sensorscope, 1998	3	14
Ugnaught, 1998	3	10

Series 14

	MNP	MIP
8-D8 Droid, 1998	3	10

Series 15

	MNP	MIP
Chewbacca as Boushh's Bounty, 1998	3	18
Death Star Trooper, 1998	3	26
Lobot, 1998	3	14

	MNP	MIP
Mon Mothma, 1998	3	16
Orrimaarko (Prune Face), 1998	3	22
Ree-Yees, 1998	3	26

Series 16

	MNP	MIP
Chewbacca (Hoth), 1998	3	8
Darth Vader, 1998	3	8
Emperor Palpatine, 1998	3	8
Luke Skywalker, 1998	3	8
Obi-Wan Kenobi, 1998	3	8
Princess Leia, 1998	3	8
R2-D2, 1998	3	8
Yoda, 1998	3	12

Series 17

	MNP	MIP
Anakin Skywalker, 1999	3	12
Aunt Beru, 1999	3	14
C-3PO, Shop Worn, 1999	3	8

Series 18

	MNP	MIP
Cantina Greedo, 1999	3	7
Cantina Han Solo, 1999	3	7
Jawa & Gonk Droid, 1999	3	7
Luke Skywalker with T16, 1999	3	7

Series 19

	MNP	MIP
Darth Vader with Interrogation Droid, 1999	5	7
Stormtrooper, 1999	5	7

Series 20

	MNP	MIP
Admiral Motti, 2000	5	9
Princess Leia (Hood Up), 2000	5	9
R2-D2 with Holographic Princess Leia, 1999	5	9

Shadows of the Empire

	MNP	MIP
Chewbacca in Bounty Hunter Disguise, 1996	3	6
Dash Rendar, 1996	3	8
Han in Carbonite, 1996	3	6
Leia in Boushh Disguise, 1996	3	6
Luke in Imperial Guard Disguise, 1996	3	8
Prince Xizor, 1996	3	6

Cantina Showdown—Obi-Wan Kenobi, Ponda Baba, Dr. Evazan, Power of the Force 2, Cinema Scene 3-Packs. Photo Courtesy Hasbro, Inc.

Cinema Scene 3-Packs

	MNP	MIP
Cantina Aliens—Labria, Nabrun Leids, Takeel	6	12
Cantina Showdown—Obi-Wan Kenobi, Ponda Baba, Dr. Evazan	6	12
Death Star Escape—Luke and Han in Stormtrooper Disguise, Chewbacca	6	22
Final Jedi Duel—Darth Vader, Luke, Emperor Palpatine	6	24
Jabba the Hutt's Dancers—Rystall, Greeata, Lyn Me	6	16
Jabba's Skiff Guards—Klaatu, Barada, Nikto, 1999	8	35
Jedi Spirits—Anakin Skywalker, Yoda, Obi-Wan Kenobi	6	10
Mynock Hunt—Han, Leia, Chewbacca	6	32
Purchase of the Droids—Luke, C-3PO, Uncle Owen	6	18
Rebel Pilots—Wedge Antilles, B-Wing Pilot (Ten Nunb), Y-Wing Pilot	6	26

Complete Galaxy

Dagobah with Yoda, 1998	6	12
Death Star with Darth Vader, 1998	6	12
Endor with Wicket, 1998	10	22
Tatooine with Luke Skywalker, 1998	10	25

Dark Empire

Clone Emperor, 1998	3	18
Imperial Sentinel, 1998	3	18
Kyle Katarn, 1998	3	35
Luke Skywalker, 1998	3	18
Princess Leia Organa Solo, 1998	3	18

Dark Forces

Darktrooper, 1998	3	30

Deluxe

Boba Fett, 1997	5	10
Crowd Control Stormtrooper, 1996	5	9
Han Solo with Smuggler's Flight Pack, 1996	5	9
Imperial Probe Droid, 1997	5	9
Luke Skywalker's Desert Sport Skiff, 1996	5	10
Snowtrooper, 1997	5	9

Deluxe 2-Packs

Boba Fett vs. IG-88, 1996	6	25
Droopy McCool and Barquin D'an	6	20
Leia and Han, 1998	6	12
Leia and Luke, 1998	6	12
Leia and R2-D2, 1998	6	12
Leia and Wicket the Ewok, 1998	6	12
Max Rebo and Doda Bodonawieedo	6	25
Prince Xizor vs. Darth Vader, 1996	6	15
Sy Snootles and Joh Yowza	6	20

Electronic Power F/X

Ben (Obi-Wan) Kenobi, 1997	5	9
Darth Vader, 1997	5	9
Emporer Palpatine, 1997	5	9
Jedi Knight Luke Skywalker, 1997	5	9
R2-D2, 1997	5	9

Fan Club Four

AT-AT Driver, 1998	3	20
Death Star Droid with Mouse Droid, 1998	3	20
Leia in Hoth Gear, 1998	3	22
Pote Snitkin, 1998	3	20

Gunner Stations

	MNP	MIP
Falcon with Han Solo, 1998	6	8
Falcon with Luke Skywalker, 1998	6	8
TIE Fighter with Darth Vader, 1998	6	15

Heir to the Empire

Grand Admiral Thrawn, 1998	3	20
Mara Jade, 1998	3	35
Spacetrooper, 1998	3	25

Millennium Minted Coin

C-3PO, with Millennium Minted Coin	5	10
Chewbacca, with Millennium Minted Coin	5	10
Emperor Palpatine, with Millennium Minted Coin	5	10
Han in Bespin Outfit, with Millennium Minted Coin	5	10
Leia in Endor Gear, with Millennium Minted Coin	5	10
Luke in Battle Poncho, with Millennium Minted Coin	5	10
Snowtrooper, with Millennium Minted Coin	5	10

Promotional 3" Figures

B'omarr Monk	10	15
Figrin D'an (Cantina Band Member)	10	15
Han in Stormtrooper Disguise	10	20
Mace Windu	5	10
Muftak and Kabe	10	16
Obi-Wan Kenobi Spirit	10	10
Oola and Salacious Crumb	10	14
STAP and Battle Droid	10	12
Theater Edition Jedi Knight Luke Skywalker, 1996	10	65

Action Figures, 12"

Star Wars

Series 1

Boba Fett, 1979	160	410
C-3PO, 1979	45	125
Chewbacca, 1979	55	175
Darth Vader, 1978	70	195
Han Solo, 1979	170	380
Jawa, 1979	80	175
Luke Skywalker, 1979	90	240
Obi-Wan Kenobi, 1979	115	220
Princess Leia, 1979	90	260
R2-D2, 1979	45	110
Stormtrooper, 1979	90	260

Empire Strikes Back

Series 2

IG-88, 1980	240	660
Boba Fett, 1979	155	420

Episode I

Action Collection

Anakin Skywalker, 1999	6	10
Battle Droid, 1999	6	15
Darth Maul, 1999	10	25
Jar Jar Binks, 1999	6	20
Obi-Wan Kenobi, 1999	6	15
Pit Droids, 1999	6	10
Qui-Gon Jinn, 1999	6	20

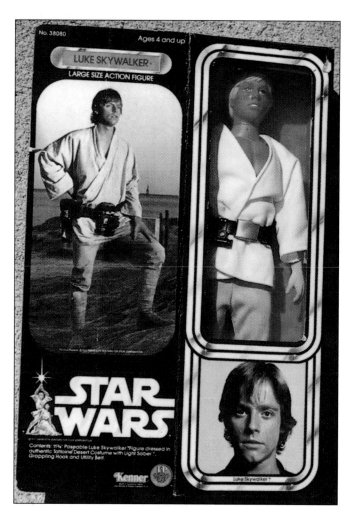

Luke Skywalker, 12", Star Wars, Series 1

Princess Leia, 12", Star Wars, Series 1

Darth Maul,
Episode I, Action
Collection

	MNP	MIP
R2-A6, 1999 6		10
Watto, 1999 6		15

Collector's Series

Series 1

Darth Vader, 1996 15		20
Han Solo, 1996 15		20
Luke Skywalker, 1996 15		20
Obi-Wan Kenobi, 1996 15		35

Series 2

Lando Calrissian, 1997 15		20
Luke in Bespin Outfit, 1997 15		35
Tusken Raider, 1997 15		35

Series 3

Boba Fett, 1997 15		70
Luke as X-Wing Pilot, 1997 15		30
Princess Leia, 1997 15		45
Stormtrooper, 1997 15		36

Series 4

Admiral Akbar, 1997 15		30
C-3PO, 1997 15		30
Chewbacca, 1997 15		75
TIE Fighter Pilot, 1997 15		28

ANH Assortment

Grand Moff Tarkin with Interrogation Droid, 1998 15		22
Greedo, 1998 15		22

Qui-Gon Jinn, Episode I, Action Collection

Greedo, Collector's Series, ANH Assortment

	MNP	MIP
Luke in Ceremonial Garb, 1998	15	15
Sandtrooper, 1998	15	15

ESB Assortment

	MNP	MIP
AT-AT Driver, 1998	15	22
Han in Hoth Gear, 1998	15	18
Luke in Hoth Gear, 1998	15	18
Snowtrooper, 1998	15	18

FAO Exclusive

	MNP	MIP
Grand Moff Tarkin and Imperial Gunner	30	60
Leia as Jabba's Prisoner and R2-D2	30	60
Wedge Antilles and Biggs Darklighter	30	60

K-B Exclusive

	MNP	MIP
Han and Luke in Stormtrooper Disguise	30	55
Luke with Poncho (Tatooine), Han with Flight Jacket, Leia in Boushh Disguise	20	65

ROJ Assortment

	MNP	MIP
Barquin D'an, 1998	15	22

	MNP	MIP
Chewbacca (Chained), 1998	15	35
Emperor Palpatine, 1998	15	18
Luke as Jedi Knight, 1998	15	18

Service Merchandise Exclusive

	MNP	MIP
Leia in Hoth Gear, 1999	15	20

Special 2-Packs

	MNP	MIP
Han in Hoth Gear with Tauntaun	25	45
Luke as Jedi Knight and Bib Fortuna	30	60
Luke in Hoth Gear with Wampa	30	80

Target Exclusive

	MNP	MIP
Han in Carbonite, 1998	15	35

Trilogy Assortment

	MNP	MIP
Jawa, 1998	15	12
R2-D2, 1998	15	12
Yoda, 1998	15	20

Wal-Mart Exclusives

	MNP	MIP
Cantina Band Aliens with six members	15	35
R2-D2, 1998	10	15
R5-D4, 1998	10	15
Wicket, 1998	10	15

Princess Leia Collection
1999 Collectors Edition

	MNP	MIP
Princess Leia in Cermonial Gown, 1999	10	25

Grand Moff Tarkin and Imperial Gunner, Collector's Series, FAO Exclusive

Han in Hoth Gear with Tauntaun, Collector's Series, Special 2-Packs

Luke in Hoth Gear with Wampa, Collector's Series, Special 2-Packs

STAR WARS – 12"

Queen Amidala Collection
Fashion Doll

	MNP	MIP
Padme (Beautiful Braids), 2000 8		16
Queen Amidala (Ultimate Hair), 1999 8		16
Queen Amidala (Royal Elegance), 1999 8		16
Queen Amidala (Hidden Majesty), 1999 8		16

1999 Portrait Edition

	MNP	MIP
Queen Amidala (Black Travel Dress), 1999 10		40
Queen Amidala (Red Senate Gown), 1999 10		40

2000 Portrait Edition

	MNP	MIP
Queen Amidala (Return to Naboo), 2000 10		45

Beasts

Star Wars
Series 1

	MNP	MIP
Patrol Dewback 20		75

Empire Strikes Back
Series 2

	MNP	MIP
Taun Taun, solid belly 14		40
Taun Taun, split belly 13		45
Wampa 14		35

Queen Amidala (Hidden Majesty), Queen Amidala Collection, Fashion Doll

Queen Amidala (Black Travel Dress), Queen Amidala Collection, 1999 Portrait Edition

Return of the Jedi
Series 3

	MNP	MIP
Rancor 30		60

Carrying Cases
Star Wars
24-Figure 30	

Empire Strikes Back
Darth Vader, 1982 40	
Mini Figure, 1980 30	

Return of the Jedi
C-3PO, 1983 25	
Darth Vader with three figures, 1983 220	
Laser Rifle, 1984 25	

Micro Series

Bespin Control Room, 1982 25	25	
Bespin Freeze Chamber, 1982 20	60	
Bespin Gantry, 1982 11	25	
Bespin World, 1982 40	90	
Death Star Compactor, 1982 20	45	
Death Star Escape, 1982 17	40	
Death Star World, 1982 40	100	
Hoth Generator Attack, 1982 14	30	
Hoth Ion Cannon, 1982 17	40	
Hoth Turret Defense, 1982 15	30	
Hoth Wampa Cave, 1982 14	30	
Hoth World, 1982 60	120	
Imperial TIE Fighter, 1982 25	60	
Millennium Falcon, 1982 140	320	
Snowspeeder, 1982 90	175	
X-Wing Fighter, 1982 20	45	

Mini Rigs

AST-5, 1983 7	20	
CAP-2 Captivator, 1982 9	25	
Desert Sail Skiff, 1984 7	20	
Endor Forest Ranger, 1984 12	25	
INT-4 Interceptor, 1982 9	25	
ISP-6 Imperial Shuttle Pod, 1983 9	20	
MLC-3 Mobile Laser Cannon, 1981 10	30	
MTV-7 Multi-Terrain Vehicle, 1981 9	30	
PDT-8 Personal Deployment Transport, 1981 10	30	
Radar Laser Cannon, 1982 8	19	
Tri-Pod Laser Cannon, 1982 8	17	
Vehicle Maintenance Energizer, 1982 8	17	

Play Sets
Star Wars
Series 1

Cantina Adventure Play Set, Sears Exclusive, 1977 180	510	
Creature Cantina, 1977 35	95	

Patrol Dewback,
Star Wars, Series 1

	MNP	MIP
Death Star Space Station, 1977	60	250
Droid Factory, 1977	35	115
Land of the Jawas, 1977	40	140

Empire Strikes Back
Series 2

	MNP	MIP
Cloud City Play Set, Sears Exclusive, 1981	100	270
Dagobah, 1982	18	75
Darth Vader's Star Destroyer	35	115
Hoth Ice Planet, 1980	35	85
Imperial Attack Base, 1980	25	80

	MNP	MIP
Rebel Command Center, 1980	60	155
Turret and Probot, 1980	35	80

Return of the Jedi
Series 3

	MNP	MIP
Ewok Village, 1983	30	75
Jabba the Hutt Dungeon	25	55
Jabba's Dungeon, with Nikto, 8D8, Klaatu, 1983	30	90

Ewoks
Series 5

	MNP	MIP
Ewoks Treehouse, 1985	16	35

Creature Cantina
Play Set, Star
Wars, Series 1

Death Star Space Station, Star Wars, Series 1

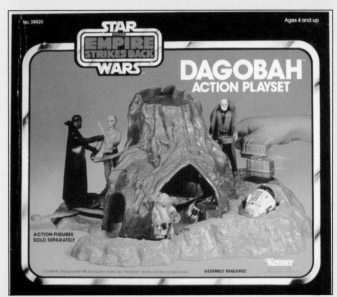

Top Right: Land of the Jawas Play Set, Star Wars, Series 1

Middle Right: Dagobah Play Set, Empire Strikes Back, Series 2

Left: Darth Vader's Star Destroyer, Empire Strikes Back, Series 2

STAR WARS - PLAY SETS

Hoth Ice Planet Play Set, Empire Strikes Back, Series 2

Imperial Attack Base Play Set, Empire Strikes Back, Series 2

Rebel Command Center Play Set, Empire Strikes Back, Series 2

Ewok Village Play Set, Return of the Jedi, Series 3

Power of the Force

Series 4

	MNP	MIP
Jabba's Dungeon, with Amanaman, EV-9D9, Barada, 1983	220	310

Vehicles

Star Wars

Series 1

Darth Vader's TIE Fighter, 1977	45	105

	MNP	MIP
Darth Vader's TIE Fighter, die-cast, 1979	11	55
Imperial TIE Fighter, 1977	30	120
Imperial Trooper Transport	30	70
Jawa Sand Crawler, battery-operated, 1977	210	540
Land Speeder, 1977	16	60
Land Speeder, die-cast, 1979	13	60
Millennium Falcon, 1977	70	210
Millennium Falcon, die-cast, 1979	30	110
Sonic Land Speeder, JC Penney Exclusive, 1977	140	470
Star Destroyer, die-cast, 1979	45	125

Jabba's Dungeon, with Amanaman, EV-9D9, Barada, Power of the Force, Series 4

STAR WARS – VEHICLES

Darth Vader's TIE Fighter,
Star Wars, Series 1

	MNP	MIP
TIE Fighter, die-cast, 1979	15	45
X-Wing Fighter, 1977	30	110
X-Wing Fighter, die-cast, 1979	18	70

Empire Strikes Back

Series 2

	MNP	MIP
AT-AT, 1980	75	190
Rebel Transport, 1980	45	100
Scout Walker, 1982	30	65
Slave I, 1980	35	100

	MNP	MIP
Slave I, die-cast, 1979	25	75
Snowspeeder	35	75
Snowspeeder, die-cast, 1979	25	80
TIE Bomber, die-cast, 1979	250	670
Twin-Pod Cloud Car, 1980	25	75
Y-Wing Fighter, 1979	40	145

Return of the Jedi

Series 3

	MNP	MIP
B-Wing Fighter, 1984	65	125

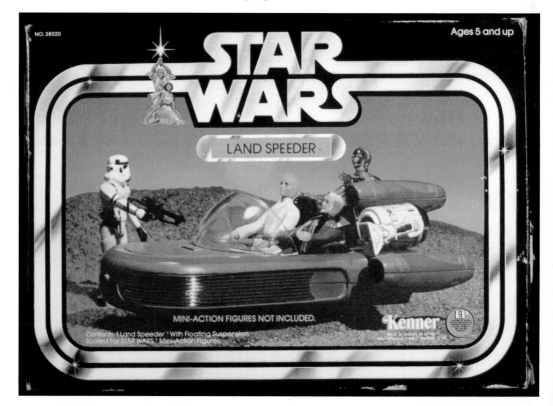

Land Speeder, Star Wars,
Series 1

TIE Fighter, die-cast, Star Wars, Series 1

Slave I, Empire Strikes Back, Series 2

Imperial Side Gunner, Droids, Series 5

A-Wing Fighter, Droids, Series 5

STAR WARS – VEHICLES

*Ewok Battle Wagon,
Power of the Force,
Series 4*

	MNP	MIP
Ewok Combat Glider, 1984	7	18
Imperial Shuttle, 1984	165	330
Speeder Bike, 1983	11	30
TIE Interceptor, 1984	50	110
Y-Wing Fighter, 1983	55	135

Droids
Series 5

A-Wing Fighter, 1983	195	400
ATL Interceptor, 1985	15	45
Imperial Side Gunner, 1985	18	60

Ewoks
Series 5

Ewoks Fire Cart, 1985	7	18
Ewoks Woodland Wagon, 1985	7	40

Power of the Force
Series 4

Ewok Battle Wagon, 1985	65	220
Imperial Sniper Vehicle, 1985	30	70
One-Man Sand Skimmer, 1985	25	65
Security Scout Vehicle, 1985	30	80
Tatooine Skiff	280	570

Weapons

Star Wars
Series 1

	MNP	MIP
Han Solo's Laser Pistol	20	90
Inflatable Lightsaber, 1977	30	135
Three-Position Laser Rifle, 1980	75	240

Empire Strikes Back
Series 2

Laser Pistol, 1980	20	80
Lightsaber, red or green, 1980	16	40
Lightsaber, yellow, 1980	16	45

Return of the Jedi
Series 3

Biker Scout's Laser Pistol, 1984	20	55
Lightsaber	20	40

Droids
Series 5

Droids Lightsaber, red or green plastic, 1985	75	190

Stargate—Anubis, Hasbro

Stargate—Horus Attack Pilot, Hasbro

Stargate—Col. O'Neil, Hasbro

Stargate—Lt. Kawalsky, Hasbro

Stargate (Hasbro, 1994)
Figures

	MNP	MIP
Anubis	2	4
Col. O'Neil	2	4
Daniel Jackson	2	5
Horus, Attack Pilot	2	4
Horus, Palace Guard	2	4
Lt. Kawalsky	2	4
Ra	2	4
Skaara	2	4

Starsky and Hutch (Mego, 1976)
8" Figures and Accessories

Captain Dobey	25	50
Car	65	125
Chopper	25	45
Huggy Bear	25	50
Hutch	20	45
Starsky	20	45

Street Fighter (Hasbro, 1994)
12" Figures

Blanka	15	25
Colonel Guile	15	25
General Bison	15	25
Ryu Hoshi	15	25

Super Hero Bendables (Mego, 1972)
5" Figures

Aquaman	50	120
Batgirl	50	120
Batman	35	90
Captain America	35	90
Catwoman	70	175
Joker	60	150

	MNP	MIP
Mr. Mxyzptlk	50	125
Penguin	60	150
Riddler	60	150
Robin	30	75
Shazam	50	125
Supergirl	70	175
Superman	30	75
Tarzan	25	60
Wonder Woman	50	100

Super Powers (Kenner, 1984-86)
5" Figures

Aquaman, 1984	15	45
Batman, 1984	35	75
Braniac, 1984	15	30
Clark Kent, mail-in figure, 1986	50	75
Cyborg, 1986	150	300
Cyclotron, 1986	35	75
Darkseid, 1985	5	15
Desaad, 1985	10	30
Dr. Fate, 1985	35	80
Firestorm, 1985	15	35
Flash, 1984	10	25
Golden Pharaoh, 1986	50	125
Green Arrow, 1985	25	55
Green Lantern, 1984	30	60
Hawkman, 1984	25	65
Joker, 1984	15	30
Kalibak, 1985	5	15
Lex Luthor, 1984	5	15
Mantis, 1985	10	30
Martian Manhunter, 1985	15	45
Mister Miracle, 1986	60	145
Mr. Freeze, 1986	25	65
Orion, 1986	25	65
Parademon, 1985	15	35

Starsky and Hutch by Mego—Left to Right: Huggy Bear; Hutch; Starsky

*Super Powers by Kenner—Left to Right:
Braniac; Wonder Woman*

*Super Powers by Kenner—
Left to Right: Cyborg;
Mister Miracle*

*Super Powers by Kenner—Left to Right:
Dr. Fate; Kalibak*

SUPER POWERS

SUPER POWERS

*Super Powers by Kenner—
Left to Right: Firestorm,
1985; Parademon, 1985*

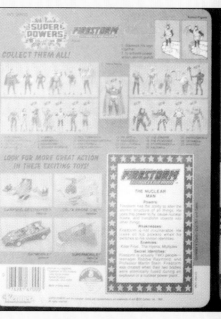

*Super Powers by Kenner—
Left to Right: The back of the
Firestorm package; Martian
Manhunter, 1985*

*Super Powers by
Kenner—Left to Right:
Orion; Cyclotron*

Super Powers—Red Tornado, 1985, Kenner

Super Powers by Kenner—Top Row, left to right: Penguin, 1984; Mr. Freeze, 1986. Bottom Row, left to right: Cyclotron, 1986; Green Lantern, 1984

Super Powers by Kenner—Left to Right: Plastic Man, 1986; Darkseid

Super Powers Robin—1984, Kenner

Super Powers by Kenner—Left to right: Samurai; Tyr; Shazam (Captain Marvel)

Super Powers by Kenner—Left to Right: Steppenwolf on card, 1985; Mantis

Super Powers by Kenner—Top Row: Batcopter. Bottom Row, left to right: Batmobile; Justice Jogger

	MNP	MIP
Penguin, 1984	20	40
Plastic Man, 1986	65	150
Red Tornado, 1985	35	85
Robin, 1984	25	50
Samurai, 1986	45	95
Shazam (Captain Marvel), 1986	25	65
Steppenwolf, in mail-in bag, 1985	15	20
Steppenwolf, on card, 1985	15	75
Superman, 1984	20	35
Tyr, 1986	40	75
Wonder Woman, 1984	15	40

Accessories

	MNP	MIP
Collector's Case, 1984	20	40

Play Sets

	MNP	MIP
Hall of Justice, 1984	75	175

Vehicles

	MNP	MIP
Batcopter, 1986	40	125
Batmobile, 1984	50	150
Darkseid Destroyer, 1985	25	50
Delta Probe One, 1985	15	30
Justice Jogger, wind-up, 1986	20	40
Kalibak Boulder Bomber, 1985	10	25
Lex-Soar 7, 1984	10	25
Supermobile, 1984	15	30

Teenage Mutant Ninja Turtles (Playmates, 1988-92)

Giant Turtles, 13", 1991

	MNP	MIP
Donatello	20	40
Leonardo	20	40
Michaelangelo	20	40
Raphael	20	40

Giant Turtles, 13", 1992

	MNP	MIP
Bebop	20	40
Movie Don	20	40
Movie Leo	20	40
Movie Mike	20	40
Movie Raph	20	40
Rocksteady	20	40

Teenage Mutant Ninja Turtles—Michaelangelo, Playmates

Series 1, 1988

	MNP	MIP
April O'Neil, no stripe	60	150
Bebop	3	8
Donatello	8	20
Donatello, with fan club form	12	50
Foot Soldier	8	20
Leonardo	8	20
Leonardo, with fan club form	12	50
Michaelangelo	8	20
Michaelangelo, with fan club form	12	50
Raphael	8	20
Raphael, with fan club form	12	50
Rocksteady	8	20
Shredder	8	20
Splinter	8	20

Series 2, 1989

	MNP	MIP
Ace Duck, hat off	5	40
Ace Duck, hat on	5	15
April O'Nei, blue stripe	12	30
Baxter Stockman	10	25
Genghis Frog, black belt	5	15
Genghis Frog, black belt, bagged weapons	5	30
Genghis Frog, yellow belt	30	75
Krang	5	15

Series 3, 1989

	MNP	MIP
Casey Jones	5	15
General Traag	5	15
Leatherhead	25	50
Metalhead	5	15

Teenage Mutant Ninja Turtles—Baxter Stockman, Playmates

Teenage Mutant Ninja Turtles—Leatherhead, Playmates

TEENAGE MUTANT NINJA TURTLES

	MNP	MIP
Rat King	5	15
Usagi Yojimbo	5	15

Series 4, 1990

	MNP	MIP
Mondo Gecko	5	15
Muckman and Joe Eyeball	5	15
Scumbag	5	15
Wingnut & Screwloose	5	15

Series 5, 1990

	MNP	MIP
Fugitoid	5	15
Slash, black belt	3	25
Slash, purple belt, red "S"	25	75
Triceraton	5	15

Series 6, 1990

	MNP	MIP
Mutagen Man	5	15
Napoleon Bonafrog	5	15
Panda Khan	5	15

Series 7, 1991

	MNP	MIP
April O'Neil	25	125
April O'Neil, "Press"	10	20
Pizza Face	5	15
Ray Fillet, purple body, red "V"	10	25
Ray Fillet, red body, maroon "V"	10	30
Ray Fillet, yellow body, blue "V"	10	15

Series 8, 1991

	MNP	MIP
Don The Undercover Turtle	5	15
Leo the Sewer Samurai	5	15

Teenage Mutant Ninja Turtles—Leo the Sewer Samurai, Playmates

	MNP	MIP
Mike the Sewer Surfer	5	15
Raph the Space Cadet	5	15

Series 9, 1991

	MNP	MIP
Chrome Dome	5	15
Dirt Bag	5	15
Ground Chuck	5	15
Storage Shell Don	5	15
Storage Shell Leo	5	15
Storage Shell Michaelangelo	5	15
Storage Shell Raphael	5	15

Series 10, 1991

	MNP	MIP
Grand Slam Raph	5	15
Hose'em Down Don	5	15
Lieutenant Leo	5	15
Make My Day Leo	5	15
Midshipman Mike	5	15
Pro Pilot Don	5	15
Raph the Green Teen Beret	5	15
Slam Dunkin' Don	5	15
Slapshot Leo	5	15
T.D. Tossin' Leonardo	5	15

Series 11, 1992

	MNP	MIP
Rahzer, black nose	5	15
Rahzer, red nose	7	25
Skateboard'n Mike	5	15
Super Shredder	5	15
Tokka, brown trim	9	25
Tokka, gray trim	5	15

Teenage Mutant Ninja Turtles—Mondo Gecko, Playmates

Teenage Mutant Ninja Turtles—Mike the Sewer Surfer, Playmates

Series 12, 1992

	MNP	MIP
Movie Don	5	15
Movie Leo	5	15
Movie Mike	5	15
Movie Raph	5	15
Movie Splinter, no tooth	5	15
Movie Splinter, with tooth	25	75

Vehicles and Accessories

Flushomatic	4	10
Foot Cruiser	14	35
Foot Ski	4	10
Mega Mutant Killer Bee	3	8
Mega Mutant Needlenose	8	20
Mike's Pizza Chopper Backpack	4	10
Mutant Sewer Cycle with Sidecar	4	10
Ninja Newscycle	5	12
Oozey	4	10
Pizza Powered Sewer Dragster	5	15
Pizza Thrower	14	35
Psycho Cycle	10	25
Raph's Sewer Dragster	6	16
Raph's Sewer Speedboat	5	12
Retrocatapult	4	10
Retromutagen Ooze	2	4
Sewer Seltzer Cannon	4	10
Sludgemobile	7	18
Technodrome, 22"	24	60
Toilet Taxi	5	12
Turtle Blimp, green vinyl, 30"	12	30

	MNP	MIP
Turtle Party Wagon	16	40
Turtle Trooper Parachute, 22"	4	10
Turtlecopter	16	40

Wacky Action, 1991

Breakfightin' Raphael	5	15
Creepy Crawlin' Splinter	5	15
Headspinnin' Bebop	5	15
Machine Gunnin' Rocksteady	5	15
Rock & Roll Michaelangelo	5	15
Sewer Swimmin' Don	5	15
Slice 'n Dice Shredder	10	25
Sword Slicin' Leonardo	8	15
Wacky Walkin' Mouser	10	20

Thundercats (LJN, 1985-87)
6" Figures

Ben-Gali	75	200
Capt. Cracker	15	40
Capt. Shiner	15	40
Cheetara	30	70
Cheetara and Wilykit	45	100
Grune the Destroyer	10	30
Hachiman	15	40
Jackalman	15	35
Lion-O	30	70
Lion-O and Snarf	25	60
Lynx-O	30	75
Mongor	30	75
Monkian	10	35
Mumm-ra	10	35
Panthro	30	70
Pumyra	25	75
Ratar-O	10	30
Safari Joe	10	35
Snowman of Hook Mountain	15	40
S-S-Slithe	15	40
Tuska Warrior	10	35
Tygra	30	70
Tygra and Wilykat	25	60
Vultureman	10	30

Berserkers

Cruncher	15	40
Hammerhead	15	40
Ram-Bam	15	40
Top-Spinner	15	40

Companions

Berbil Belle	15	50
Berbil Bill	15	50
Ma-Mut	10	45
Snarf	10	45
Wilykat	15	50
Wilykit	15	50

Ram-Pagers

Driller, the	25	75
Mad Bubbler, The	25	75
Stinger, The	25	75

Tick, The (Bandai, 1994-95)
Accessories

Steel Box	8	20

The Tick—Grasping El Seed, Bandai

The Tick—Steel Box, Bandai, Photo Courtesy Bandai

The Tick—Death Hug Dean, Bandai

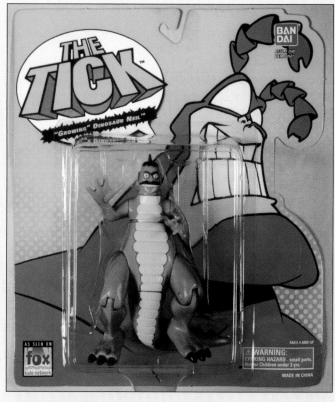

The Tick—Growing Dinosaur Neil, Bandai

The Tick—Man Eating Cow, Bandai

Series I, 6" figures

	MNP	MIP
Bounding Tick	8	20
Death Hug Dean	8	20
Exploding Dyne-Mole	6	15
Fluttering Arthur	8	20
Grasping El Seed	8	20
Growing Dinosaur Neil	8	20
Man Eating Cow	15	50
Pose Striking Die Fledermaus	15	50

Tomb Raider—Lara Croft in wet suit with harpoon and two pistols, Playmates

	MNP	MIP
Projectile Human Bullet	8	20
Sewer Spray Sewer Urchin	8	20

Series II, 6" figures

Color Changing Chameleon	15	45
Hurling Stop Sign Tick	8	20
Propellerized Skippy the Dog	8	20
Sliming Mucus Tick	10	30
Thrakkorzog	10	30
Twist and Chop American Maid	10	35

Tomb Raider (Playmates, 1999)

12" Figure

Talking Lara Croft	8	25

9" Figures

Lara Croft in Area 51 outfit with hand guns and an M-16, on base	8	20
Lara Croft in jungle outfit with two guns, on base	8	20
Lara Croft in wet suit with harpoon and two pistols, on base	8	20

Adventures of Lara Croft, 6" Figures

Lara Croft escapes a Bengal, on diorama base	3	10
Lara Croft escapes the yeti, on diorama base	3	10
Lara Croft faces a Bengal, on diorama base	3	10

Total Chaos (McFarlane, 1996-97)

Series 1, Figures

Al Simmons	5	15
Al Simmons, blue uniform	3	12
Al Simmons, red uniform with "Spawn" on visor, available through conventions only	15	45
Conqueror	5	15
Dragon Blade vs. Conqueror, Puzzle Zoo exclusive	6	18
Dragon Blade, black tunic	4	12
Dragon Blade, white tunic	5	15
Gore	5	15
Hoof, black body with khaki armor	3	12

Total Chaos—Poacher, McFarlane Toys. Photo Courtesy McFarlane Toys

TOTAL CHAOS

*Total Chaos—Quartz,
McFarlane Toys.
Photo Courtesy
McFarlane Toys*

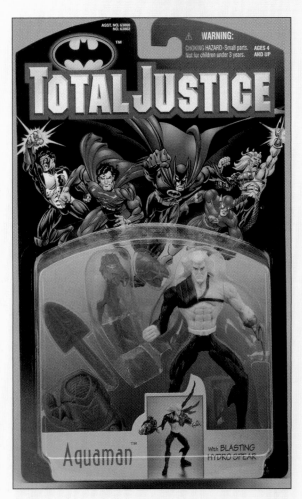

*Total Justice—Aquaman, with Hydro-Blasting Spear,
gold armor, Kenner*

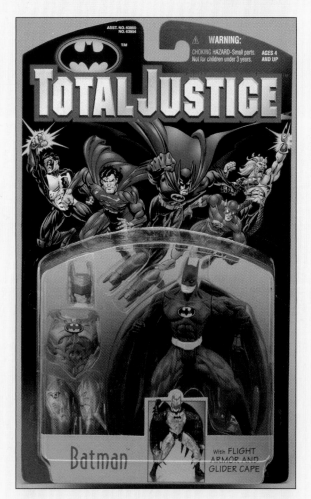

Total Justice—Batman, Kenner

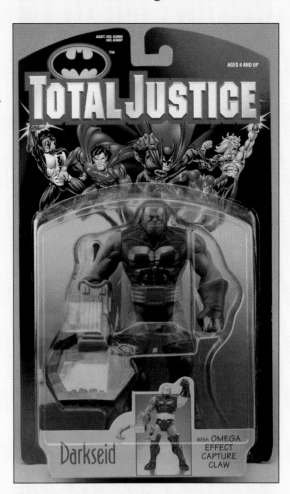

Total Justice—Darkseid, Kenner

Total Justice—The Flash, Kenner

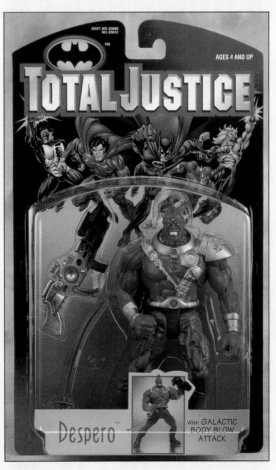

Total Justice—Despero, Kenner

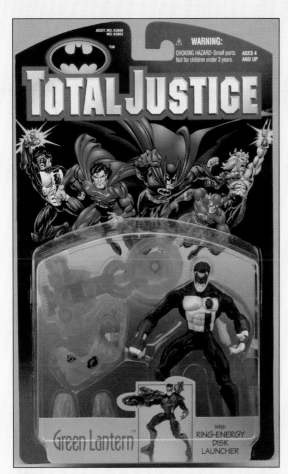

Total Justice—Green Lantern, Kenner

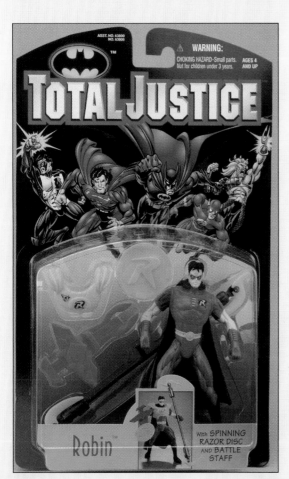

Total Justice—Hawkman, Kenner

Total Justice—Robin, Kenner

Total Justice—Superman, Kenner

	MNP	MIP
Despero	5	10
Flash, The	5	15
Green Arrow	5	15
Green Lantern	5	15
Hawkman	5	15
Huntress	5	15
Parallax	5	15
Robin	5	15
Superman	5	15

Toy Story (Thinkway, 1996)

5" Figures

	MNP	MIP
Alien	5	15
Boxer Buzz	4	8
Crawling Baby Face	3	9
Fighting Woody	3	9
Flying Buzz (Rocket)	4	8
Hamm	4	8
Karate Buzz	4	8
Kicking Woody	4	8
Quick-Draw Woody	4	8
Rex	4	8
Super Sonic Buzz	3	9

Large Figures

	MNP	MIP
Talking Buzz Lightyear	15	50
Talking Woody	15	60

	MNP	MIP
Hoof, gray body with brown armor	5	15
Thorax, black and yellow	3	12
Thorax, green and red	4	12
Thresher, light blue skin	5	15
Thresher, violet skin	3	10

Series 2, Figures

	MNP	MIP
Blitz	3	10
Brain Drain	3	10
Corn Boy	3	10
Poacher	3	10
Quartz	3	10
Smuggler	3	10

Total Justice (Kenner, 1996)

5" Figures

	MNP	MIP
Aquaman, black armor	5	15
Aquaman, with Hydro-Blasting Spear, gold armor	7	20
Batman	5	20
Black Lightning	7	15
Darkseid	5	10

Toy Story—Kicking Woody, Thinkway

TOY STORY

Transformers (Kenner, 1984-95)

Generation 1, Series 1, 1984

	MNP	MIP
Bluestreak, blue	100	350
Bluestreak, silver	90	250
Brawn	10	40
Bumblebee, red	40	100
Bumblebee, yellow	20	50
Cliffjumper, red	10	40
Cliffjumper, yellow	20	50
Gears	10	40
Hound	100	275
Huffer	10	40
Ironhide	75	250
Jazz	75	250
Megatron	100	300
Mirage	90	250
Optimus Prime with gray or blue roller	100	300
Prowl	90	250
Ratchet with cross	75	150
Ratchet without cross	75	200
Sideswipe	100	275
Skywarp	50	120
Soundwave and Buzzsaw	50	120

	MNP	MIP
Starscream	60	150
Sunstreaker	100	275
Thundercracker	50	120
Trailbreaker	75	150
Wheeljack	90	250
Windcharger	20	50

Generation 1, Series 2, 1985

	MNP	MIP
Astrotrain	10	50
Beachcomber	5	15
Blaster	20	50
Blitzwing	20	50
Brawn	8	20
Brawn with Minispy	10	40
Bumblebee with Minispy, yellow	20	50
Bumblebee, red	10	30
Bumblebee, yellow	10	30
Cliffjumper with Minispy, red	50	125
Cliffjumper, red	8	20
Cliffjumper, yellow	10	30
Cosmos	8	20
Dirge	40	100
Gears	10	30
Gears with Minispy	10	30
Grapple	50	125

Transformers—Megatron, Generation 1, Series 1, Kenner, 1984

Transformers—Jetfire, Generation 1, Series 2, Kenner, 1985

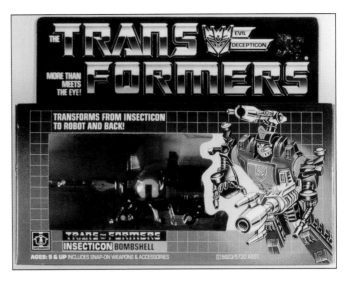

Transformers—Bombshell, Generation 1, Series 2, Kenner, 1985

	MNP	MIP
Hoist	50	125
Huffer	10	30
Huffer with Minispy	10	40
Inferno	40	100
Jazz	5	40
Jetfire	100	325
Omega Supreme	75	200
Optimus Prime	75	250
Perceptor	40	100
Powerglide	8	20
Ramjet	40	80
Red Alert	60	175
Roadbuster	50	100
Seaspray	8	20
Shockwave	75	200
Skids	60	175
Smokescreen	50	150
Thrust	40	80
Tracks	60	175
Warpath	8	20
Whirl	50	150
Windcharger	20	50
Windcharger with Minispy	20	50

Constructicons

Bonecrusher	10	40
Hook	10	40
Long Haul	10	40
Mixmaster	10	40
Scavenger	10	40
Scrapper	10	40

Deluxe Insecticons

Barrage	20	55
Chop Shop	10	55
Ransack	20	55
Venom	20	55

Dinobots

Grimlock	20	125
Slag	40	100
Sludge	40	100
Snarl	40	100

Insecticons

Bombshell	8	25

Transformers—Kickback, Generation 1, Series 2, Kenner, 1985

Transformers—Shrapnel, Generation 1, Series 2, Kenner, 1985

TRANSFORMERS

TRANSFORMERS

	MNP	MIP
Kickback	8	25
Shrapnel	8	25

Generation 1, Series 3, 1986

	MNP	MIP
Beachcomber	5	15
Beachcomber with patch	8	20
Blurr	30	80
Blurr with poster	20	60
Bumblebee	5	15
Bumblebee with patch	20	50
Cosmos	5	15
Cosmos with patch	8	20
Hot Rod with poster, plastic toes	100	250
Hot Rod, metal toes	50	150
Hubcap	5	15
Hubcap with patch	5	15
Kup, plastic tires and wheels	20	60
Kup, rubber tires and metal wheels	20	60
Outback	5	15
Outback with patch	5	15
Pipes	5	15
Pipes with patch	5	15
Powerglide	5	15
Powerglide with patch	8	20
Rodimus Prime, metal toes	50	130
Rodimus Prime, plastic toes	50	130
Seaspray	5	15
Seaspray with patch	8	20
Swerve	5	15
Swerve with patch	5	15
Tailgate	5	15
Tailgate with patch	5	15
Warpath	5	15
Warpath with patch	8	20
Wheelie	5	15
Wheelie with patch	5	15
Wreck-gar	20	60
Wreck-gar with poster	30	80

Aerialbots

	MNP	MIP
Air Raid	10	30
Air Raid with patch	10	30
Fireflight	10	30
Fireflight with patch	10	30
Silverbolt	10	40
Skydive	10	30
Skydive with patch	10	30
Slingshot	10	30
Slingshot with patch	10	30

Combaticons

	MNP	MIP
Blast Off, metal treads	10	30
Blast Off, plastic chest	10	30
Brawl, metal treads	10	30
Brawl, plastic treads	10	30
Onslaught	10	40
Swindle, gray plastic chest	10	30
Swindle, metal treads	10	30
Vortex, metal treads	10	30
Vortex, plastic chest	10	30

Predacons and Sharkticon

	MNP	MIP
Divebomb with poster, plastic body	30	80
Divebomb, metal body	30	80
Divebomb, plastic body	40	100
Headstrong, metal body	40	100
Rampage, metal body	20	75
Rampage, plastic body	20	75
Razorclaw, metal body	20	75
Razorclaw, plastic body	20	75
Tantrum with poster, plastic body	30	80
Tantrum, metal body	40	100
Tantrum, plastic body	30	80

Protectobots

	MNP	MIP
Blades	10	30
Blades, plastic chest	10	30
First Aid	10	30
First Aid, plastic chest	10	30
Groove	10	30
Groove, silver chest	10	30
Hot Spot	10	40
Streetwise	10	30

Stunticons

	MNP	MIP
Breakdown	10	30
Breakdown with patch	10	30
Dead End	10	30

Transformers—Groove, Generation 1, Series 3, Kenner, 1986

	MNP	MIP
Dead End with patch	10	30
Drag Strip	10	30
Drag Strip with patch	10	30
Motormaster	10	40
Wildrider	10	30
Wildrider with patch	10	30

Triple Changers

Broadside	20	60
Broadside with poster	20	50
Octane	30	75
Octane with poster	20	50
Sandstorm, metal or plastic toes	50	150
Sandstorm, plastic toes	30	75
Springer, metal or plastic front	50	100

Generation 1, Series 3, 1987

Predacons and Sharkticon

Headstrong, plastic body	30	80

Generation 1, Series 4, 1987

Battletrap	8	25
Flywheels	8	25

Aerialbots

Air Raid	5	15
Air Raid with decoy	10	35
Fireflight	5	15
Fireflight with decoy	8	20
Skydive	5	15
Skydive with decoy	10	35
Slingshot	5	15
Slingshot with decoy	10	35

Combaticons

Blast Off with decoy, plastic chest	8	25
Brawl with decoy, plastic treads	8	20
Swindle with decoy, gray plastic chest	8	25
Vortex with decoy, plastic chest	8	25

Headmaster

Apeface	20	55
Brainstorm	20	50
Chromedome	30	75
Fortess Maximus	300	900
Hardhead	20	50
Highbrow	20	50
Mindwipe	20	50
Skullcruncher	20	50
Snapdragon	20	55
Weirdwolf	20	50

Monsterbots

Doublecross	20	45
Grotusque	20	45
Repugnus	20	45

Protectobots

Blades with decoy, plastic chest	8	20
Blades, plastic chest	5	15
First Aid with decoy, plastic chest	8	20
First Aid, plastic chest	5	15
Groove with decoy, silver chest	8	20
Groove, silver chest	5	15

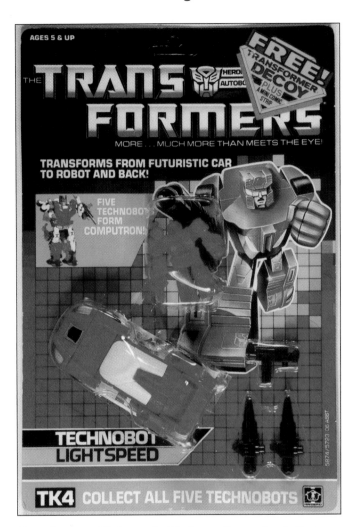

Transformers—Lightspeed with decoy, Generation 1, Series 4, Kenner, 1987

	MNP	MIP
Streetwise	5	15
Streetwise with decoy	8	20

Stunticons

Breakdown with decoy	8	20
Dead End with decoy	8	20
Drag Strip with decoy	8	20
Wildrider with decoy	8	20

Targetmaster

Blurr	50	150
Crosshairs	50	150
Cyclonus	50	130
Hot Rod	100	300
Kup	50	150
Misfire	30	80
Pointblank	30	70
Scourge	50	130
Slugslinger	30	80
Sureshot	30	70
Triggerhappy	30	80

Technobots

Afterburner	8	25
Afterburner with decoy	10	30
Lightspeed	8	20
Lightspeed with decoy	8	25

TRANSFORMERS

TRANSFORMERS

	MNP	MIP
Nosecone 8		25
Nosecone with decoy 10		30
Strafe...8		20
Strafe with decoy 10		35

Terrorcons

	MNP	MIP
Blot with decoy 8		20
Cutthroat with decoy 8		35
Rippersnapper with decoy 8		20
Sinnertwin with decoy 8		20

Throttlebots

	MNP	MIP
Chase 8		20
Chase with decoy.....................................8		35
Freeway 8		20
Freeway with decoy 10		35
Goldbug 8		20
Goldbug with decoy 10		35
Rollbar 10		35
Rollbar with decoy 8		20
Searchlight 8		20
Searchlight with decoy 10		35
Wideload 8		20
Wideload with decoy 10		35

Generation 1, Series 5, 1988

Firecons

	MNP	MIP
Cindersaur 4		10
Flamefeather 4		10
Sparkstalker 4		10

Headmaster

	MNP	MIP
Fangry 20		50
Horri-bull 20		50
Hosehead 20		50
Nightbeat 20		60
Siren 20		50
Squeezeplay 20		50

Powermaster

	MNP	MIP
Darkwing 20		50
Dreadwind 20		50
Getaway 10		40
Joyride 10		40
Slapdash 10		40

Pretenders

	MNP	MIP
Bomb-burst, clear insert 20		60
Bugly 20		60
Carnivac 10		40
Catilla..20		50
Chainclaw 10		40
Cloudburst, clear insert 20		50
Finback 20		65
Groundbreaker 20		65
Gunrunner 20		55
Iguanus 10		40
Landmine, clear insert 10		40
Roadgrabber...20		55
Skullgrin, clear insert 20		50
Sky High 10		40
Snarler 20		50
Splashdown 20		50
Submarauder, clear insert 20		50

	MNP	MIP
Waverider, clear insert 20		50

Seacons

	MNP	MIP
Nautilator 10		30
Overbite 10		30
Seawing 10		30
Skalor 10		30
Tentakil 10		30

Sparkabots

	MNP	MIP
Fizzle 4		15
Guzzle 4		15
Sizzle 4		15

Targetmaster

	MNP	MIP
Landfill 8		20
Needlenose 10		30
Quake 10		30
Quickmix 8		25
Scoop 8		25
Spinister 10		30

Technobots

	MNP	MIP
Afterburner 5		15
Lightspeed 5		15
Nosecone 5		15
Strafe 5		15

Terrorcons

	MNP	MIP
Blot 8		20
Cutthroat 8		20
Rippersnapper 8		20
Sinnertwin 8		20

Triggerbots

	MNP	MIP
Backstreet 5		15
Dogfight 5		15
Override 5		15

Triggercons

	MNP	MIP
Crankcase..5		15
Ruckus 5		15
Windsweeper 5		15

Transformers—Nightbeat, Generation 1, Series 5, Kenner, 1988

Generation 1, Series 6, 1989

Mega Pretenders

	MNP	MIP
Crossblades	10	40
Thunderwing	10	40
Vroom	10	40

Micromaster Bases

Groundshaker	10	30
Skyhopper	10	30

Micromaster Battle Stations

Airwave	8	20
Greasepit	8	20
Hot House	8	20
Ironworks	8	20

Micromaster Patrols

Air Strike Patrol	3	10
Battle Patrol	3	10
Off Road Patrol	3	10
Race Car Patrol	3	10
Rescue Patrol	3	10
Sports Car Patrol	3	10

Micromaster Transports

Erector	5	15
Flattop	5	15
Overload	5	15
Roughstuff	5	15

Pretenders

Birdbrain	5	15
Bludgeon	10	30
Bomb-burst	10	30
Bristleback	5	15
Cloudburst	10	30
Doubleheader	8	20
Landmine	20	50
Longtooth	8	20
Octopunch	8	20
Pincher	8	20
Roadblock	20	50
Scowl	5	15
Skullgrin	10	35
Skyhammer	20	50
Slog	5	15
Stranglehold	8	20
Submarauder	10	30
Waverider	10	30
Wildfly	5	15

Generation 1, Series 7, 1990

Action Master Action Vehicles

Gutcruncher	10	45
Megatron	20	60
Sprocket	10	35
Wheeljack	10	35

Action Masters

Axer	8	20
Banzai-Tron	8	20
Blaster	4	12
Bumblebee	4	12

	MNP	MIP
Devastator	4	12
Grimlock	4	12
Inferno	8	20
Jackpot	4	12
Jazz	4	12
Kick-Off	8	20
Krok	4	12
Mainframe	4	12
Over-Run	8	20
Prowl	8	20
Rad	4	12
Rollout	4	12
Shockwave	8	20
Skyfall	8	20
Snarl	8	20
Soundwave	5	15
Treadshot	4	12

Micromaster Combiner Squads

Astro Squad	5	15
Battle Squad	5	15
Constructor Squad	5	15
Metro Squad	5	15

Micromaster Combiner Transports

Cannon Transport	8	20
Missile Launcher	8	20
Tanker Truck	8	20

Micromaster Patrols

Air Patrol	4	10
Construction Patrol	4	10
Hot Rod Patrol	4	10
Military Patrol	4	10
Monster Trucks Patrol	4	10
Race Track Patrol	4	10

Micromaster Transports

Erector	5	12
Flattop	5	12
Overload	5	12
Roughstuff	5	12

Generation 2, Series 1, 1993

Afterburner	3	12
Bumblebee	5	15
Deluge, changes colors	5	15
Drench, changes colors	5	15
Eagle Eye	3	12
Gobots, changes colors	5	15
Hubcap	5	15
Inferno	8	25
Jazz	35	100
Jetstorm, changes colors	5	15
Ramjet, missiles grouped	8	20
Ramjet, missiles separate	10	35
Rapido	3	12
Seaspray	5	15
Sideswipe	8	25
Skram	5	15
Starscream, missiles grouped	8	20
Starscream, missiles separate	10	35
Terradive	5	15

TRANSFORMERS

	MNP	MIP
Turbofire	5	15
Windbreaker	5	15
Windrazor	5	15

Constructicons

	MNP	MIP
Bonecrusher, orange	5	17
Bonecrusher, yellow	3	12
Hook, orange	5	15
Hook, yellow	3	12
Long Haul, orange	5	15
Long Haul, yellow	3	12
Mixmaster, orange	5	15
Mixmaster, yellow	3	12
Scavenger, orange	5	15
Scavenger, yellow	3	12
Scrapper, orange	5	15
Scrapper, yellow	5	15

Dinobots

	MNP	MIP
Grimlock, dark blue	8	20
Grimlock, silver	20	65
Grimlock, turquoise	35	100
Slag, green	8	30
Slag, red	20	55
Slag, silver	20	55
Snarl, green	20	55
Snarl, red	8	30
Snarl, silver	20	55

Generation 2, Series 2, 1994

	MNP	MIP
Megatron, purple and black camouflage	5	15
Optimus Prime, red and white	10	30

Aerialbots

	MNP	MIP
Air Raid	5	15
Fireflight	5	15
Skydive	5	15
Slingshot	5	15

Combaticons

	MNP	MIP
Blast Off	5	15
Brawl	8	20
Onslaught	10	40
Swindle	5	15
Vortex	5	15

Laser Rods

	MNP	MIP
Electro	5	15
Jolt	5	15
Sizzle	5	15
Volt	5	15

Rotor Force

	MNP	MIP
Leadfoot	3	12
Manta Ray	3	12
Powerdive, black rotors	8	20
Powerdive, red rotors	3	12
Ransack, black rotors	8	20
Ransack, red rotors	3	12

Generation 2, Series 3, 1995

	MNP	MIP
Dirtbag	3	12
Roadblock	3	12

Cyberjets

	MNP	MIP
Air Raid	2	6

Transformers—Megatron, purple and black camouflage, Generation 2, Series 2, Kenner, 1994

	MNP	MIP
Hooligan	2	6
Jetfire	2	6
Skyjack	2	6
Space Case	2	6
Strafe	2	6

Go-Bots

	MNP	MIP
Blowout	3	10
Bumblebee	3	10
Double Clutch	3	10
Firecracker	3	10
Frenzy	3	10
Gearhead, clear	3	10
Gearhead, solid	3	10
High Beam	3	10
Ironhide	3	10
Megatron	3	10
Mirage	3	10
Motormouth, clear	3	10
Motormouth, solid	3	10
Optimus Prime	3	10
Sideswipe	3	10
Soundwave	3	10

Transformers: Beast Wars (Kenner, 1996-99)

Basic Beast, 1996

	MNP	MIP
Airazor	10	30
Armordillo	5	15
Claw Jaw	8	25
Drill Bit	8	25
Iguanus	10	30
Insecticon	5	15

Transformers—Dirtbag, Generation 2, Series 3, Kenner, 1995

Transformers—Roadblock, Generation 2, Series 3, Kenner, 1995

Transformers—Generation 2, Series 3 by Kenner, 1995. Left to Right: Gearhead; Blowout

TRANSFORMERS – BEAST WARS

TRANSFORMERS - BEAST WARS

Transformers—Generation 2, Series 3 by Kenner, 1995. Left to Right: Firecracker; High Beam

	MNP	MIP
Lazorbeak	8	25
Rattrap	15	50
Razorbeast	15	45
Razorclaw	10	30
Snapper	8	20
Snarl	8	25
Terrorsaur	15	50

Basic Beast, 1997

Powerpinch	8	25
Spittor	8	25

Basic Fuzors, 1998

Air Hammer	5	15
Bantor	3	8
Buzzclaw	3	8
Noctorro	3	8
Quickstrike	5	15
Terragator	4	12

Basic Transmetal 2, 1999

Optimus Minor	8	25
Scarem	3	8
Sonar	3	8
Spittor	3	10

Comic 2-Pack, 1996

Megatron	15	50
Optimus Primal	15	50

Transformers: Beast Wars—Razorbeast, Basic Beast, Kenner, 1996

Transformers: Beast Wars—Razorclaw, Basic Beast, Kenner, 1996

Transformers: Beast Wars—Torca, Deluxe Fuzors, Kenner, 1998

Transformers: Beast Wars—Injector, Deluxe Fuzors, Kenner, 1998

Deluxe Beast, 1996

	MNP	MIP
Blackarachnia	40	115
Bonecrusher	15	50
Buzz Saw	25	75
Cheetor, blue eyes	50	150
Cheetor, red eyes	40	120
Cybershark	30	90
Dinobot	40	110
Jetstorm	15	45
Rhinox	40	110
Tarantulas	40	125
Tigatron	30	100
Waspinator	40	125
Wolfang	40	110

Deluxe Beast, 1997

Grimlock	25	75
K-9	8	25
Manterror	15	50
Retrax	8	25

Transformers: Beast Wars—Rattrap, Deluxe Transmetals Fuzors, Kenner, 1998

Transformers: Beast Wars—Tarantulas, Deluxe Transmetals, Kenner, 1998

Transformers: Beast Wars—Scavenger, Mega Transmetals, Kenner, 1998

TRANSFORMERS – BEAST WARS

Deluxe Fuzors, 1998

	MNP	MIP
Injector	4	12
Silverbolt	8	25
Sky Shadow	4	12
Torca	3	10

Deluxe Transmetal 2, 1999

Iguanus	3	10
Jawbreaker	3	10
Ramulus	5	15
Scourge	4	12

Deluxe Transmetals, 1998

Airazor	8	20
Cheetor	8	25
Rattrap	10	30
Rhinox	15	35
Tarantulas	8	20
Terrorsaur	5	15
Waspinator	8	25

Mega Beast, 1996

B'Boom	8	25
Polar Claw	20	65
Scorponok	15	45

Transformers: Beast Wars—Airazor, Video Pack-in, Kenner, 1998

Transformers: Beast Wars—Magnaboss (Maximal Team): Ironhide, Silverbolt, Prowl, Ultra Team, Kenner, 1997

Mega Beast, 1997

	MNP	MIP
Inferno	15	45
Transquito	8	20

Mega Transmetal 2, 1999

Blackarachnia	15	45
Cybershark	5	15

Mega Transmetals, 1998

Megatron	8	20
Optimus Primal	8	25
Scavenger	5	15

Super Beast, 1998

Optimal Optimus	8	20

Ultra Beast, 1996

Megatron	15	50
Optimus Primal	20	60

Ultra Team, 1997

Magnaboss (Maximal Team)óIronhide, Silverbolt, Prowl	8	25
Tripredacus (Predacon Team)-Ram Horn, Sea Clamp, Cicadacon	8	25

Ultra Transmetal 2, 1999

Megatron	8	25
Tigerhawk	5	15

Ultra Transmetals, 1998

Depth Charge	8	20
Rampage	8	25

Video Pack-in, 1998

Airazor	8	25
Razorclaw	8	25

Universal Monsters—Bride of Frankenstein, Sideshow Toys

Universal Monsters—Creature from the Black Lagoon, Sideshow Toys

Tuff Talkin' Wrestlers
(Toy Biz, 1999)
Figures

	MNP	MIP
Goldberg/Kevin Nash	20	40
Sting/Diamond Dallas Page	20	40

Universal Monsters
(Remco, 1979)
8" Figures

Creature from the Black Lagoon	75	200
Dracula	40	100
Frankenstein	20	40
Mummy, The	20	40
Phantom of the Opera	100	250
Wolfman, The	55	130

Universal Monsters
(Sideshow Toys, 1998-Present)
Series I, 8" Figures

Frankenstein	6	15
Mummy, The	8	20
Wolfman, The	8	20

Series II, 8" Figures

	MNP	MIP
Bride of Frankenstein	8	20
Creature from the Black Lagoon	8	20
Phantom of the Opera	8	20

Series III, 8" Figures

Hunchback of Notredame	7	15
Invisible Man	7	15
Metaluna Mutant	7	15

Universal Monsters: Hasbro Signature Series
(Hasbro, 1998)
Figures

Frankenstein	10	25
The Bride of Frankenstein	10	25
The Mummy	10	25
The Wolf Man	10	25

Vault, The
(Toy Biz, 1998)
6" Figures

Stegron	3	6
Typhoid Mary	3	6
Ultron	3	6

Universal Monsters—Phantom of the Opera, Sideshow Toys

Universal Monsters—Invisible Man, Sideshow Toys

Universal Monsters—Hunchback of Notredame, Sideshow Toys

UNIVERSAL MONSTERS

Universal Monsters—Metaluna Mutant, Sideshow Toys

Vikings—Brave Eric the Viking, Marx

Vikings (Marx, 1960s)
Figures

	MNP	MIP
Brave Eric the Viking	150	300
Mighty Viking Horse	150	300
Odin the Viking Chieftan	150	300

Voltron (Matchbox, 1985-86)
3-3/4" Figures

Doom Commander	5	15
Haggar the Witch	5	15
Hunk	8	20
Keith	8	20
King Zarkon	5	15
Lance	5	15
Pidge	5	15
Prince Lotor	8	20
Princess Allura	8	20
Robeast Mutilor	4	10

	MNP	MIP
Robeast Scorpious	4	12
Voltron Robot	10	30

Accessories

Coffin of Darkness	8	20
Coffin of Doom	8	20
Doom Blaster	12	25
Skull Tank	12	25
Zorkon Zapper	12	25

Gift Sets

Deluxe Gift Set I	65	225
Deluxe Gift Set II	55	200
Deluxe Gift Set III	55	200

Waltons (Mego, 1975)
8" Figures

Grandma and Grandpa	25	50
John Boy and Ellen	25	50
Mom and Pop	25	50

VIKINGS

WCW/NWO Two Packs—Chris Jericho vs. Dean Malenko, Toy Biz

WCW/NWO Two Packs—Goldberg vs. Hollywood Hogan, Toy Biz

WCW/NWO GRIP 'N FLIP

Accessories

	MNP	MIP
Barn 50		100
Country Store 50		100
Truck 40		80

Play Sets

	MNP	MIP
Farm House 75		150
Farm House with Six Figures 150		300

Warrior Beasts, The (Remco, 1983)
Figures

Craven 15		50
Gecko 15		60
Guana 15		50
Hydraz 15		60
Ramar 15		50
Skullman 25		90
Snake Man 25		90
Stegos 15		50
Wolf Warrior 30		90
Zardus 15		50

WCW Bash at the Beach (Toy Biz, 2000)
6" Figures

Diamond Dallas Page 3		8
Goldberg 3		8
Hulk Hogan 3		8
Lex Luger 3		8
Sting 3		8

WCW Collector Series (Toy Biz, 2000)
12" Figures

Goldberg 5		15
Hulk Hogan 5		15
Sting 5		15

WCW Cyborg Wrestlers (Toy Biz, 2000)
6" Figures

Bret Hart 3		8
Goldberg 3		8
Kevin Nash 3		8
Sid Vicious 3		8
Sting 3		8

WCW Nitro Active Wrestlers (Toy Biz, 2000)
6" Figures

Buff Bagwell 3		8
Goldberg 3		8
Jeff Jarrett 3		8
Sid Vicious 3		8
Vampiro 3		8

WCW Power Slam Wrestlers I (Toy Biz, 2000)
6" Figures

Goldberg 3		8
Hak 3		8
Hulk Hogan 3		8
Rodman 3		8
Sid Vicious 3		8

WCW Power Slam Wrestlers II (Toy Biz, 2000)
6" Figures

Buff Bagwell 3		8
Kanyon 3		8

WCW Power Slam Wrestlers II—Roddy Piper, Toy Biz. Photo Courtesy Toy Biz

	MNP	MIP
Kevin Nash 3		8
Roddy Piper 3		8
Sting 3		8

WCW S.L.A.M. Force (Toy Biz, 2000)
6" Figures

Benoit with comic book 3		8
Bret Hart with comic book 3		8
Goldberg with comic book 3		8
Kevin Nash with comic book 3		8
Sting with comic book 3		8

WCW Thunder Slam Twin Packs (Toy Biz, 2000)
6" Figures

Bam Bam Bigelow and Goldberg 3		10
Kevin Nash and Scott Hall 3		10
Sting and Bret Hart 3		10

WCW World Championship Wrestling Ring Fighters (Toy Biz, 1999)
6" Figures

Booker T 3		10
Bret Hart 3		10
Chris Benoit 3		10
Scott Steiner 3		10

WCW World Championship Wrestling Smash 'n Slam (Toy Biz, 1999)
6" Figures

Hollywood Hogan 5		15

WCW S.L.A.M. Force—Goldberg, Toy Biz. Photo Courtesy Toy Biz

WCW S.L.A.M. Force—Kevin Nash, Toy Biz. Photo Courtesy Toy Biz

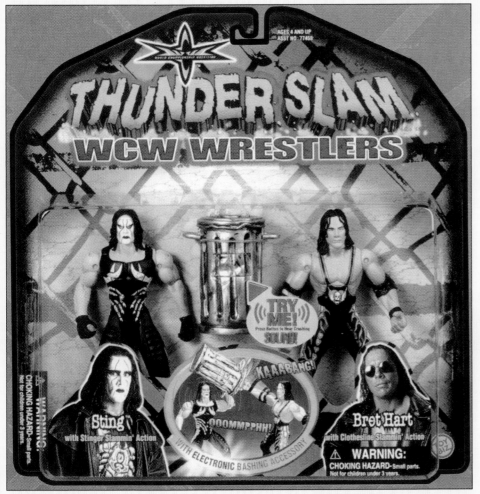

WCW Thunder Slam Twin Packs— Sting and Bret Hart, Toy Biz. Photo Courtesy Toy Biz

WCW SLAM

	MNP	MIP
Kevin Nash	5	15
Macho Man Randy Savage	4	12
Scott Hall	5	15

WCW World Championship Wrestling Smash 'n Slam II (Toy Biz, 1999)
6" Figures

	MNP	MIP
D.D.P.	3	10
Giant & Rey Mysterio Jr.	3	10
Goldberg & Masked Wrestler	3	10
Lex Luger	3	10
Sting	3	10

WCW/NWO Ring Masters (Toy Biz, 1998)
6" Figures

	MNP	MIP
Bret Hart	3	10
Chris Jericho	3	10
Goldberg	3	10
Lex Luger	3	10

WCW/NWO Slam 'n Crunch (Toy Biz, 1998)
6" Figures

	MNP	MIP
Buff Bagwell	3	10
Goldberg	3	10
Konnan	3	10
Sting	3	10

WCW/NWO Two Packs (Toy Biz, 1999)
Battle of the Giants, 6" Figures

	MNP	MIP
Giant vs. Kevin Nash	3	10

Clash of the Champions, 6" Figures

	MNP	MIP
Sting vs. Hollywood Hogan	5	15

Grip 'n Flip Wrestlers II, 6" Figures

	MNP	MIP
Kevin Nash vs. Bret Hart	3	10
Scott Steiner vs. Rick Steiner	3	10
Sting vs. Lex Luger	3	10

Grip 'n Flip Wrestlers, 6" Figures

	MNP	MIP
Chris Jericho vs. Dean Malenko	3	10
Goldberg vs. Hollywood Hogan	5	15
Raven vs. Diamond Dallas Page	3	10

Power and Beauty, 6" Figures

	MNP	MIP
Macho Man & Elizabeth	3	10

Welcome Back, Kotter (Mattel, 1976)
Figures

	MNP	MIP
Barbarino	40	80
Epstein	20	50
Horshback	20	50

Wetworks (prototype figure)—Dane, McFarlane. Photo Courtesy McFarlane Toys

Wetworks (prototype figure)—Mother-1, McFarlane. Photo Courtesy McFarlane Toys

*Wetworks (prototype figure)—Dozer, McFarlane. Photo
Courtesy McFarlane Toys*

*Wetworks (prototype figure)—Grail, McFarlane. Photo
Courtesy McFarlane Toys*

*Wetworks (prototype figure)—Vampire, McFarlane. Photo
Courtesy McFarlane Toys*

*Wetworks (prototype figure)—Werewolf, McFarlane. Photo
Courtesy McFarlane Toys*

WETWORKS

Welcome Back, Kotter—Deluxe Play Set, Mattel

	MNP	MIP
Mr. Kotter	20	50
Washington	20	50

Play Sets

	MNP	MIP
Welcome Back Kotter Play Set, Deluxe	50	150
Welcome Back, Kotter Play Set	40	100

Wetworks (McFarlane, 1995-96)

Series 1

	MNP	MIP
Dane	3	10
Dozer	3	10
Grail	3	10
Mother-One	5	15
Vampire, dark green	5	15
Vampire, gray	5	15
Werewolf, light blue	5	15
Werewolf, reddish brown	8	20

Series 2

	MNP	MIP
Assasin One, blue	3	10
Assasin One, red	3	10

	MNP	MIP
Blood Queen, all black	8	20
Blood Queen, all black with red trim	8	20
Delta Commander, flesh tones	3	10
Delta Commander, gold	3	10
Frankenstein, brown	3	10
Frankenstein, green	3	10
Mendoza, flesh colored	3	10
Mendoza, half gold	3	10
Pilgrim, flesh tones	5	15
Pilgrim, gold	8	20

Witchblade
(Moore Action Collectibles, 1998-present)

Series I, figures

	MNP	MIP
Ian Nottingham	3	12
Kenneth Irons	3	12
Medieval Witchblade	3	12
Sara Pezzini/Witchblade	3	12

Witchblade—Sara Pezzini/Witchblade, Moore Action Collectibles. Photo Courtesy Moore Action Collectibles

Witchblade—Aspen Mathews/Fathom, Moore Action Collectibles. Photo Courtesy Moore Action Collectibles

WITCHBLADE

WITCHBLADE

Series II, figures

	MNP	MIP
Aspen Mathews/Fathom	3	12
Sara Pezzini in Red Dress	3	12

Wizard of Oz (Mego, 1974)
4" Boxed Figures

Munchkin Dancer	75	150
Munchkin Flower Girl	75	150
Munchkin General	75	150
Munchkin Lollipop Kid	75	150
Munchkin Mayor	75	150

8" Boxed Figures

Cowardly Lion	25	50
Dorothy with Toto	25	50
Glinda the Good Witch	25	50
Scarecrow	25	50
Tin Woodsman	25	50
Wicked Witch	50	100
Wizard of Oz	35	250

Play Sets

Emerald City with eight 8" figures	125	350
Emerald City with Wizard of Oz	45	100
Munchkin Land	150	300
Witch's Castle, Sears Exclusive	250	450

Wizard of Oz (Multi-Toys, 1989)
50th Anniversary, 12" figures

Cowardly Lion	5	15
Dorothy and Toto	5	15
Glinda	5	15
Scarecrow	5	15
Tin Man	5	15

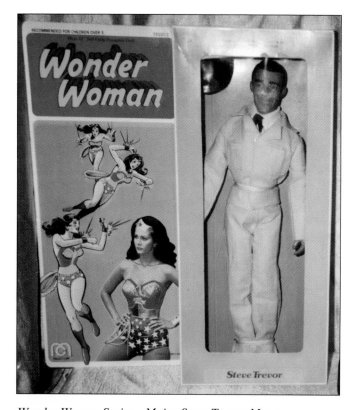

Wonder Woman Series—Major Steve Trevor, Mego

Wonder Woman Series—Wonder Women with Fly Away Action, Mego

	MNP	MIP
Wicked Witch	5	15
Wizard	5	15

Wonder Woman Series (Mego, 1977-80)
Figures

Major Steve Trevor, 1978	26	65
Queen Hippolyte, 1978	40	100
Queen Nubia, 1978	40	100
Wonder Woman with Diana Prince Outfit, 1978	100	200
Wonder Women with Fly Away Action	125	250

World's Greatest Super Knights (Mego, 1975)
8" Figures

Black Knight	90	355
Ivanhoe	65	275
King Arthur	60	200
Sir Galahad	80	300
Sir Lancelot	80	300

World's Greatest Super Pirates (Mego, 1974)
Figures

Blackbeard	200	500
Captain Patch	175	300
Jean Lafitte	250	550
Long John Silver	250	550

World's Greatest Super-Heroes (Mego, 1972-78)
12-1/2" Figures

Amazing Spider-Man, 1978	40	100
Batman, 1978	60	125
Batman, magnetic, 1978	75	100
Captain America, 1978	75	150
Hulk, 1978	30	60

*World's Greatest Super-Heroes—
Captain America, 1978, Mego*

World's Greatest Super Knights—Ivanhoe, Mego

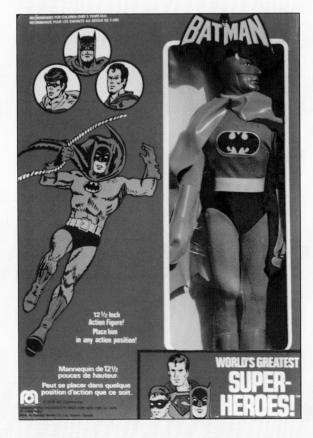

*World's Greatest Super-Heroes—
Batman, 1978, Mego*

WORLD'S GREATEST SUPER HEROES

Left: World's Greatest Super-Heroes—Captain America, boxed, 1972, Mego

Right: World's Greatest Super-Heroes—Catwoman, boxed, 1973, Mego

World's Greatest Super-Heroes by Mego—Left to Right: Robin, magnetic; Batman, magnetic, 1978

World's Greatest Super-Heroes— Amazing Spider-Man, 1978, Mego

World's Greatest Super-Heroes—Batman with painted mask, carded, 1972, Mego

World's Greatest Super-Heroes—Isis, carded, 1976, carded, Mego

WORLD'S GREATEST SUPER HEROES

WORLD'S GREATEST SUPER HEROES

World's Greatest Super-Heroes—Falcon, boxed, 1974, Mego

World's Greatest Super-Heroes—Joker, boxed, 1973, Mego

World's Greatest Super-Heroes—Superman, boxed, 1972, Mego

World's Greatest Super-Heroes by Mego—Left to Right: Robin with painted mask, boxed, 1972; Robin with painted mask, carded, 1972

	MNP	MIP
Robin, magnetic, 1978	75	100
Spider-Man, web shooting	75	150

8" Figures

	MNP	MIP
Aquaman, 1972, boxed	50	150
Aquaman, 1972, carded	50	150
Batgirl, 1973, boxed	125	300
Batgirl, 1973, carded	125	250
Batman, fist fighting, 1975, boxed	150	350
Batman, painted mask, 1972, boxed	60	150
Batman, painted mask, 1972, carded	60	100
Batman, removable mask, 1972, boxed	200	350
Batman, removable mask, 1972, Kresge card only	200	450
Bruce Wayne, 1974, boxed, Montgomery Ward exclusive	1200	2000
Captain America, 1972, boxed	60	200
Captain America, 1972, carded	60	150
Catwoman, 1973, boxed	150	350
Catwoman, 1973, carded	150	450
Clark Kent, 1974, boxed, Montgomery Ward exclusive	1200	2000
Conan, 1975, boxed	150	400
Conan, 1975, carded	150	500
Dick Grayson, 1974, boxed, Montgomery Ward exclusive	1200	2000
Falcon, 1974, boxed	60	150
Falcon, 1974, carded	60	450
Green Arrow, 1973, boxed	150	450
Green Arrow, 1973, carded	150	550
Green Goblin, 1974, boxed	90	275
Green Goblin, 1974, carded	90	650
Human Torch, Fantastic Four, 1975, boxed	25	90
Human Torch, Fantastic Four, 1975, card	25	50
Incredible Hulk, 1974, boxed	20	100
Incredible Hulk, 1974, carded	20	50
Invisible Girl, Fantastic Four, 1975, boxed	30	150
Invisible Girl, Fantastic Four, 1975, card	30	60
Iron Man, 1974, boxed	75	125
Iron Man, 1974, carded	75	450
Isis, 1976, boxed	75	250
Isis, 1976, carded	75	125
Joker, 1973, boxed	60	150
Joker, 1973, carded	60	150
Joker, fist fighting, 1975, boxed	150	400
Lizard, 1974, boxed	75	200
Lizard, 1974, carded	75	450
Lizard, fist fighting, 1974, boxed	200	600
Mr. Fantastic, Fantastic Four, 1975, boxed	30	140
Mr. Fantastic, Fantastic Four, 1975, carded	30	60
Mr. Mxyzptlk, open mouth, 1973, boxed	50	75
Mr. Mxyzptlk, open mouth, 1973, carded	50	150
Mr. Mxyzptlk, smirk, 1973, boxed	60	150
Penguin, 1973, boxed	60	150
Penguin, 1973, carded	60	125
Peter Parker, 1974, boxed, Montgomery Ward exclusive	1200	2000
Riddler, 1973, boxed	100	250
Riddler, 1973, carded	100	400
Riddler, fist fighting, 1975, boxed	150	400
Robin, fist fighting, 1975, boxed	125	350
Robin, painted mask, 1972, boxed	60	150
Robin, painted mask, 1972, carded	60	90
Robin, removable mask, 1972, boxed	250	400
Robin, removable mask, 1972, solid box	250	1500
Shazam, 1972, boxed	75	200
Shazam, 1972, carded	75	150
Spider-Man, 1972, boxed	20	100

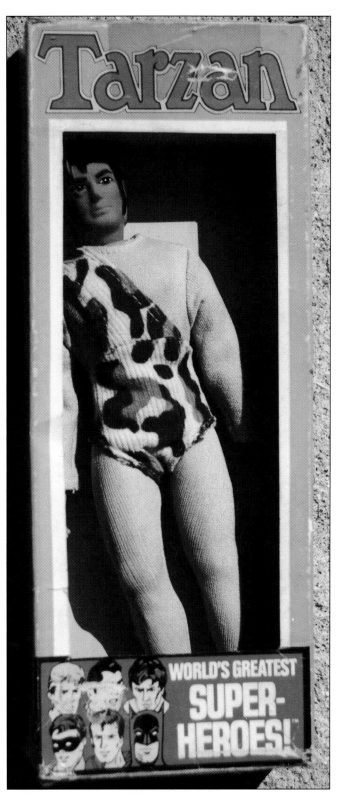

World's Greatest Super-Heroes—Tarzan, boxed, 1972, Mego

	MNP	MIP
Spider-Man, 1972, carded	20	50
Supergirl, 1973, boxed	300	450
Supergirl, 1973, carded	300	450
Superman, 1972, boxed	50	125
Superman, 1972, carded	50	100
Tarzan, 1972, boxed	50	150
Tarzan, 1976, Kresge card only	60	225

	MNP	MIP
Thing, Fantastic Four, 1975, boxed	40	150
Thing, Fantastic Four, 1975, carded	40	60
Thor, 1975, boxed	150	300
Thor, 1975, carded	150	300
Wonder Woman, boxed	100	350
Wonder Woman, Kresge card only	100	450
Wondergirl	125	400

Accessories

	MNP	MIP
Super Hero Carry Case, 1973	40	100
Supervator, 1974	60	120

Play Sets

	MNP	MIP
Aquaman vs. The Great White Shark, 1978	300	750
Batcave Play Set, 1974, vinyl	150	300
Batman's Wayne Foundation Penthouse, 1977, fiberboard	600	1200
Hall of Justice, 1976, vinyl	125	250

Superman Series

	MNP	MIP
General Zod, 1978	50	100
Jor-El, 1978	50	100
Lex Luthor, 1978	50	100
Superman, 1978	50	125

Teen Titans, 6-1/2" Figures

	MNP	MIP
Aqualad	175	350
Kid Flash	175	300
Speedy	300	500
Wondergirl	200	450

Vehicles

	MNP	MIP
Batcopter, 1974, boxed	75	150
Batcopter, 1974, on display card	55	110
Batcycle, black, 1975, boxed	75	185
Batcycle, black, 1975, carded	60	150
Batcycle, blue, 1974, boxed	75	170
Batcycle, blue, 1974, carded	75	135
Batmobile and Batman	40	100
Batmobile, 1974, artwork box	75	325
Batmobile, 1974, carded	50	120
Batmobile, 1974, photo box	75	395
Captain America, 1976	125	275
Green Arrowcar, 1976	175	350
Jokermobile, 1976	150	300
Mobile Bat Lab, 1975	125	250
Spidercar, 1976	50	125

WWF (Jakks Pacific, 1997-present)

2-Tuff, Series 1

	MNP	MIP
D.O.A. 8-Ball	4	12
Goldust and Marlena	4	12
HHH and Chyna	4	12
Truth Commission	4	12

2-Tuff, Series 2

	MNP	MIP
Brian Christopher and Jerry Lawler	4	15
D-Lo Brown and Kama	4	15
Kurrgan and Jackyl	4	15
New Age Outlaws	4	15

2-Tuff, Series 3

	MNP	MIP
Kane and Mankind	4	15
Legion of Doom 2000	4	15
Rocky Maivia (The Rock) and Owen Hart	8	20
Stone Cold Steve Austin/Undertaker	4	15

2-Tuff, Series 4

	MNP	MIP
Billy Gunn and Val Venis	3	12
Mankind and The Rock	3	12
Stone Cold Steve Austin and Big Bossman	3	12
Undertaker and Kane	3	12

2-Tuff, Series 5

	MNP	MIP
Debra and Jarrett	3	10
Road Dogg and Billy Gunn	3	10
Stone Cold Steve Austin and The Rock	8	20
Undertaker and Viscera	3	10

Best of 1997, Series 1

	MNP	MIP
Ahmed Johnson	3	10
Bret Hart	3	10
British Bulldog	3	10
Owen Hart	5	15
Stone Cold Steve Austin	3	12
Undertaker	3	10

Best of 1997, Series 2

	MNP	MIP
Crush	3	10
Goldust	3	10
HHH	3	10
Ken Shamrock	3	10

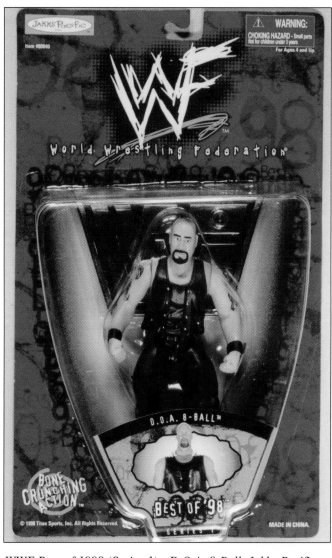

WWF Best of 1998 (Series 1)—D.O.A. 8-Ball, Jakks Pacific

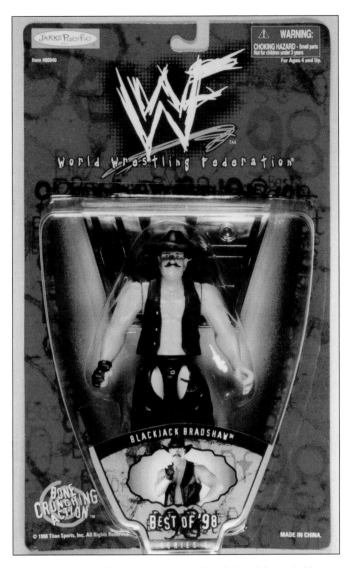

WWF Best of 1998 (Series 1)—Blackjack Bradshaw, Jakks Pacific

WWF Best of 1998 (Series 1)—Brian Christopher, Jakks Pacific

	MNP	MIP
Marc Mero	3	10
Rocky Maivia (The Rock)	5	15
Shawn Michaels	3	10
Undertaker	3	10

Best of 1998, Series 1

8-Ball	3	8
Blackjack Bradshaw	3	8
Brian Christopher	3	8
Chyna	3	8
Shawn Michaels	3	8
D.O.A. Skull	3	8
Stone Cold Steve Austin	4	10
Vader	3	8

Best of 1998, Series 2

Dan Severn	3	8
Dude Love	3	8
HHH	3	8
Jeff Jarrett	3	8
Ken Shamrock	3	8
Mark Henry	3	8
Stone Cold Steve Austin	4	10
Undertaker	3	8

Bone Crunchin' Buddies, Series 1

	MNP	MIP
Dude Love	5	15
Shawn Michaels	5	15
Stone Cold Steve Austin	5	15
Undertaker	5	15

Bone Crunchin' Buddies, Series 2

Animal	5	15
Hawk	5	15
Rock, The	8	20
Stone Cold Steve Austin	5	15
Undertaker	5	15

Bone Crunchin' Buddies, Series 3

HHH	5	15
Kane	5	15
Rock, The	8	20
Stone Cold Steve Austin in shirt and pants	5	15
Stone Cold Steve Austin in tights and vest	5	15
Undertaker	5	15

Fully Loaded, Series 1

Al Snow	3	8
Billy Gunn	3	8

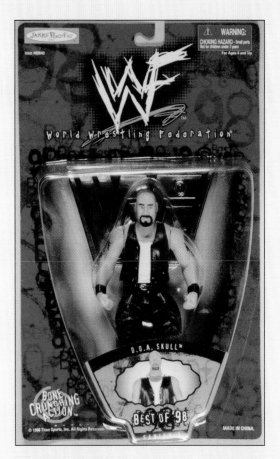

WWF Best of 1998 (Series 1)—D.O.A. Skull, Jakks Pacific

WWF Best of 1998 (Series 1)—Shawn Michaels, Jakks Pacific

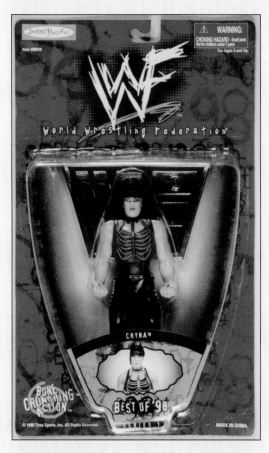

WWF Best of 1998 (Series 1)—Chyna, Jakks Pacific

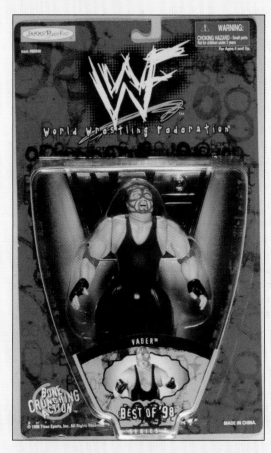

WWF Best of 1998 (Series 1)—Vader, Jakks Pacific

	MNP	MIP
Hunter Hearst Hemsley	3	8
Kane	3	8
Road Dog Jesse James	3	8
Rocky Maivia (The Rock)	5	15

Fully Loaded, Series 2

	MNP	MIP
Road Dog Jesse James	2	6
Rock, The	5	15
Shane McMahon	2	6
Stone Cold Steve Austin	3	10
Test	2	6
X Pac	3	8

Grudge Match

	MNP	MIP
Brian Christopher vs. TAKA	5	15
Dan Severn vs. Ken Shamrock	5	15
HHH vs. Owen Hart	5	15
HHHvs HBK	5	15
Jeff Jarrett vs. X Pac	5	15
Kane vs. Undertaker	5	15
Marc Mero vs. Steve Blackman	5	15
Mark Henry vs. Vader	5	15
McMahon vs. Stone Cold Steve Austin	5	15
Road Dog Jesse James vs. Al Snow	5	15
Sable vs. Luna Vachon	5	15
Shamrock vs. Billy Gunn	5	15
Shawn Michaels vs. Stone Cold Steve Austin	8	20
Stone Cold Steve Austin vs. The Rock	8	20

Legends, Series 1

	MNP	MIP
Andre The Giant	3	12
Captian Lou Albano	3	12
Classie Freddie Blassie	3	12
Jimmy Snuka	3	12

Livewire, Series 1

	MNP	MIP
Chyna	3	8
Ken Shamrock	3	8
Mankind	3	8
Stone Cold Steve Austin	4	10
Undertaker	3	8
Vader	3	8

Livewire, Series 2

	MNP	MIP
Marc Mero	2	6
Mark Henry	2	6
Rock, The	5	15
Shawn Michaels	2	6
Val Venis	2	6
X Pac	2	6

Manager, Series 1

	MNP	MIP
Backlund and Sultan	3	12
Bearer and Mankind	3	12
Mason and Crush	3	12
Sable and Mero	3	12

Maximum Sweat, Series 1

	MNP	MIP
HHH	3	8
Kane	3	8
Rock, The	5	15
Shawn Michaels	3	8
Stone Cold Steve Austin	3	10
Undertaker	3	8

Maximum Sweat, Series 2

	MNP	MIP
Billy Gunn	2	6
Edge	2	6
Ken Shamrock	2	6
Road Dogg Jesse James	2	6
Stone Cold Steve Austin	3	10
Undertaker	2	6

Maximum Sweat, Series 3

	MNP	MIP
Big Bossman	2	6
Billy Gunn	2	6
Gangrel	2	6
Mankind	2	6
Rock, The	5	15
Stone Cold Steve Austin	3	10

Ringside, Series 1

	MNP	MIP
Referee	3	8
Sable	3	8
Sunny	3	8
Vince McMahon	3	8

Ringside, Series 2

	MNP	MIP
Honky Tonk Man	2	6
Jim Cornette	2	6
Jim Ross	2	6

WWF Ringside (Series 2)—Honky Tonk Man, Jakks Pacific

WWF

Left: WWF Ringside (Series 2)—Jim Cornette, Jakks Pacific

Right: WWF Ringside (Series 2)—Jim Ross, Jakks Pacific

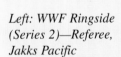
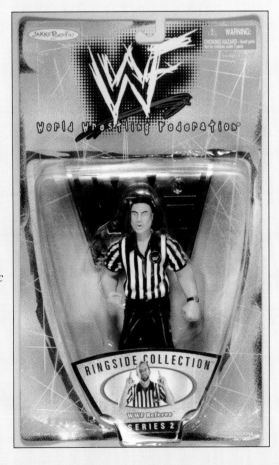
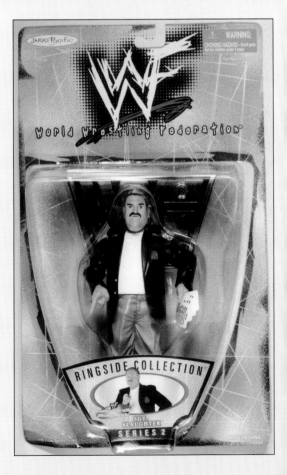

Left: WWF Ringside (Series 2)—Referee, Jakks Pacific

Right: WWF Ringside (Series 2)—Sgt. Slaughter, Jakks Pacific

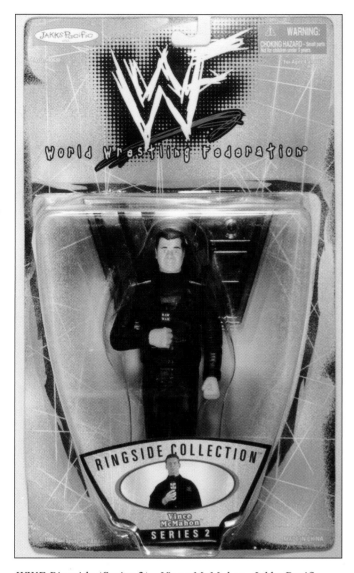

WWF Ringside (Series 2)—Vince McMahon, Jakks Pacific

WWF S.T.O.M.P. (Series 1)—Stone Cold Steve Austin, Jakks Pacific

	MNP	MIP
Referee	2	6
Sgt. Slaughter	2	6
Vince McMahon	2	6

Ripped and Ruthless, Series 1

Goldust	3	8
Mankind	3	8
Stone Cold Steve Austin	4	10
Undertaker	3	8

Ripped and Ruthless, Series 2

HHH	3	10
Kane	5	15
Sable	5	15
Shawn Michaels	3	10

S.T.O.M.P., Series 1

Ahmed Johnson	3	8
Brian Pillman	3	8
Crush	3	8
Ken Shamrock	3	8
Stone Cold Steve Austin	3	10
Undertaker	3	8

S.T.O.M.P., Series 2

	MNP	MIP
Chyna	3	8
Mosh	3	8
Owen Hart	3	8
Rocky Maivia (The Rock)	5	15
Stone Cold Steve Austin	3	10
Thrasher	3	8

S.T.O.M.P., Series 3

Animal	3	8
Hawk	3	8
Kane	3	8
Marc Mero	3	8
Sable	3	8
Undertaker	3	8

S.T.O.M.P., Series 4

Billy Gunn	2	6
Chyna	2	6
HHH	2	6
Road Dog Jesse James	2	6
Stone Cold Steve Austin	3	8
X Pac	2	6

WWF

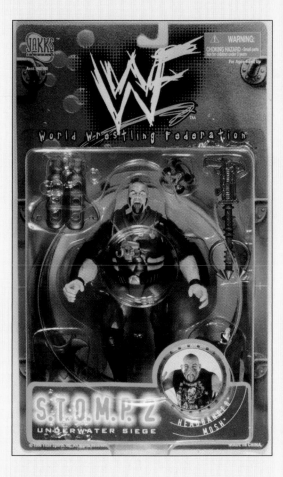

Left: WWF S.T.O.M.P. (Series 2)—Chyna, Jakks Pacific

Right: WWF S.T.O.M.P. (Series 2)—Mosh, Jakks Pacific

Left: WWF S.T.O.M.P. (Series 2)—Owen Hart, Jakks Pacific

Right: WWF S.T.O.M.P. (Series 2)—Rocky Maivia (The Rock), Jakks Pacific

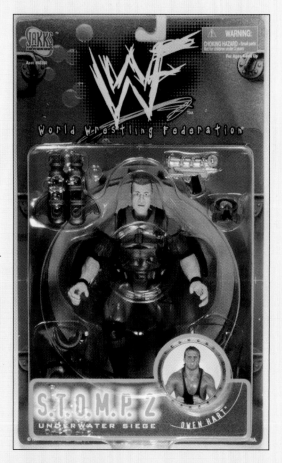

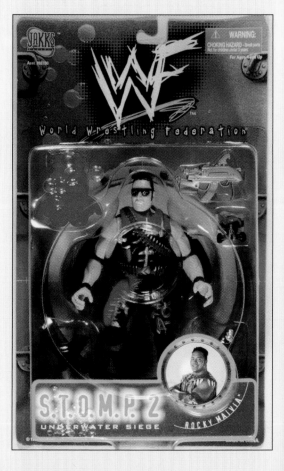

WWF S.T.O.M.P. (Series 2)—Thrasher, Jakks Pacific

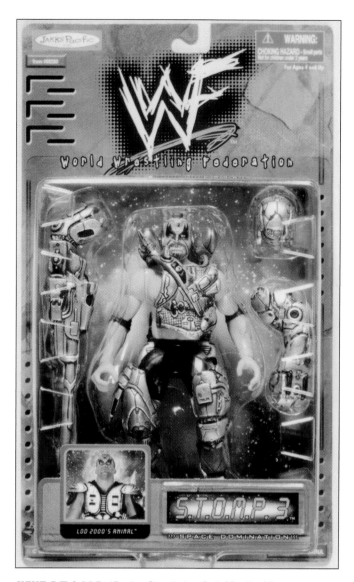

WWF S.T.O.M.P. (Series 3)—Animal, Jakks Pacific

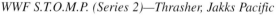

Shotgun Saturday Night, Series 1

	MNP	MIP
Animal	3	8
Hawk	3	8
Henry O. Godwinn	3	8
Phineas I. Godwinn	3	8
Rocky Maivia (The Rock)	5	15
Savio Vega	3	8
Stone Cold Steve Austin	3	10
Undertaker	3	8

Shotgun Saturday Night, Series 2

	MNP	MIP
Billy Gunn	2	6
Jeff Jarrett	2	6
Kane	2	6
Road Dog Jesse James	2	6
Sable	3	8
Shawn Michaels	2	6

Signature, Series 1

	MNP	MIP
Animal	3	8
Goldust	3	8
Hawk	3	8

	MNP	MIP
Hunter Hearst Hemsley	3	8
Mankind	3	8
Stone Cold Steve Austin	5	15

Signature, Series 2

	MNP	MIP
Billy Gunn	3	8
Dude Love	3	8
Kane	3	8
Road Dog Jesse James	3	8
Shawn Michaels	3	8
Undertaker	3	8

Signature, Series 3

	MNP	MIP
Edge	3	8
HHH	2	6
Jackie	3	8
Rock, The	5	15
Stone Cold Steve Austin	5	15
Undertaker	3	8

Sunday Night Heat

	MNP	MIP
Billy Gunn	3	8
Road Dog Jesse James	3	8
Rock, The	5	15

WWF

WWF

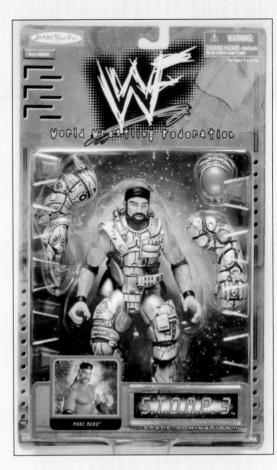

*Left: WWF S.T.O.M.P.
(Series 3)—Kane,
Jakks Pacific*

*Right: WWF
S.T.O.M.P. (Series 3)—
Marc Mero, Jakks
Pacific*

*Left: WWF S.T.O.M.P.
(Series 3)—Sable,
Jakks Pacific*

*Right: WWF
S.T.O.M.P. (Series 3)—
Undertaker, Jakks
Pacific*

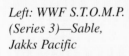

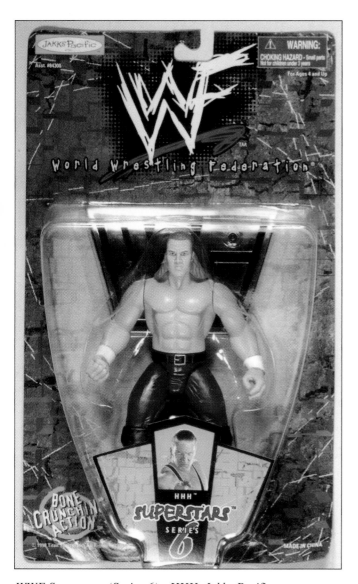

WWF Superstars (Series 6)—HHH, Jakks Pacific

WWF Superstars (Series 6)—Jeff Jarrett, Jakks Pacific

	MNP	MIP
Sable	2	6
Stone Cold Steve Austin	3	10
Undertaker	3	8

Superstars, Series 1

	MNP	MIP
Bret Hart	8	20
Diesel	10	40
Goldust	8	20
Razor Ramon	15	50
Shawn Michaels	5	15
Undertaker	8	20

Superstars, Series 2

	MNP	MIP
Bret Hart	5	15
Owen Hart	8	30
Shawn Michaels	5	15
Ultimate Warrior	8	30
Undertaker	10	30
Vader	5	15

Superstars, Series 3

	MNP	MIP
Ahmed Johnson	3	10
Bret Hart	3	10
British Bulldog	5	15

	MNP	MIP
Diesel, reissue	5	15
Goldust, reissue	5	15
Mankind	3	10
Shawn Michaels	3	10
Sycho Sid	3	10

Superstars, Series 4

	MNP	MIP
Farooq	3	10
Hunter Hearst Hemsley	3	10
Jerry The King Lawler	3	10
Justin Hawk Bradshaw	3	10
Stone Cold Steve Austin	5	15
Vader	3	10

Superstars, Series 5

	MNP	MIP
Flash Funk	3	10
Ken Shamrock	3	10
Rocky Maivia	3	10
Savio Vega	3	10
Stone Cold Steve Austin	5	15
Sycho Sid	3	10

Superstars, Series 6

	MNP	MIP
HHH	3	10

WWF

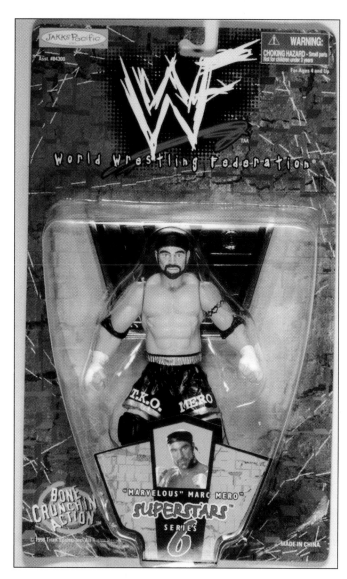

WWF Superstars (Series 6)—Marc Mero, Jakks Pacific

WWF Superstars (Series 6)—Owen Hart, Jakks Pacific

	MNP	MIP
Jeff Jarrett	2	6
Marc Mero	2	6
Mark Henry	2	6
Owen Hart	5	15
Steve Blackman	2	6

Superstars, Series 7

	MNP	MIP
Dr. Death Steve Williams	2	6
Edge	2	6
Stone Cold Steve Austin	3	10
Undertaker	3	10
Val Venis	2	6
X Pac	3	8

Superstars, Series 8

	MNP	MIP
Big Boss Man	2	6
Ken Shamrock	2	6
Rock, The	5	15
Shane McMahon	2	6
Shawn Michaels	2	6

Superstars, Series 9

	MNP	MIP
Bob Holly	2	6
Christian	2	6

	MNP	MIP
Gangrel	2	6
Paul Wright	2	6
Undertaker with robe	2	6
Vince McMahon	2	6

Tag Team, Series 1

	MNP	MIP
Godwinns	4	15
Headbangers	4	15
Legion of Doom	4	15
New Blackjacks	4	15

Titan Tron Live

	MNP	MIP
Kane	2	6
Mankind	2	6
Road Dogg Jesse James	2	6
Rock, The	5	15
Stone Cold Steve Austin	3	10
Undertaker	2	6

WWF World Wrestling Federation (Hasbro, 1990-94)

Figures

1-2-3 Kid	30	75

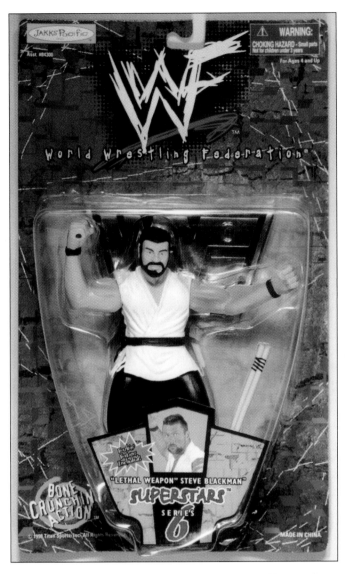

WWF Superstars (Series 6)—Steve Blackman, Jakks Pacific

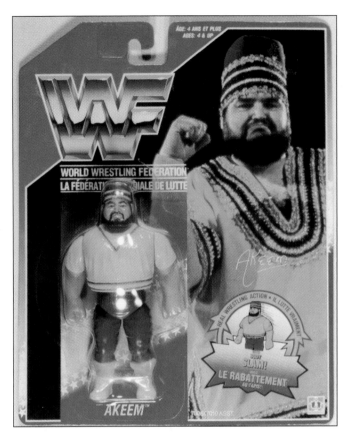

WWF World Wrestling Federation—Akeem, Hasbro

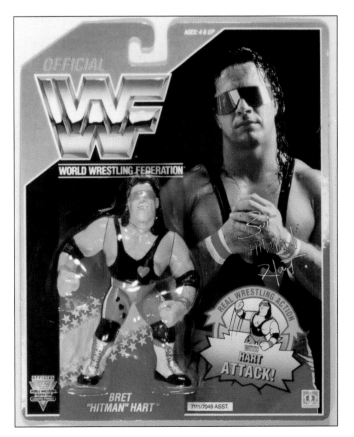

WWF World Wrestling Federation—Bret "Hitman" Hart with Hart Attack, Hasbro

	MNP	MIP
Adam Bomb	20	35
Akeem	30	75
Andre the Giant	50	150
Ax	10	30
Bam Bam Bigelow	12	30
Bart Gunn	20	35
Berzerker	6	15
Big Bossman with Jailhouse Jam, 1992	7	15
Big Bossman, 1990	8	16
Billy Gunn	20	35
Bret "Hitman" Hart with Hart Attack, 1992	10	25
Bret Hart, 1993 mail-in	75	n/a
Bret Hart, 1994	7	15
British Bulldog with Bulldog Bash, 1992	7	15
Brutus "the Barber" Beefcake with Beefcake Flattop, 1992	12	25
Brutus the Barber, 1990	12	25
Bushwackers, two-pack	10	20
Butch Miller	5	15
Crush, 1993	12	25
Crush, 1994	6	15
Demolition, two-pack	20	45
Doink the Clown	7	15

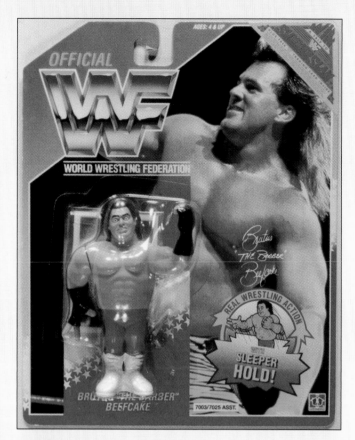

WWF World Wrestling Federation—Brutus "The Barber" Beefcake, Hasbro

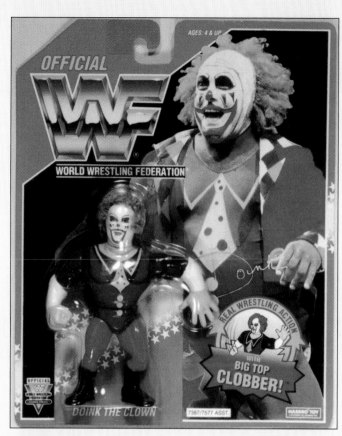

WWF World Wrestling Federation—Doink the Clown, Hasbro

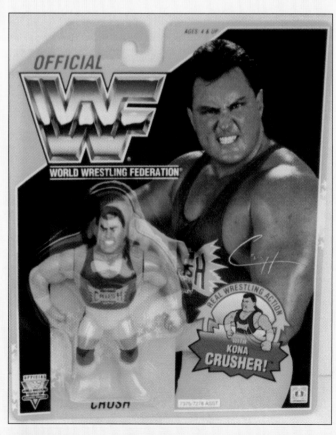

WWF World Wrestling Federation—Crush, Hasbro

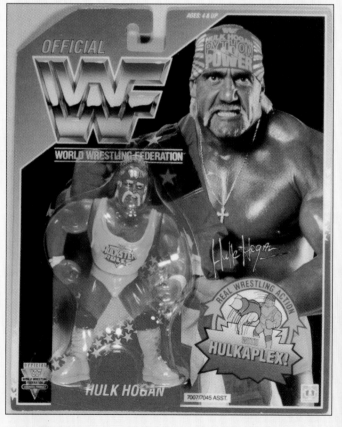

WWF World Wrestling Federation—Hulk Hogan with Hulkaplex, Hasbro

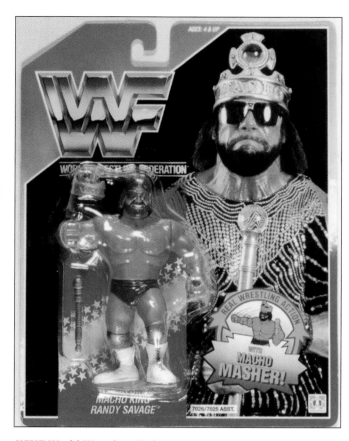

WWF World Wrestling Federation—Macho Man Randy
Savage with Macho Masher, Hasbro

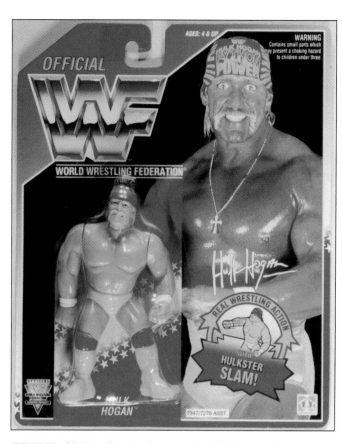

WWF World Wrestling Federation—Hulk Hogan with
Hulkster Slam, Hasbro

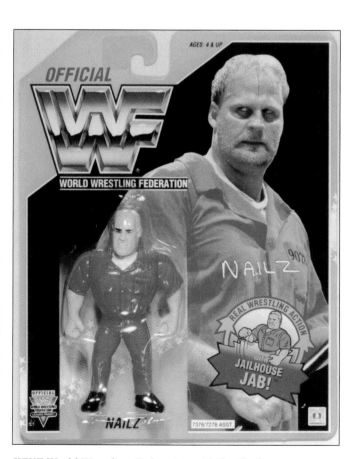

WWF World Wrestling Federation—Nailz, Hasbro

	MNP	MIP
Dusty Rhodes	125	300
Earthquake	15	30
Earthquake with Aftershock	8	25
El Matador	6	15
Fatu	5	15
Giant Gonzales	5	15
Greg "the Hammer" Valentine with Hammer Slammer (1992)	9	30
Hacksaw Jim Duggan, 1991	5	15
Hacksaw Jim Duggan, 1994	5	15
Honky Tonk Man	25	50
Hulk Hogan with Hulkaplex, 1992	10	20
Hulk Hogan, 1990	12	25
Hulk Hogan, 1991	10	20
Hulk Hogan, 1993, mail-in	75	100
Hulk Hogan, 1993, no shirt	10	20
I.R.S.	7	15
Jake the Snake Roberts	9	20
Jim Neidhart	6	15
Jimmy Superfly Snuka	12	25
Kamala	10	25
Koko B. Ware with Bird Man Bounce, 1992	20	60
Legion of Doom, two-pack	20	40
Lex Luger	15	30
Ludwig Borga	20	35
Luke Williams	5	15
Macho Man Randy Savage with Macho Masher, 1992	15	35
Macho Man, 1990	12	25
Macho Man, 1991	15	35
Macho Man, 1993	7	15
Marty Jannetty	5	15

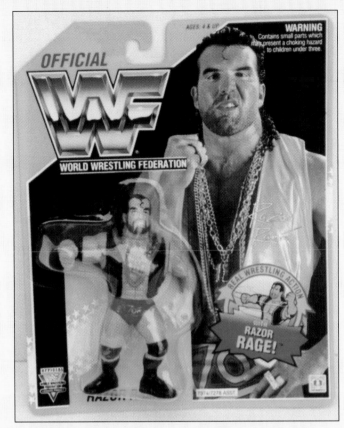

WWF World Wrestling Federation—Razor Ramone, Hasbro

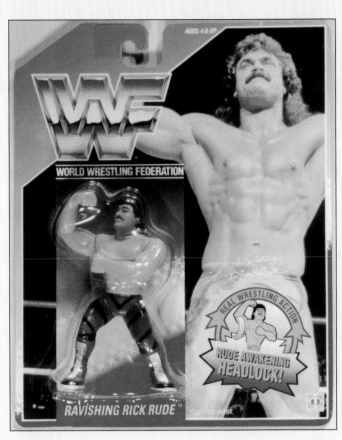

WWF World Wrestling Federation—Rick Rude, Hasbro

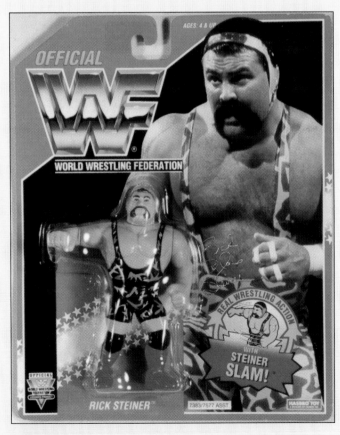

WWF World Wrestling Federation—Rick Steiner, Hasbro

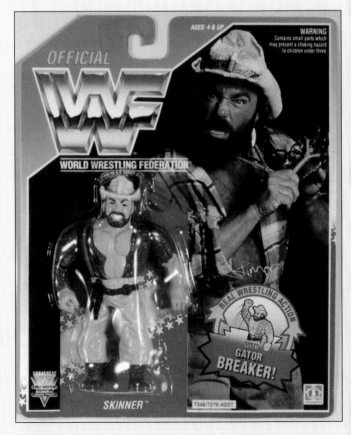

WWF World Wrestling Federation—Skinner, Hasbro

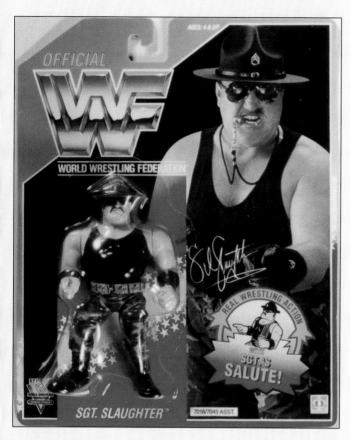

WWF World Wrestling Federation—Sgt. Slaughter, Hasbro

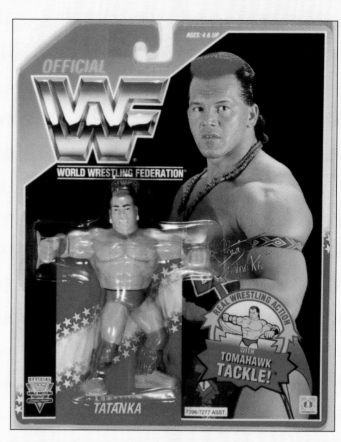

WWF World Wrestling Federation—Tatanka, Hasbro

WWF World Wrestling Federation—Ultimate Warrior, Hasbro

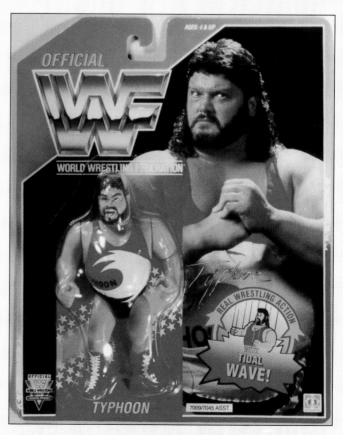

WWF World Wrestling Federation—Typhoon, Hasbro

WWF WORLD WRESTLING FEDERATION

WWF World Wrestling Federation—Yokozuna, Hasbro

WWF World Wrestling Federation by Hasbro—Top row, left to right: Ted Diabiase; Scott Steiner. Bottom Row, left to right: Hacksaw; Jim Duggan; Rick Steiner; Brutus "The Barber" Beefcake with Beefcake Flattop; Doink the Clown. Photo Courtesy Hasbro

	MNP	MIP
Mountie	6	15
Mr. Perfect with Perfect Plex, 1992	8	20
Mr. Perfect with Texas Twister, 1992	15	35
Mr. Perfect, 1994	12	25
Nailz	12	25
Nasty Boys, two-pack	15	80
Owen Hart	15	45
Papa Shango	7	15
Razor Ramon, 1993	15	30
Razor Ramon, 1994	9	18
Repo Man	7	15
Ric Flair	7	15
Rick Martel	5	15
Rick Rude	15	30
Rick Steiner	9	18
Ricky "The Dragon" Steamboat with Steamboat Springer, 1992	7	15
Rockers, two-pack	10	20
Rowdy Roddy Piper	15	30
Samu	5	15
Scott Steiner	8	18
Sgt. Slaughter with Sgt.'s Salute, 1992	15	30
Shawn Michaels, 1993	10	25
Shawn Michaels, 1994	6	15
Sid Justice	6	15
Skinner	6	15
Smash	12	25
Tatanka, 1993	7	15
Tatanka, 1994	7	15
Ted Diabiase, 1990	10	20
Ted Diabiase, 1991	7	15
Ted Diabiase, 1994	7	15

X-Files by McFarlane Toys—Left to Right: Scully; Mulder. Photo Courtesy McFarlane Toys

	MNP	MIP
Texas Tornado with Texas Twister, 1992	10	50
Typhoon with Tidal Wave, 1992	15	30
Ultimate Warrior with Warrior Wham, 1992	20	40
Ultimate Warrior, 1990	12	25
Ultimate Warrior, 1991	10	20
Undertaker with Graveyard Smash, 1992	9	18
Undertaker, 1993, mail-in	25	50
Undertaker, 1994	15	25
Virgil	7	15
Warlord	6	15
Yokozuna	15	30

Xena Warrior Princess (Toy Biz, 1998-99)
6" Figures

	MNP	MIP
Callisto Warrior Goddess with Hope	3	10
Grieving Gabrielle	3	10
Xena Conqueror of Nations	3	10
Xena Warrior Huntress	3	10

Series I, 12" Figures

	MNP	MIP
Callisto	8	25
Gabrielle	8	25
Xena	8	25

Series II, 12" Figures

	MNP	MIP
Ares	8	25

	MNP	MIP
Gabrielle Amazon Princess	8	25
Roman Xena	8	25
Warlord Xena	8	25

Series III, 12" Figures

	MNP	MIP
Empress Gabrielle	8	25
Shamaness Xena	8	25
Xena the Evil Warrior	8	25

X-Files (McFarlane, 1998)
Figures

	MNP	MIP
Fireman with Cryolitter	10	25
Mulder in Arctic wear	4	8
Mulder with docile alien	4	8
Mulder with Human Host and Cryopod Chamber	4	8
Mulder with victim	4	8
Primitive Man with Attack Alien	4	8
Scully in Arctic wear	4	8
Scully with docile alien	4	8
Scully with Human Host and Cryopod Chamber	4	8
Scully with Victim	4	8

X-Men (Toy Biz, 1991-96)
Figures

	MNP	MIP
Ahab, 1994	5	15
Apocalypse I, 1991	7	15

X-Men by Toy Biz—Left to Right: Archangel II, 1995; Ravaged Wolverine, 1995

*X-Men by Toy Biz—
Left to Right: Havok,
1995; Sabretooth,
1995*

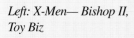

*Left: X-Men— Bishop II,
Toy Biz*

*Right: X-Men—Omega
Red II, Toy Biz*

X-Men—Polaris, 1996, Toy Biz

X-Men—Savage Land Wolverine, 1996, Toy Biz

	MNP	MIP
Apocalypse I, 1993	4	15
Apocolypse, 1996	3	8
Archangel II, 1995	4	15
Archangel, 1991	7	15
Archangel, 1996	3	8
Banshee I, 1992	7	15
Battle Ravaged Wolverine, 1995	4	8
Beast, 1994	10	20
Bishop II, 1993	7	15
Bishop II, 1996	3	8
Blob, 1995	5	15
Cable Cyborg, 1995	4	15
Caliban, 1995	4	15
Cameron Hodge, 1995	4	15
Captive Sabretooth, 1995	4	15
Colossus, 1991	10	20
Colossus, 1993	6	15
Colossus, 1996	3	8
Corsair, 1995	3	15
Cyclops I, blue, 1991	10	20
Cyclops I, stripes, 1991	5	15
Cyclops II, 1993	5	15
Cyclops, 1996	3	8
Deadpool, 1995	6	15
Domino, 1995	5	15

	MNP	MIP
Forge, 1992	10	25
Gambit, 1992	10	20
Gambit, 1993	7	15
Gladiator, 1995	3	15
Havok, 1995	4	15
Ice Man II, 1995	4	15
Ice Man, 1992	20	45
Juggernaut, 1991	10	25
Juggernaut, 1993	4	15
Lady Deathstrike, 1996	3	8
Magneto I, 1991	6	15
Magneto II, 1992	5	15
Magneto, 1996	3	8
Morph, 1994	10	20
Mr. Sinister, 1992	7	15
Nightcrawler, 1993	10	25
Nimrod, 1995	4	15
Omega Red II	3	8
Omega Red, 1993	6	15
Phoenix, 1995	10	25
Polaris, 1996	3	8
Professor X, 1993	6	15
Raza, 1994	3	15
Sabretooth, 1996	3	8
Sauron, 1992	3	15

X-Men Classics (Light-up Weapons)—Gambit with Light-up Plasma Energy Weapon, 1996, Toy Biz

X-Men Classics (Light-up Weapons)—Juggernaut with Light-up Jewel Weapon, 1996, Toy Biz

	MNP	MIP
Savage Land Wolverine, 1996	3	8
Spiral, 1995	4	15
Storm, 1991	20	40
Strong Guy, 1993	3	15
Sunfire, 1995	4	15
Trevor Fitzroy, 1994	3	15
Tusk, 1992	5	15
Warstar, 1995	6	15
Weapon X, 1996	3	8
Wolverine Fang, 1995	4	15
Wolverine I, 1991	10	20
Wolverine I, 1993	7	15
Wolverine II, 1992	7	15
Wolverine III, 1992	12	25
Wolverine V, 1993	7	15
Wolverine, 1996	3	10
Wolverine, space armor, 1995	6	15
Wolverine, street clothes, 1994	5	15
X-Cutioner, 1995	4	15

X-Men (Toy Biz, 1996-98)

Age of Apocalypse, 5" Figures, 1996

	MNP	MIP
Apocalypse, Removable Armor and Transforming Limbs	3	8

	MNP	MIP
Cyclops, Cybernetic Guardian and Laser Blaster	2	6
Gambit, Blast-throwing Action	2	6
Magneto, Removable Helmet and Shrapnel	2	6
Sabretooth, Wild Child Sidekick Figure	2	6
Weapon X, Interchangeable Weaponry	2	6

Classics, Light-up Weapons, 5" Figures, 1996

	MNP	MIP
Gambit, Light-up Plasma Energy Weapon	3	10
Juggernaut, Light-up Jewel Weapon	3	10
Nightcrawler, Light-up Sword	3	10
Psylock, light-up Psychic Knife	3	10
Wolverine Stealth, Light-up Plasma Weapon	3	10

Missle Flyers, 5" Figures, 1997

	MNP	MIP
Apocalypse, Trap-door Chest	3	8
Bishop, Fold-out Armor Wing Blasters	3	8
Cable, Attack Wings	3	8
Shard, Spring Loaded Firing Wing Extensions	3	8
Wolverine, Head Launching Bird of Prey	3	8

Monster Armor, 5" Figures, 1997

	MNP	MIP
Cyclops with Snap-on Cyclaw Armor	2	6
Mr. Sinister with Snap-on Cyber Tech Armor	2	6
Mystique with Snap-on She-Beast Armor	2	6

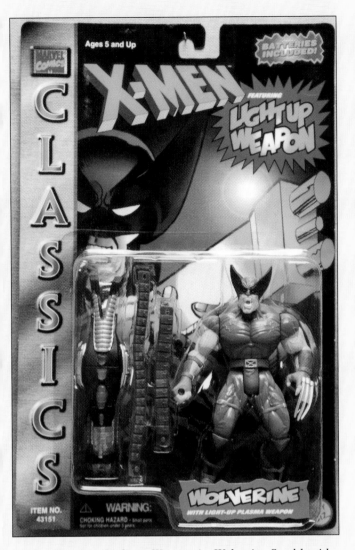

X-Men Classics (Light-up Weapons)—Wolverine Stealth with
Light-up Plasma Weapon, 1996, Toy Biz

X-Men Classics (Light-up Weapons)—Nightcrawler with
Light-up Sword, 1996, Toy Biz

X-Men Savage Land—Angel with Wing Flapping Sauron-Dino, 1997, Toy Biz

*X-Men Savage Land—
Kazar with Jumping Zabu
Tiger, 1997, Toy Biz*

*X-Men Savage Land—
Savage Storm with Head
Ramming Colossus Dino,
1997, Toy Biz*

*X-Men Savage Land—
Savage Wolverine with
Jaw Chomping Crawler-
Rex, 1997, Toy Biz*

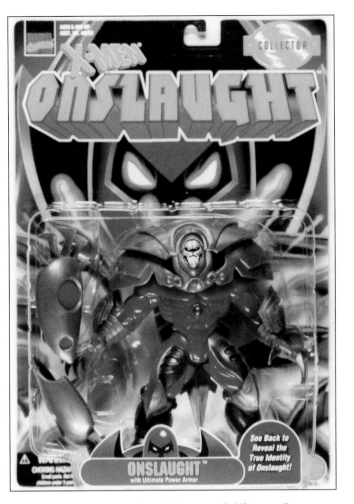

X-Men Onslaught—Onslaught figure with Ultimate Power Armor, 1997, Toy Biz

	MNP	MIP
Rogue with Snap-on Leech Bat Armor	2	6
Wolverine with Snap-on Fangor Armor	2	6

New Mutants, 5" Figures, 1998

Magik	2	6
Warlock	2	6
Wolfsbane	2	6

Ninja Force, 5" Figures, 1997

Dark Nemesis with Spear Shooting Staff	3	8
Ninja Sabretooth with Clip-on Claw Armor	3	8
Ninja Wolverine with Warrior Assault Gear	3	8
Psylocke with Extending Power Sword	3	8
Space Ninja Deathbird with Fold-Out Ninja Wings	3	8

Onslaught, 6" figures, 1997

Apocalypse Rising, Ozymandias	3	11
Jean Grey, Psychic Claw	3	11
Onslaught, Ultimate Power Armor	3	10
Wolverine Unleashed, Franklin Richards	3	10

Robot Fighters, 5" Figures, 1997

Cyclops, Apocalypse Droid with Gattling Gun Arm	3	8
Gambit, Attack Robot Droid with Projectile Missile	3	8
Jubilee, Grabbing Sentinel Hand with Projectile Finger	4	12
Storm, Spinning Weather Station with Lightning Projectile	4	12
Wolverine, Slashing Sabretooth Droid with Missile Claw	3	8

Savage Land, 5" Figures, 1997

	MNP	MIP
Angel with Wing Flapping Sauron-Dino	2	6
Kazar with Jumping Zabu Tiger	2	6
Magneto with Water Spitting Amphibious	2	6
Savage Storm with Head Ramming Colossus Dino	2	6
Savage Wolverine with Jaw Chomping Crawler-Rex	2	6

Secret Weapon Force Battle Bases, 5" Figures, 1998

Cyclops with War Tank Blaster	2	6
Jean Grey with Catapult Tank Blaster	2	6
Magneto Battle Base	2	6
Omega with Spinning Rocket Blaster	2	6
Wolverine Battle Base	2	6
Wolverine with Claw Cannon Blaster	2	6

Secret Weapon Force Flying Fighters, 5" Figures, 1998

Cyclops with High-Flying Hazard Gear	3	8
Jean Grey with Fire Bird Flyer	3	8
Maggot with Expanding Assault Wings	3	8
Mr. Sinister with Bio-Tech Attack Wings	3	8

X-Men Secret Weapon Force Battle Bases—Omega with Spinning Rocket Blaster, 1998, Toy Biz. Photo Courtesy Toy Biz

X-MEN

X-Men Secret Weapon Force Shape Shifters—Wolverine forms into Mutant Wolf, 1998, Toy Biz. Photo Courtesy Toy Biz

Secret Weapon Force Power Slammers, 5" Figures, 1998

	MNP	MIP
Gambit with Rapid Fire Card Cannon Slammer	2	6
Master Mold with Rapid Fire Sentinels	2	6
Rogue with Double Barrel Slammer	3	8
Wolverine with Rapid Fire Disk Slammer	2	6

Secret Weapon Force Shape Shifters, 7" Figures, 1998

Juggernaut forms into Titanic Tank	2	6
Morph forms into Mega Missile	2	6
Wolverine forms into Mutant Wolf	2	6

Secret Weapon Force Super Shooter, 5" Figures, 1998

Apocalypse	3	10
Beast	3	8
Colossus	3	8
Wolverine	3	8

Shattershot, 5" Figures, 1996

Age of Apocalypse Beast, Wind-up Chain Saw	2	6
Archangel, Wing-flapping Action	2	6
Colossus, Super Punch Gauntlets	2	6

	MNP	MIP
Lady Death Strike, Transforming Reaver Armor	2	6
Patch Wolverine, Total Assault Arsenal	2	6

Special Edition Series, 12" Figures, 1998

Gambit	8	25
Storm	8	25
Wolverine	8	25

X-Men 2099 (Toy Biz, 1996)
5" Figures

Bloodhawk	2	6
Breakdown, Dominick Sidekick Figure	2	6
Brimstone Love	2	6
Halloween Jack	2	6
Junkpile, Snap-on Battle Armor	2	6
La Lunatica, Futuristic Jai-Lai	2	6
Meanstreak	2	6
Metalhead	2	6
Shadow Dancer	2	6
Skullfire, Glowing Fire Skeleton	2	6

X-Men vs. Street Fighter (Toy Biz, 1998)
5" Figures

Apocalypse vs. Dhalism	2	6
Cyclops vs. M. Bison	5	15

X-Men/X-Force—Cable, Toy Biz. Photo Courtesy Toy Biz

X-Men/X-Force—Cannonball, pink, 1993, Toy Biz

	MNP	MIP
Cable V, 1994	5	15
Cannonball, pink, 1993	15	35
Cannonball, purple, 1993	10	20
Commando, 1995	3	8
Deadpool, 1992	15	35
Deadpool, 1995	3	10
Domino, 1995	3	10
Exodus, 1995	3	8
Forearm, 1992	10	20
Genesis, 1995	3	8
Gideon, 1992	5	15
Grizzly, 1993	5	15
Kane I, 1992	7	15
Kane II, 1993	4	15
Killspree II, 1996	4	8
Killspree, 1994	7	15
Krule, 1993	3	15
Kylun, 1994	3	15
Longshot, 1994	7	15
Mojo, 1995	3	8
Nimrod, 1995	3	8
Pyro, 1994	5	15
Quark, 1994	3	15
Random, 1994	3	15

	MNP	MIP
Gambit vs. Cammy	2	6
Juggernaut vs. Chunu	2	6
Magneto vs. Ryu	5	15
Rogue vs. Zangief	2	6
Sabretooth vs. Ken	5	15
Wolverine vs. Akuma	5	15

X-Men/X-Force (Toy Biz, 1991-96)

Deluxe 10" Figures

Cable	8	20
Kane	8	20
Shatterstar	8	20

Figures

Arctic Armor Cable, 1996	3	8
Avalanche, 1995	3	8
Black Tom, 1994	5	15
Black Tom, 1995	5	15
Blob, The, 1995	5	15
Bonebreaker, 1994	3	15
Bridge, 1992	5	15
Brood, 1993	4	15
Cable Cyborg, 1995	3	8
Cable I, 1992	6	15
Cable II, 1993	4	15
Cable III, 1993	4	15
Cable IV, 1994	3	15
Cable Stealth, 1996	3	8

X-Men/X-Force—Killspree II, 1996, Toy Biz

YELLOW SUBMARINE

Yellow Submarine—George with Yellow Submarine, McFarlane Toys

Yellow Submarine—John with Jeremy, McFarlane Toys

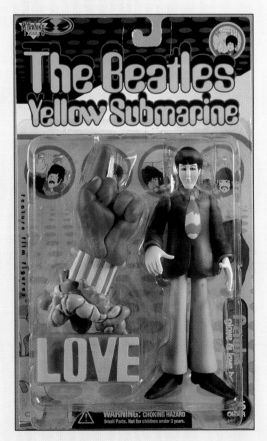

Yellow Submarine—Paul with Glove and Love base, McFarlane Toys

Yellow Submarine—Ringo with Blue Meanie, McFarlane Toys

Youngblood (prototype figure)—Crypt, McFarlane. Photo Courtesy McFarlane Toys

Youngblood (prototype figure)—Sentinel, McFarlane. Photo Courtesy McFarlane Toys

Youngblood (prototype figure)— Dutch, McFarlane. Photo Courtesy McFarlane Toys

YOUNGBLOOD

Youngblood (prototype figure)—Shaft, McFarlane. Photo Courtesy McFarlane Toys

Youngblood (prototype figure)—Troll, McFarlane. Photo Courtesy McFarlane Toys

	MNP	MIP
Rictor, 1994	3	15
Rogue, 1994	10	25
Sabretooth I, 1992	7	15
Sabretooth II, 1994	6	15
Shatterstar I, 1992	4	12
Shatterstar II, 1994	4	12
Shatterstar III, 1996	3	8
Silver Samurai, 1994	3	15
Slayback, 1994	3	15
Stryfe, 1992	10	25
Sunspot, 1994	3	15
Urban Assault, 1995	3	8
Warpath I, 1992	7	15
Warpath II, 1994	5	15
X-Treme, 1994	5	15

X-Men: The Movie (Toy Biz, 2000)
Figures

	MNP	MIP
Cyclops	3	10
Jean Grey	5	15
Logan	3	10
Magneto	3	10
Mystique	3	10
Professor X	4	12
Rogue	3	10
Sabretooth	3	10
Storm	4	12
Toad	3	10
Wolverine	3	10

Two Packs

	MNP	MIP
Logan and Rogue	5	15
Magneto and Logan	5	15
Wolverine and Sabre	5	15

Yellow Submarine (McFarlane, 1999)
Figures

	MNP	MIP
George with Yellow Submarine	3	10
John with Jeremy	3	10
Paul with Glove and Love base	4	12
Ringo with Blue Meanie	3	10

Youngblood (McFarlane, 1995)
Figures

	MNP	MIP
Crypt	5	10
Die Hard	4	8
Dutch	4	8
Sentinel	4	8
Shaft	4	8
Troll	10	20

Zorro (Gabriel, 1982)
Figures

	MNP	MIP
Amigo	10	25
Captain Ramon	10	25
Picaro	15	35
Sergeant Gonzales	10	25
Tempest	10	25
Zorro	15	25

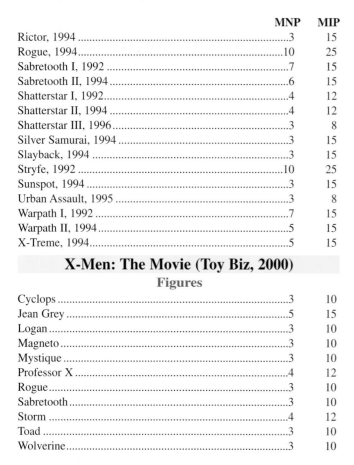

2001 Toys & Prices
8th Edition
edited by Sharon Korbeck and Elizabeth A. Stephan

One of today's hottest collecting areas - TV Toys - now has its own chapter, highlighting your favorites from the 1940s through the 1990s. Space toys fans will now have an easier-to-use section, including a spotlight on ultra-hot robots. Both the casual collector and veteran enthusiast will find over 58,000 values on more than 20,000 toys including cast-iron banks, lunch boxes, board games, Barbie, PEZ, space toys, Fisher-Price, Hot Wheels, restaurant toys and more. More than 20 chapters make this compact guide indispensable as a reference guide.

Softcover • 6 x 9 • 936 pages
700 b&w photos • 8-page color section
Item# TE08 • $18.95

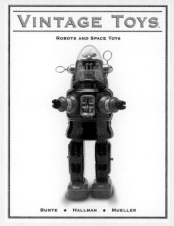

Vintage Toys
Robots and Space Toys
by Jim Bunte, Dave Hallman, and Heinz Mueller

Packed with beautiful, large color photographs and encyclopedic-style details, this volume focuses on tin toys manufactured from World War I through the 1970s. American, British, French, German and Spanish robots and space toys are featured, but special coverage is given to Japanese tin toys. More than 300 different items are illustrated and profiled, along with up-to-date collector values.

Softcover • 8-1/2 x 11 • 192 pages
400 color photos
Item# AT1025 • $26.95

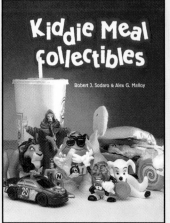

Kiddie Meal Collectibles
by Alex G. Malloy and Robert J. Sodaro

In the world of fast food premium collectibles, three key questions beg answering: What was offered? When was it offered? What's it worth today? This new book, compiled by two leading experts in contemporary collectibles, answers those questions, and more, in 208 pages filled with facts, photos, descriptions, and current marketplace prices. Premiums offered by more than thirty restaurant franchises are covered in detail, complete with current values for mint-in-package items, mint-out-of-package items, individual objects, and complete sets.

Softcover • 8-1/2 x 11 • 208 pages
400+ b&w photos • 32-page color section, 100 color photos
Item# AT5161 • $24.95

American Games
Comprehensive Collector's Guide
by Alex G. Malloy

Here's the first-ever accurate and detailed accounting of American games ever published. Compiled by the nation's foremost games collector, this new volume provides everything the savvy enthusiast needs to know in the form of comprehensive listings, detailed descriptions, and up-to-date marketplace values for more than 9,000 individual games in two grades of condition. As an added benefit, Alex Malloy shares his knowledge and experience with expert tips on how to collect, grade, and value games of all types, including board games, card games, and action games.

Softcover • 8-1/2 x 11 • 352 pages
500+ b&w photos • 400 color photos
Item# AT5609 • $26.95

Marx Toys Sampler
Playthings from an Ohio Valley Legend
by Michelle Smith

If "Marx mania" has you in its grasp, here's a new book that's sure to capture your attention and interest. In this first behind-the-scenes look at the internal operations and production output of the Marx Toys plant in Glen Dale, West Virginia, you'll learn about Marx toys and the people who produced them. And, you'll find a comprehensive listing, supported by more than 150 photographs, representing over thirty years of lithographed metal and cast plastic toy production-a valuable tool for identifying and dating items in your own collection of Marx Playsets, doll houses, figures, and other toys.

Softcover • 8-1/2 x 11 • 192 pages
150 b&w photos • 32-page color section, 100 color photos
Item# MXTS • $26.95

Today's Hottest™ Collectibles
2nd Edition
by the Publishers of *Toy Shop* and *Warman's Today's Collector*

This must-have reference for collecting offers the perfect introduction to the novice, and is a valuable tool to experienced collectors. Updated with 50 new chapters to reflect today's hottest trends, the book offers introductory histories of many collecting specialties, general collecting guidelines, 10,000 values for representative collectibles in over 90 categories, tips on buying and selling on the Internet, and club information for the specialty collector.

Softcover • 8-1/2 x 11 • 356 pages
1,300 b&w photos
Item# CGA02 • $24.95

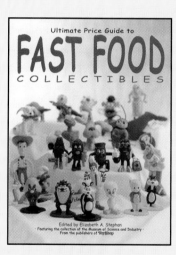
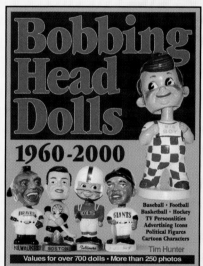
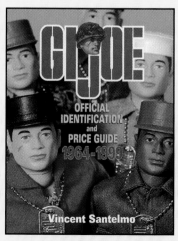

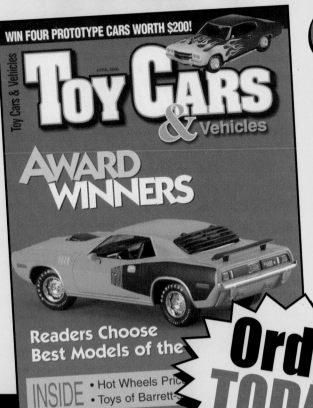